Program Planning for
Adult Christian Education

Program Planning for Adult Christian Education

By

REV. JAMES R. SCHAEFER, S.T.L., PhD.

with a Foreword by
D. CAMPBELL WYCKOFF, PhD.

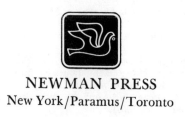

NEWMAN PRESS
New York/Paramus/Toronto

Nihil Obstat:
Rev. Msgr. Carroll E. Satterfield, S.T.D.
Censor Librorum

Imprimatur:
✠ Lawrence Cardinal Shehan
Archbishop of Baltimore

March 8, 1972

The Nihil Obstat and Imprimatur are official declarations that a book or pamphlet is free of doctrinal or moral error. No implication is contained therein that those who have granted the Nihil Obstat and Imprimatur agree with the contents, opinions or statements expressed.

Library of Congress
Catalog Card Number: 72-88324

ISBN 0-8091-0175-0 (cloth)   ISBN 0-8091-1755-X (paper)

Published by Newman Press
Editorial Office: 1865 Broadway, New York, N.Y. 10023
Business Office: 400 Sette Drive, Paramus, N.J. 07652

Printed and bound in the
United States of America

ACKNOWLEDGMENTS

Acknowledgment is gratefully made to the publishers for their permission to quote from the following works:

Foundations for Curriculum. American Baptist Approved Documents for Curriculum Building (Valley Forge, Pa.: American Baptist Board of Education and Publication. © Harold W. Richardson, 1966).

The Church and Christian Education, ed. by Paul H. Vieth (St. Louis, Mo.: The Bethany Press, 1947).

"Natural Knowledge of God," in *Proceedings of the Twenty-Third Annual Convention* by The Catholic Theological Society of America, 1969.

"The God of Revelation," by Gabriel Moran, in *Commonweal,* LXXXV, No. 18 (February 10, 1967).

"Horizon Analysis and Eschatology," by David Tracy, in *Continuum,* VI (Summer, 1968).

"Mystērion," in *Theological Dictionary of the New Testament,* Vol. IV by Gunther Bornkamm (Grand Rapids, Mich.: Wm. B. Eerdmans Publishing Co., 1967).

The Documents of Vatican II, ed. by Walter M. Abbott, S.J. (London: Geoffrey Chapman, 1966).

Objectives in Religious Education by Paul H. Vieth (New York: Harper & Row Publishers, Inc., 1930).

New Frontiers in Theology: Discussions among Continental and American Theologians. Vol. II: *The Hermeneutic,* ed. by James M. Robinson and John B. Cobb, Jr. (New York: Harper & Row Publishers, Inc., 1964).

Salvation in History by Oscar Cullmann, tr. by Sidney G. Sowers (New York: Harper & Row Publishers, Inc., 1967).

"Dimensions of Meaning," in *Collection: Papers by Bernard Lonergan,* ed. by F. E. Crowe (New York: Herder and Herder, 1967).

"Theology in Its New Context," by Bernard Lonergan, in *Theology of Renewal,* Vol. I, ed. by L. K. Shook (New York: Herder and Herder, 1968).

The Structure of Catechetics by Marcel van Caster (New York: Herder and Herder, 1965).

Curriculum Planning for Better Teaching and Learning by J. Galen Saylor and William M. Alexander (New York: Holt, Rinehart and Winston, Inc., 1954).

"Redemptive Event and History, by Wolfhart Pannenberg, in *Essays on Old Testament Hermeneutics,* ed. by Claus Westermann (Richmond: John Knox Press, 1963).

Realms of Meaning: A Philosophy of the Curriculum for General Education, by Philip H. Phenix, copyright © 1964 (New York: McGraw-Hill Book Company).

The Objective of Christian Education for Senior High Young People by the Commission on General Christian Education of the National Council of Churches of Christ in the U.S.A., 1958.

The Church's Educational Ministry: A Curriculum Plan, by the Cooperative Curriculum Project of the National Council of Churches in the U.S.A., 1965.

The Law of Christ: Moral Theology for Priests and Laity, Vol. I, by Bernard Häring (New York and Paramus: Newman Press, 1967).

"Instruction, the Person and the Group," by D. Campbell Wyckoff, in *Religious Education,* LXI (January-February, 1966) (New York: The Religious Education Association).

Catholic Adult Education, by Vaile Scott, from N.C.E.A. Papers, No. 4, 1968 (Washington, D.C.: National Catholic Educational Association).

"Design in Protestant Curriculum," by D. Campbell Wyckoff, in *Religious Education,* LXI (May-June, 1966) (New York: The Religious Education Association).

"Toward a Definition of Religious Education as a Discipline," by D. Campbell Wyckoff, in *Religious Education,* LXII (September-October, 1967) (New York: The Religious Education Association).

Old and New in Interpretation: A Study of the Two Testaments, by James Barr (London: SCM Press).

Christ the Sacrament of the Encounter with God, by Edward Schillebeeckx, © Sheed & Ward Ltd., 1963.

"Questions To Ask in Planning a Program," in *PACE* 1, ed. by Sheila Moriarty. Copyright © 1970 (Winona, Minn.: St. Mary's College Press).

Theories of Learning in Christian Education, by Robert R. Boelke. Copyright © MCMLXII, W. L. Jenkins (Philadelphia: The Westminster Press).

Lay Education in the Parish, by Robert H. Kempes, ed. by Edward K. Trefz. Copyright © MCMLXVIII (Philadelphia: The Geneva Press).

Christian Faith and Action/Designs for an Educational System, by The Board of Christian Education of the United Presbyterian Church in the U.S.A., 1967 (Philadelphia: The Westminster Press).

A Dynamic Approach to Church Education, by Gerard H. Slusser. Copyright © MCMLXVIII (Philadelphia: The Geneva Press).

Theory and Design of Christian Education Curriculum, by D. Campbell Wyckoff. Copyright © MCMLXI, W. L. Jenkins (Philadelphia: The Westminster Press).

The Gospel and Christian Education, by D. Campbell Wyckoff. Copyright © MCMLIX (Philadelphia: The Westminster Press).

Liturgical Piety, by Louis Bouyer (University of Notre Dame Press, 1955).

Wider Horizons in Christian Adult Education, ed. by Lawrence C. Little (Pittsburgh: University of Pittsburgh Press, © 1962).

School, Curriculum, and the Individual, by John I. Goodlad. Copyright © 1966 (Lexington, Mass: Xerox Corporation).

Personal Acknowledgments

Without the encouragement and support of many persons, this book and the dissertation from which it grew could not have reached completion. I am indebted to Father Gerard S. Sloyan who provided as leading an influence in this work as he has in Catholic Religious Education in the United States these past two decades. Father Berard Marthaler, his capable successor as head of Catholic University's Department of Religion and Religious Education, suggested several critical improvements. Sister Mary Charles Bryce lent the encouragement of careful reading and approval.

To Professor D. Campbell Wyckoff of Princeton Theological Seminary, I am more than grateful for schooling me in the ways of doing curriculum in Protestant Christian Education. The methodology which this work adopts and refines is largely his own. Careless of time and energy, he unselfishly shared with me his rich experience in designing Protestant curricula. He made available, too, his personal library and files. He offered judicious critiques each step of the way. I do not exaggerate to say that without his guidance I would not have known where to begin, how to proceed, or when to end.

I deeply appreciate, too, the close collaboration of the members of the Baltimore Archdiocesan Steering Committee who suffered under my adherence to this methodology in designing GIFT (Growth in Faith Together) and who tested the viability of these principles in the live arena of learning. They are Bishop T. Austin Murphy, D.D., Chairman; Rev. Francis X. Callahan, Brother Henry Werner, F.S.C., and Cornelius J. Feehley, PhD., Reflection Groups Consultants; Rev. Michael J. Spillane, S.T.L., Liturgical Consultant; Rev. Paul M. Asselin, C.S.P., Catechetical Consultant; Mr. William F. Tiefenwerth, Publicity Consultant; and Mr. Joseph M. Hargadon, Continuing Response Consultant.

I am also indebted to Rev. Philip T. Snouffer for his thorough and painstaking indexing of this volume.

To my competent and extraordinarily patient secretary, Mrs. Margaret Cox, I am grateful for typing and correcting the final copy. How she managed to accomplish the feat along with her overload of office work is a mystery. I am also grateful to Mrs. Teresa Satterfield for her careful proofreading.

JAMES R. SCHAEFER
Baltimore, January, 1972

To His Eminence
LAWRENCE CARDINAL SHEHAN
for whom *omnia in caritate*
more than a motto
is a way of life

Table of Contents

Foreword

In Christian education, theory and practice are inseparably bound together, and the person worth listening to is the one who combines the thoughtfulness of the theoretician with the skill of the practitioner. Dr. Schaefer is such a person, and his contribution is all the more to be valued in that he is completely at home with the most significant ideas in Christian education and its theological and behavioral sources, has a genuine feel for Christian education as it takes place at the parish level, and in addition brings to the question the understandings and experience of planning and supervising Christian education at the diocesan level.

In *Program Planning for Adult Christian Education* we have a substantial book in Christian education theory centering on the problem of responsible and thorough-going curriculum design. The first chapter, almost a book in itself, develops a method for thinking about Christian education and arriving at informed decisions at the practical level. Theological and educational materials are handled skilfully in arriving at those fundamental points of inquiry with which the adult Christian educator must deal. It is indicated to him that he will be able to function intelligently when he seeks and frames answers to certain basic questions, answers that take the form of principles that guide considered practice. The principles group themselves in the categories of the objective of Christian education, the personnel involved and their roles, the scope of subject matter and experience to be taken into account, the process of teaching and learning, the context for education, and its timing. In addition, three general curriculum concerns that always take these six categories into account are identified: the need for a principle for organizing the curriculum, guides and procedures for evaluation, and models of administration.

The body of the book, chapters II-VII, consists of a careful weighing of various options in each of the six categories. Here the ecumenical yet discriminating character of the study comes through clearly. Four existing curriculum plans were thoroughly studied in preparation for the decisions to be made on the content of the various principles. The curriculum of the American Baptist Convention was selected

1

as a good representative of the curriculum developed in Protestant circles on the basis of the National Council of Churches' Cooperative Curriculum Project. The adult program of lay education of the United Presbyterian Church in the U.S.A. was chosen as a prime example of the use of the "situational approach" in adult Christian education. The programs of two different Roman Catholic dioceses were also analyzed, those of Lansing and Baltimore. Incidentally, the four bodies studied were quite cooperative and appreciative of what was being done. The two Protestant groups were eager, I know personally, to have the results of the analysis, which were available first in dissertation form, and went over them very carefully for the benefit of their own thought and planning. The analyses were so thorough and penetrating that the author was able to identify quite clearly from internal evidence a number of those inevitable points of compromise in planning which, once arrived at, are glossed over with rhetorical devices.

In each of these chapters the analytical and comparative study yields material from which a discriminating decision may be made on the content of the principles themselves. In each case a principle is enunciated, for instance, the objective is stated as "that mature persons learn the mystery of Christ." Then subordinate principles, necessary implications, are delineated. The study is thus a fine example of the use of these formal categories, and the way in which they can guarantee theoretical integrity and at the same time provide the handles for grasping the necessities of practice. By the time the subordinate principles are set down, the design of adult Christian education becomes quite clear. Not that this means any rigidity or narrowness in the conception. Quite the contrary, what is produced is "sure ground" upon which a variety of plans may be built.

The last chapter is in the nature of a summary of the content of the six categories, restating the six principles and their subordinate principles, plus a summary of decisions on the organizing principle, evaluation, and administration.

Several years ago an age-level committee of the National Council of Churches produced a document entitled, *The Objective of Christian Education for Senior High Young People*. (New York: National Council of the Churches of Christ in the U.S.A., 1958.) Designed as it was for guidance of Christian education at one age level, it actually served to break open the whole question of curriculum theory and design in Christian education at every age level, because of the fact that it dealt with its age-level decisions in such basic terms. The same may well be true of this book. It is specifically written as an

introduction and guide to adult work, but it treats its subject in a way
that provides clarification, stimulus, and guidance for Christian educators at any age level. Actually we have here an ecumenical volume
addressed to every thoughtful Christian educator.

Important as are the formal aspects of the construction of the book,
they do not overshadow the substantive. What stands out in particular
is the way in which the book is throughout a discussion of Christian
education as "learning the mystery of Christ." For adult education
this is the epecially challenging task of *mature* persons engaging in
such learning, and doing so on the basis of the meaning of the
Church's experience of this mystery. The key is "interpersonal appropriation" in the community of faith.

As is to be expected in today's adult education, self-development
and planning of programs are stressed. But the "situational approach"
is to be solidly backed by a body of common, carefully considered
principles. And back of it all is the experience of the author himself
in the setting up, conduct, and evaluation of the GIFT (Growth
in Faith Together) program in his own Archdiocese of Baltimore. For
the practitioner there are included valuable instruments for planning
and evaluation developed in connection with this program.

D. CAMPBELL WYCKOFF

Princeton Theological Seminary
Princeton, New Jersey
March 8, 1972

Introduction

OPPORTUNITY

The mounting crisis in Catholic faith and discipline is alive with educational opportunities. This is especially true regarding adult education. It usually takes severe shock to convince a settled adult to learn —to learn, that is, in a way that is more personal than informational. Personal learning involves risk. Frequently, it is only when complacency entails greater risk, that an adult will dare to learn. The current crisis shatters complacency. The religious questions being asked, the initiatives being acted upon, the departures being taken are too threatening to the personal integrity of adult believers to be ignored. Unexamined faith is a luxury no longer available. Consequently, the opportunity is ripe for adult Christian learning of the most profound and engaging kind. The present situation, then, is not to be damned for its disturbing confusion but seized upon for its potential.

Fortunately, many parishes and schools are capitalizing upon the opportunity. Parishes sponsor lectures and discussion groups for interested adults. High schools provide programs for parents upset by what their sons and daughters are learning. Colleges offer credit and non-credit evening courses in religious studies.

PURPOSE

This book will not suggest specific programs for these various settings. It is not a book of recipes. Rather it will try to unlock the planning process itself. It will explore the art of program design so that persons on the local scene can plan programs themselves to meet the growing opportunity of adult Christian education.

I am convinced that adult education in any field must be planned as close to the grassroots as possible. "Canned" and imported programs have had little success in attracting adults. The reason is that

5

adults do not usually pursue learning unless they perceive a need for it, set their own learning goals, and feel a sense of responsibility for the success of the program itself.[1]

This book is written as a guide to grassroot planners. It presents a methodology of designing programs and offers principles to guide practical planning.

Technically speaking, this book provides a curriculum design for adult Christian education. Describing what each of those terms means will enlarge upon the purpose. These terms will receive further precision in the first chapter. Here they receive only preliminary explanation.

By *curriculum design* is meant, a set of consistent principles to guide program or curriculum planning. *Principles,* in turn, may initially be described as "rules of thumb" to guide practical curriculum decisions.

Curriculum, in itself, deserves clarification. In this study it means the sum of all learning experiences provided for in a program or a curriculum plan. It does not mean, then, textbooks or lesson plans. These latter may be referred to as curriculum materials or resources. *Curriculum plan* is also a carefully chosen term. Here it means an intentional and explicit provision of learning opportunities. Curriculum, as used in this book, then, might be differentiated from *"live" curriculum.* "Live" curriculum is the result of a spontaneous interaction of persons, persons and events, persons and things. "Live" curriculum happens without planning. Frequently, it provides the most significant learnings persons achieve. Curriculum consists rather of those learnings which are the result of intentional and explicit planning.

Moreover, we are dealing with *adult* education. By adults, I mean persons roughly of the age of twenty-five years and over who have commensurate maturity. The description is as arbitrary as it is loose. The only reason for selecting the age of twenty-five is that by that time most young men and women have completed formal schooling, wrestled through the identity crises of later youth, and chosen the life commitments that will usually occupy the rest of their adult years. Of set purpose, then, we shall not deal with the critical and creative years of eighteen to twenty-five. Nor shall we consider the special

---

[1] This theory is amply explained and tested in Paul Bergevin and John Mc-Kinley, *Design for Adult Education in the Church* (Greenwich, Conn.: The Seabury Press, 1958). For the psychology of adult learning upon which this theory is based, see Malcolm S. Knowles, "Androgogy, Not Pedagogy!" *Adult Leadership,* XVI, No. 10 (April, 1968), 350-52 and 386.

learnings which older age invites. We deal especially with the years from twenty-five to sixty-five.[2]

"With commensurate maturity" is purposely vague. There seem to be few measurements of maturity. Both random samplings of common sense measurements and the behavioral sciences agree that maturity is a continuing growth in autonomy and altruism. It is growth in auto-direction and in concern for others.[3] Commensurate maturity here means that the person has already achieved a degree of human stability and responsibility and will continue to grow in these qualities with or without Christian education. Hopefully, Christian education will facilitate his human maturation.

The title also specifies *Christian education* as the distinct enterprise for which this study develops principles. The term cannot be used lightly. Adapting D. Campbell Wycoff's definition,[4] I consider Christian education the ways and means by which, in accord with the character of Christianity and the process of education, persons freely participate in teaching and learning the Christian faith and life. This definition leaves undefined as much as it defines. *Education* itself needs to be defined. I consider education any continuous undertaking through which the participants intend consciously and primarily to learn. Learning goes on in many situations where learning is not the primary and conscious intention of the participants. It goes on in rearing a family, in working, in political endeavor, in social action. Education, however, is an undertaking designed precisely for learning.

This suggestion is deceptively obvious. But it may help us to differentiate Christian education from other agencies and programs in the diocesan and parochial structure which have educational aspects. Liturgical commissions, parish councils, family life bureaus, social action groups, to name but a few, are agencies in which much Christian learning goes on. But in most cases the conscious and primary intention of their participants is not to learn. It is, respectively, to guide worship, to order parochial life, to encourage family happiness, and to change social structures and relationships. It is true that each of these agencies may sponsor workshops, institutes, sessions, courses to

---

[2] This is not to say that many changes of life do not take place during these years and that these changes are not significant for learning. See at length, J. Roby Kidd, *How Adults Learn* (New York: Association Press, 1959), pp. 58-92.

[3] See Jeffrey Keefe, "Considerations on Maturity and the Catholic Priest," *Worship*, XLIII, No. 2 (February, 1969), 82-99.

[4] "Christian Education Redefined" in *The Church in the Modern World: Essays in Honor of James Sutherland Thomson*, ed. by George Johnston and Wolfgang Roth (Toronto: The Ryerson Press, 1967), pp. 222-23.

learn about liturgy, parish life, family concerns, and social needs. When they do, they sponsor programs of Christian education. In such instances, the purpose of the participants has become primarily to learn. The *intention* of the participants, then, both planners and members, is, I submit, what differentiates Christian education from other kindred services in the Church.

What renders education distinctively *Christian* is an even more problematic issue. I shall try throughout this work to identify the various points at which God, Christ, and the Church bear upon Christian education. I am persuaded, however, that it is especially with regard to scope (content or subject-matter) that the Christian aspect of Christian education is most determinate. Process (methods), too, has a distinctively Christian aspect; but, it can only be affirmed and not explained.[5]

I also think it possible to differentiate Christian education from religious and general education with respect to the scope of each. Anticipating the later argumentation of this study,[6] I see the scope of Christian education as the meaning of the Church's experience of the mystery of Christ. I see the scope of religious education more broadly as the meaning of mankind's experience of the mystery of God. More broadly still, I see the scope of general education as the meaning of mankind's experience of the mystery of man. These three delineations can be visualized as concentric circles. General education includes religious education; religious education, in turn, includes Christian education. Moreover, the distinctions are notional. They serve to set priorities among curriculum choices. The distinctions do not pretend that there is a trichotomy in learning, and still less in life, between some sort of human, religious, and Christian "realities."

With this clarification of terms, the purpose of the study should become more obvious. To propose a curriculum design for adult Christian education is to develop a set of consistent principles to guide the intentional and explicit provision of Christian learning for persons of twenty-five years and older which can be used in a variety of local situations.

BACKGROUND

This book grew out of a doctoral dissertation.[7] To disguise that fact

5 *Infra,* 150-52.

6 *Infra,* 109-16.

7 James R. Schaefer, *"A Proposed Curriculum Design for Adult Christian Education for Use in Catholic Dioceses,"* an unpublished doctoral dissertation, The Catholic University of America, Washington, D.C., 1971 (cited hereafter as *Dissertation.*)

is pointless. The academic style breaks through at enough junctures to make the fact obvious.

However, the Dissertation has been completely reorganized and re-written for this publication. Moreover, two years of practical experience in adult education [8] and several workshops wherein the results of the Dissertation were demonstrated and criticized have changed the content and form of the original significantly.

Knowing of the Dissertation may, however, be useful to the reader. I shall refer to it frequently in the notes (cited simply as *Dissertation*) when fuller justification for broad statements seems desirable.

Knowing its procedure is even more useful. The Dissertation follows a different order than this work.[9] It proceeds in four steps: a methodology of curriculum design (Part I); analyses of Protestant designs (Part II); analyses of Catholic diocesan curriculum planning (Part III); and the development of a curriculum design from the previous analyses and the foundational disciplines (Part IV).

Since a methodology for designing adult Christian education programs was lacking when the Dissertation was begun,[10] it was necessary to develop one. Then the methodology was used to analyze Protestant and Catholic designs and was reevaluated in light of its use. The methodology which appears in the first Chapter of this book is not the same as the methodology in the first Chapter of the Dissertation but the one resulting from use and reevaluation which comes at the end of the Dissertation.

The analyses of Protestant and Catholic designs which occupy four Chapters and two hundred and sixty-six pages of the Dissertation do not survive in this book save by way of incidental examples. The analyses were necessary to arrive at practical and tested principles to guide adult Christian education planning. This book only gives the refinement of those principles.

The two Protestant designs analyzed were those of the American

[8] The author is director and chief designer of the GIFT (Growth *In* Faith *T*ogether) program developed in the Archdiocese of Baltimore and published by Paulist Press. See James R. Schaefer, "Baltimore's GIFT Program," *Today's Parish*, July/August, 1971, pp. 3-5, and *idem* "GIFT—An Adult Program that Works," *The Living Light*, VIII, No. 3 (Fall, 1971), 77-88.

[9] The table of contents of the *Dissertation* appears in Appendix A, *infra*, 203-06.

[10] Happily, methodologies of program design in adult Christian education are now developing rapidly. See *An Overview of the Steps in Program Planning* (distributed by United Church of Christ, Council for Lay Life and Work, P. O. Box 7286, St. Louis, Mo. 65177. [n.d.]). *Planning Curriculum Locally—A Situational Approach to Lay Education—A Training Design for Presbyterians and Synods* (distributed by Board of Christian Education, Presbyterian Church, U.S., Richmond, Va. 1970). John McKinley and Robert M. Smith, *Guide to Program Planning* (New York: Seabury Press, 1965). Eloise Roth Rhodes, *Planning in the Local Setting* (distributed by Central Distribution Service, Box 7286, St. Louis, Missouri, 1970).

Baptist Convention and of the United Presbyterian Church in the U.S.A. The first is a centrally-designed curriculum for adults based upon the Cooperative Curriculum Project of the National Council of Churches.[11] It reveals both the advantages and disadvantages of a program developed at a national headquarters for use in local congregations and based upon an explicit methodology and careful research.[12]

The second design adopts a "situational approach" to adult Christian education. Although the United Presbyterian Church was the first to develop a comprehensive curriculum [13] for member congregations, it changed to a policy of encouraging local churches to plan their own adult education in 1968.[14] The experiment provides useful lessons for Catholic adult education which almost without exception is planned "situationally."

The Dissertation also studies two Catholic diocesan approaches to adult education planning—those of Baltimore, Maryland and of Lansing, Michigan. First the adult programs sponsored by each are described. Then the replies of diocesan staff persons to a questionnaire are presented and analyzed.[15] The questionnaire has been revised in light of my changed methodology and may be found in Appendix C.[16] The questionnaire may be useful for testing the consistency of

---

[11] The Cooperative Curriculum Project is the work of sixteen Protestant denominations to devise a central curriculum resource from which denominations might construct curriculum plans for all age groups. They labored for four years (1960-64). The product is published in *The Church's Educational Ministry: A Curriculum Plan*, the Work of the Cooperative Curriculum Project of the National Council of Churches in the U.S.A. (St. Louis: The Bethany Press, 1965). (Cited hereafter as *CCP*). In 1964, sixteen more denominations, eleven of the original and five new members, worked together for two and a half years (1964-66) to make the results of CCP more applicable to denominations and local congregations. The product of their efforts may be found in *Tools of Curriculum Development for the Church's Educational Ministry*, the work of Cooperative Curriculum Development (Anderson, Ind.: Warner Press, Inc., 1967) and in *Specialized Resources for National Curriculum Developers in the Church's Educational Ministry*, the work of Cooperative Curriculum Development (New York: Division of Christian Education, National Council of Churches of Christ in the United States of America, 1967). For more on the Cooperative Curriculum Project and Cooperative Curriculum Development, see *Dissertation*, 117-21.

[12] See *Dissertation*, Chapter II, 117-89.

[13] In Protestant circles, a comprehensive curriculum is a set of systematically planned learnings for all age groups (infancy through old age) and all settings (Sunday school, church school, camp, etc.) together with their materials and resources.

[14] See *Dissertation*, Chapter III, 190-277.

[15] In the *Dissertation*, Chapter IV, 282-333 analyzes Lansing's planning approach and Chapter V, 334-80, analyzes Baltimore's.

[16] *Infra*, 217-25.

adult program designs, the principles that govern them, and the assumptions that underlie those principles.

It was necessary to use a questionnaire to study the Catholic planning approaches because unlike the Protestant Boards of Christian Education, Catholic diocesan offices seldom publish principles of design and their presuppositions upon which programs are based. Yet these principles and their foundations are precisely what the Dissertation wished to unearth and this present book wishes to explicate.

After analyzing the four adult designs, the Dissertation compares all their principles and presuppositions and constructs from them a single master design. Only the principles which I consider most validly justified remain in this work. Readers who desire to explore the argumentation further may consult Chapter VI (pp. 383-456) of the Dissertation.

In many instances, however, I found no single principle nor a combination of them from the designs adequate to resolve a particular curriculum problem. In these instances I framed new principles. Then I offered theological and educational justification for these new principles. This effort occupies Chapter VII (pp. 457-555) of the Dissertation and represents the most original work of the whole thesis. To a great extent this present work is an expansion of Chapter VII punctuated and illustrated by data from Chapters II through VI.

OUTLINE

How then does this book proceed? The first Chapter provides a methodology for designing adult Christian education programs. The methodology identifies six invariant factors which must be dealt with somehow or other in program design. They are objective, personnel, scope, process, context, and timing. It also articulates the major and subordinate questions to be faced regarding each of those factors. The methodology further indicates the data sources from which those questions can be answered.

Each succeeding Chapter takes one of those factors and presents both the principles and their justification which I think best answer the questions posed by the methodology. Thus the second Chapter treats the objective, the third personnel, the fourth scope, the fifth process, the sixth context, and the seventh timing.

An eighth Chapter presents a summary of the principles and demonstrates how all of them are mutually consistent with one another.

The resulting design may be used as a kind of master model from which to derive a variety of practical designs for grassroots programs.

ANALYTIC PLANNING

The enterprise upon which this study embarks relies upon a premise which may not enjoy broad agreement. The premise is that curriculum design should be done analytically and systematically. The counter premise may appeal to many: "Why not just let adult Christian education happen?" "Why analyze it to death?" "Why suffocate it with system?" The counter premise seems convinced that adult Christian education will be more creative to the degree that it is more spontaneous.

The counter premise may be true. One gets the impression that the United Presbyterian Division of Lay Education abandoned systematic curriculum design for adults [17] precisely because system stifled initiative. One also finds support for the counter premise in the imagination and resourcefulness of many Catholic adult programs.

However, I remain convinced that analytic and systematic planning holds more promise than a "creative mess" approach to adult Christian education. Moreover, the promise which analytic planning holds is precisely that of higher and more sustained creativity. Once the factors are identified which interact in any learning situation, once principles can be thought through to guide one's choice of variables among those factors, once the data sources of adult Christian education are known and their relevance to curriculum traced, it becomes possible to discern whether a "new" technique is new or old, whether a "different" program is innovative or imitative, whether a change in procedure will frustrate or facilitate a desired outcome. The proof of this statement, however, must await the unfolding of the study itself. The reader will have to judge for himself at the end whether analytic and systematic planning of curriculum is a help or a hindrance to creative adult Christian education.

There is another way of putting the matter. In his survey paper *Catholic Adult Education*,[18] Vaile Scott offers "guidelines for the movement toward a genuine adult education program in the Church." His guidelines are:

17 Not altogether, however; see *Dissertation*, 192 and 232-33.
18 N.C.E.A. Papers, No. 4 (distributed by N.C.E.A. Papers, Box 667, Dayton, Ohio, 1968).

1) a study of the broad field of adult education, background, theory, and practice, to gain from the experience and research of others; 2) a critical appraisal of the traditional forms of adult involvement in the Church which considers their underlying philosophy, methods and impact; followed by an exploration of how best to accomplish the goals for a renewed Church set forth in the Vatican II documents; and culminating in the formulation of a rationale for Catholic adult education; 3) adequate provision for multiple experiments by agencies and institutions with diversified points of view; and 4) a plan for achieving maximum communication on a local and national level among those who are engaged in adult education, including theologians, educators, clergy, religious, and lay people.[19]

The Dissertation addressed itself to the second guideline. It undertook a critical appraisal of present forms of adult Christian education at least in terms of their philosophy and methods. It culminated in the formulation of a rationale for Catholic adult education, if by rationale, Mr. Scott approximates my meaning of curriculum design. Although the critical appraisal of present forms of adult education does not find a place in this book, a curriculum design for the future does.

Furthermore, the methodology of curriculum design which is here explained may provide the necessary vehicle for the communication which Scott insists upon in his fourth guideline. For unless there is basic agreement among "theologians, educators, clergy, religious, and lay people" as to a common identification of curriculum factors, a common articulation of questions regarding each factor, and a common way of framing principles from the experience of Christian education and from the foundational disciplines—in short, unless there is a common language of adult Christian education, then the most extensive conversations among all parties will compound confusion rather than cooperation.

I offer the methodology of this study as one vehicle of communication and the resultant curriculum design as a developed rationale for adult Christian education. I hope that adult Christian educators will find both useful and will contribute their insights to this work of program design which is in its infancy.

[19] *Ibid.,* 7.

CHAPTER I

The Elements and Dynamics of Curriculum Design

THE PROBLEM

ANYONE WHO HAS a part in planning adult Christian education programs faces literally hundreds of questions. "Should courses be offered?" "What kinds of courses?" "How long should they run?" "Should they take the form of lectures?" "Should discussion be encouraged?" "How?" "Would it be best to forsake formal courses and use happenings or social involvement as learning opportunities?" "How do adults learn most effectively?" "What kinds of learning should be given high priority?" "What are adults most interested in?" "Which adults?" "Is a programmed sequence of learnings desirable?" "Should existing reading materials be utilized or new ones developed?" "Who is going to administer the program?" "Should it be conducted in parishes, in special centers, in homes?" "What is the purpose of adult Christian education?" "Why not use movies as a teaching medium?" "Who should deal with these questions: learners? teachers? sociologists? psychologists? theologians? the parish priest? a diocesan director?"

This is but a random sampling of the myriad questions that program designers face.[1] Each decision taken will eliminate several promising options that might have been pursued. Yet, curriculum planning is essentially a matter of making such choices.

Necessary, then, are categories of inquiry which will organize the questions in a manageable way, reveal their interdependency, suggest priorities among them, and differentiate the questions that arise immediately out of the practical task of curriculum planning from those

[1] For a lengthy list of questions confronting adult Christian education, see *Wider Horizons in Christian Adult Education*, Selected Addresses and Papers Presented in a Workshop on the Curriculum of Christian Education for Adults, Pittsburgh, Pennsylvania, June 19-30, 1961, ed. by Lawrence C. Little (Pittsburgh: University of Pittsburgh Press, 1962).

which search after assumptions underlying their answers. The purpose of this chapter is to delineate such categories of inquiry and to demonstrate their adequacy in organizing the major questions which program designers must meet. It wishes also to indicate the kinds of answers they require and the sources from which those answers may be derived. This chapter seeks, then, to outline what might be called a conceptual system or a methodological model or an heuristic structure by which to deal with unavoidable curricular questions in adult Christian education.

RESOURCES FOR ESTABLISHING CATEGORIES OF INQUIRY [2]

Adult Christian education is not alone in facing the task of establishing categories by which to organize curricular questions. John Goodlad awards the same problem primacy of importance in general education curriculum research.

Out of a multitude of topics worthy of research, a few are proposed to suggest the richness of the potential harvest awaiting the eager researcher's whetted scythe:
1. Conceptual systems which identify the major questions to be answered in developing a curriculum must be rigorously formulated. The elements that tie these questions together in a system must be classified; subordinate questions must be identified and classified properly in relation to the major questions; sources of data to be used must be revealed in answering the questions posed by the system; and the relevance of data extracted from these sources must be suggested.[3]

Especially in developing categories of inquiry, theorists of adult Christian education curriculum find themselves facing a similar task to that of theorists in general education curriculum. They can profit much from the latters' organization of curricular questions.[4] An illus-

---

[2] From here on this chapter may prove tedious to the reader who is uninterested in the origins of curriculum methodology. If uninterested one might read Appendix B, QUESTIONS TO ASK IN PLANNING A PROGRAM, 207-16, which is a brief and popular summary of this chapter. It would also be helpful to read at least the summary of this chapter, 64-69, before proceeding to the subsequent chapters.

[3] John I. Goodlad, *School, Curriculum, and the Individual* (Waltham, Mass.: Blaisdell Publishing Company, 1966), p. 137.

[4] I have found helpful, besides Goodlad, Vernon E. Anderson, *Principles and Procedures of Curriculum Improvement* (2d ed.: New York: The Ronald Press Company, 1965); J. Galen Saylor and William M. Alexander, *Curriculum Planning*

trative example is the organization of questions that can be found in
the first chapter of *Developing a Curriculum for Modern Living* developed by the Horace Mann-Lincoln Institute of Teachers College,
Columbia University. The following are identified as major curricular
questions: "What shall be the role of the school in achieving educational goals?" "What to teach—toward what knowledge, understandings, and skills shall experience be guided?" "How shall the curriculum
be organized?" "How to teach—how shall curriculum experiences be
guided?" "Who should be taught what under a curriculum that provides for all pupils?" "How shall pupil growth and progress be
evaluated?" "How shall curriculum improvement be assured?" [5]
Several subordinate questions follow each major one. Three foundational areas are identified from which answers may be found. They
are the fields of sociology, psychology, and philosophy.[6]

Helpful as such a conceptual system is in differentiating questions
and identifying foundational areas from which they might be answered, adult Christian education can adopt it only partially.

General education curriculum design begins with a determined context, the public school system, where a classroom or laboratory is
the traditional setting, where a teacher-pupil relationship is fairly
well defined, where pupils are usually divided into grades by age and
achievement, and where the duration of the school year is established
by civil law. In short, general education usually addresses itself to an
inherited context and prearranged settings. Catholic adult education is
largely without either. Therefore, its categories of inquiry must incorporate questions of context and setting. Nothing would be more
inimical to an imaginative and varied adult Christian education program than the untested assumption that it belongs of necessity in the
classroom or lecture hall.

Moreover, general education curriculum planning provides learning
opportunities for pupils roughly from the ages of six through eighteen whose readiness levels and measureable growth in learning can

for Better Teaching and Learning (New York: Rinehart & Company, Inc., 1954);
B. Othanel Smith, William O. Stanley, and J. Harlan Shores, *Fundamentals of
Curriculum Development* (rev. ed.; Yonkers on Hudson, N.Y.: World Book Com-
pany, 1957); and especially Florence B. Stratemeyer *et al., Developing a Curriculum
for Modern Living* (2d ed. rev. and enlarged; New York: Bureau of Publications,
Teachers College, Columbia University, 1957).

[5] Stratemeyer *et al., Developing a Curriculum. . . ,* 3-25. For a different ordering
of basic curricular questions, cf. Saylor and Alexander, *Curriculum Planning. . . ,*
39-70.

[6] Stratemeyer *et al., Developing a Curriculum. . . ,* 22-23.

be predicted and evaluated with fair success.[7] The adult years do not seem to be similarly characterized by readiness levels common to most persons of the same age and background. At least, current research has not been significantly successful in identifying them.[8] Consequently, adult Christian education lacks one of the important factors which determines to a large extent the sequence of learning opportunities in general education, that of the psychological readiness of the learner.

Despite these differences, adult Christian education can borrow from general education theory a methodological model including categories of major and subordinate questions, many of which will be relevant to adult education. It can also profit from the identification of foundational sources from which the answers to those questions can be derived.

Such "a theory of Christian-Adult education methodology" was called for by Professor Malcolm Knowles at a Workshop on the Curriculum of Christian Education for Adults held at the University of Pittsburgh, June 19-30, 1961.[9] He outlined the practical functions and conditions it would have to meet.

A good theory provides a conceptual structure for understanding a given body of phenomena and for predicting how these phenomena will respond to various influences. . . .

The practical effect of a good theory is to provide a set of guiding principles for the selection of means that will most effectively accomplish given ends. An adequate theory of Christian adult education methodology would, therefore, help Christian adult educators in several ways: (1) by enabling them to define educational objectives more precisely and realistically; (2) by guiding them in planning sequences of learning experiences that would

---

[7] See Erik H. Erikson, *Childhood and Society* (2d ed. rev. and enlarged; New York: W. W. Norton & Company, Inc., 1963); *idem, Identity: Youth and Crisis* (New York: W. W. Norton & Company, Inc., 1968); John H. Flavell, *The Developmental Psychology of Jean Piaget,* The University Series in Psychology, ed. David C. McClelland (Princeton, N.J.: D. Van Nostrand Company, Inc., 1963); Robert J. Havighurst, *Human Development and Education* (New York: David McKay Company, Inc., 1953); and L. Joseph Stone and Joseph Church, *Childhood and Adolescence: A Psychology of the Growing Person* (2d ed.; New York: Random House, 1968).

[8] See Kidd, *How Adults Learn,* 33-57. A more promising venture than describing readiness levels by age is that of identifying adult developmental tasks through which significant learnings occur. See Havighurst, *Human Development. . . ,* 257-83 and Malcolm S. Knowles, "Program Planning for Adults as Learners," *Adult Leadership,* XV (Feb., 1967), 268 and 278-79.

[9] Selected addresses and papers delivered at the workshop are published in Little (ed.), *Wider Horizons. . . .*

move consistently toward ultimate goals; (3) by providing a basis for selecting (or inventing) methods that would most effectively accomplish each objective; and (4) by providing criteria against which the results of their efforts can be tested.

At least some of the more obvious conditions that an adequate theory of Christian adult education methodology would have to meet are the following:

1. It is based on a coherent conception of the purpose of education.
2. Its methodological principles are consistent with existing knowledge about the nature of the learning process.
3. Its methodological principles take into account the unique charac-teristics of adult learners.
4. It provides criteria for selecting methods appropriate to different objectives.
5. It provides a basis for measuring outcomes.[10]

Professor Knowles is correct in naming the provision of guiding principles as the practical effect of theory. He is correct also in giving primary importance to objectives (purpose) in the planning of educa-tional experiences and methods for adults. He does well to insist that the methodological principles be consistent with the nature of the learning process and take into account the unique characteristics of adult learners. Professor Knowles does not, however, offer categories of inquiry nor does he differentiate major from subordinate questions nor does he supply a method of deriving from foundational sources the answers to those questions.[11] He does not, in short, offer the kind of conceptual system that John Goodlad calls for in general education curriculum research and which Florence Stratemeyer and her coauthors work out to some degree for general education curriculum design. For a methodological model which will include both the categories of in-quiry and the method of deriving answers from data or foundational sources one must look elsewhere.

First, it is necessary to understand in greater detail what Professor Goodlad means by a conceptual system.

By conceptual system, I mean a carefully engineered framework designed to identify and reveal relationships among complex, related, interacting phenomena; in effect, to reveal the whole where wholeness might not other-

10 *Ibid.*, 74-75.

11 At the time of revising this chapter, I was inexcusably ignorant of Professor Knowles' *The Modern Practice of Adult Education: Androgogy versus Pedagogy* (New York: Association Press, 1970). In that excellent work Knowles provides a more complete system of program design.

wise be thought to exist. Such a system consists of categories abstracted from the phenomena that the system is designed to describe and classify, categories which can be readily discussed and manipulated at consistent, clearly identifiable levels of generality and which can be developed from different perspectives.

. . . .

Just as a conceptual system has structure, so does it perform functions. In curriculum, then, it facilitates the following: (1) the identification of problems and questions presumably having relevance to planning any instructional program; (2) the clarification of the types of inquiry likely to be productive in dealing with these problems and questions (i.e., empirical inductive or theoretical deductive or some combination of the two); (3) the revelation of possible connections among these problems and questions; (4) the identification of promising data-sources for dealing with these problems and questions; and (5) the initiation of processes designed to reveal the relevance of these sources and of data extracted from them to the problems and questions classified by the system.[12]

After a brief review of the curriculum inquiry of the last fifty years; a sampling of research questions from courses labeled "curriculum" and "curriculum theory"; and the lament, "we know not what *curriculum*—in contrast to a curriculum—is, and choose not to name it"; [13] Goodlad adopts Ralph Tyler's four questions as a productive beginning toward answering functions (1) and (3) above.

1. What educational purposes should the school seek to attain?
2. What educational experiences can be provided that are likely to attain these purposes?
3. How can these educational experiences be effectively organized?
4. How can we determine whether these purposes are being attained? [14]

Goodlad wisely sees these questions as but the beginning of framing curriculum categories. They describe adequately, Goodlad seems to infer,[15] the "substantive categories" of curriculum planning. They do not identify the "levels of decision-making, specified according to remoteness from the learner." [16] He suggests three levels of decision-making in general education curriculum design: "Instructional (with decisions primarily the responsibility of a teacher or team of teachers

12 Goodlad, *School, Curriculum.* . . , 141-42.
13 *Ibid.,* 142-44.
14 *Ibid.,* 144. Smith, Stanley, and Shores, *Fundamentals of Curriculum Development,* vii, adopt the same four categories.
15 Goodlad, *School, Curriculum.* . . , 144-45.
16 *Ibid.,* 146.

guiding a specific group of learners); institutional (with decisions primarily the responsibility of total faculty groups under the leadership of administrators); and societal (with decisions the responsibility of lay boards and legislators at local, state, and Federal levels of government)".[17]

This identification of levels of decision-making is obviously tailored for general public school education, but the very model is a reminder to adult Christian educators that in addition to "substantive" categories of inquiry it must provide for a personnel category which will identify levels of curriculum decision-making. What place do learner, teacher, pastor, diocesan coordinator, and the College of Bishops have in the process of curriculum design? Not only is it necessary to identify these levels of curriculum decision-making, it is also necessary, in Goodlad's judgment, to specify the types of decision involved on each level, their processes (transactional or deductive), and the interdependency of one level's decision upon the other.[18]

In addition to identifying four "substantive" categories and three levels of decision-making, Goodlad also addresses himself to the problem of the influence of data sources upon curriculum decisions.

A conceptual system identifies data sources to be consulted in seeking to answer problems and questions identified by the system and in conducting processes implied by that system. Ideally, one would expect curriculum workers to turn exclusively to the best knowledge available—that is, the data source of funded knowledge—in making curriculum decisions. But observation of practice reveals otherwise. . . . Conventional wisdom rather than funded knowledge becomes the prime data source. For some decision, it is desirable to seek out what the body politic or subpublics of it believe to be true or to be good and desirable. For other decisions, it is desirable to seek out the viewpoints of specialists in given fields of knowledge. A conceptual system in curriculum should point to the data source or sources likely to be most relevant to the kind of decision to be made.[19]

Having adopted four "substantive" categories, identified three levels of decision-making, and indicated two kinds of data sources for decisions, Dr. Goodlad summarizes his conceptual system for general education curriculum study.

Sketched in broad strokes, then, a conceptual system . . . would include at least the following:

17 *Ibid.*, 145.
18 *Ibid.*, 145-46.
19 *Ibid.*, 146.

1. An identification of levels of decision-making, specified according to remoteness from the learner. Three possible categories, moving successively away from the learner are instructional, institutional, and societal.

2. An elaboration of the substantive curriculum decisions and subdecisions at each level.

3. A specification of the *type* of decisions to be effected at each level and between levels of the system. This specification would include the processes involved in studying and effecting these decisions; hence, transactional decisions lend themselves nicely to empirical analysis, deductive decisions lend themselves to logical analysis, although such a neat separation oversimplifies.

4. An identification of appropriate data sources to be consulted for each type of decision; *e.g.*, funded knowledge in contrast to conventional wisdom.

5. A clarification of authority and responsibility for decisions based on office and of authority and responsibility based on proximity of individuals or classes of individuals to appropriate data.[20]

Though developed as a conceptual system to assess critically the decisions underlying general education curriculum, Dr. Goodlad's outline provides a valuable set of criteria to measure the validity and comprehensiveness of the categories of inquiry in curriculum planning for adult Christian education. It should be noted, however, that Goodlad's summary above deals directly with the responses to questions within the categories of inquiry, i.e., with curricular *decisions*. The prior interest of this chapter is to establish the categories of *questions* which underly the decisions to be made. In that interest it is necessary to return to Goodlad's starting point and build precisely for adult Christian education curriculum the steps which brought him to his summary. In other words, it is necessary to begin afresh (1) rigorously to formulate the major questions to be answered in developing a curriculum for adult Christian education, (2) to identify and classify subordinate questions properly in relation to the major ones, (3) to classify elements that tie these questions together in a system, (4) to reveal sources of data to be used in answering the questions, and (5) to suggest the relevance of data extracted from these sources.

In my judgment, the most comprehensive, manageable, and sharply defined categories of inquiry available to serve as a methodological model for the major and subordinate questions which Christian education curriculum design must face are those developed by the Cooperative Curriculum Project.[21] These categories are especially useful as explained and further developed by Dr. D. Campbell Wyckoff, Pro-

20 *Ibid.*
21 See *supra*, 10.

fessor of Christian Education, Princeton Theological Seminary.[22] Wyckoff's categories of inquiry are intended for a theory of Christian education curriculum for the whole life span. Consequently they apply to adult Christian education.

Beginning with his first book, *The Task of Christian Education*,[23] Wyckoff's concern with developing categories of inquiry has increased measureably with his participation in the efforts of the National Council of Churches which culminated in the Cooperative Curriculum Project. His *The Gospel and Christian Education* [24] and especially his *Theory and Design of Christian Education Curriculum* [25] evidence both his growing interest in the enterprise and success in defining the categories themselves. This task remains the absorbing preoccupation of his publications and seminars today.[26]

In a recent address, February, 1967, Dr. Wyckoff articulated his present thinking on the genesis and functions of curriculum categories of inquiry. His remarks are directed toward developing Christian education as a discipline, but they are equally relevant to a methodological model for handling curriculum questions.

The construction and reconstruction of theory is first of all a matter of establishing basic categories for inquiry, and hammering those categories into a framework for thought about the field. Once the framework is established (subject, of course, to refinement and reworking), the Christian educator will know where to go in the related disciplines, and what to ask of them. With these resources gathered and organized, principles may be formulated, fleshing out the skeletal framework of the discipline. These principles are to be used in setting up, guiding, and correcting the enterprise, and in the process tested, experimented with, and subjected to research.

The establishment of religious education as a discipline, . . would not in any sense imply divorce from the practicalities of the enterprise. I see religious education as a practical discipline, deriving its categories from the questions that inevitably arise in the process of trying to carry on the enterprise effectively and intelligently. I see the derivation and substantiation

---

[22] Dr. Wyckoff was an active consultant to the Cooperative Curriculum Project especially with respect to its theoretical design and planning stages (*CCP*, iv). For an appreciation of his services, see L. Harold DeWolf, *Teaching Our Faith in God* (Nashville: Abingdon Press, 1963), p. 5.

[23] (Philadelphia: The Westminster Press, 1955).

[24] (Philadelphia: The Westminster Press, 1959).

[25] (Philadelphia: The Westminster Press, 1961).

[26] I am grateful to Dr. Wyckoff for participation in his course "Principles of Christian Education" during the second semester of the scholastic year, 1967-68; for a guided reading program in Christian education curriculum design during the same semester; and for numerous interviews while researching and writing this study.

of theory as undergirding an informed and valid practice in religious education.[27]

Later in the address he named and briefly described six categories of inquiry.

I have elsewhere spent considerable effort in trying to establish that the basic categories for the discipline of Christian education are: objective, scope, context, process, personnel, and timing. In other words, a theory encompassing our purpose, the essential content and experience involved in our education enterprise, the setting in which it can most integrally take place, the procedures and methods to be used, the partners to the enterprise and their various roles, and the sequence anticipated and planned for, will provide the conceptual guidance required for the planning, conducting, and evaluation of the practical enterprise.[28]

Those familiar with the categories developed by the Cooperative Curriculum Project will recognize Wyckoff's first three: objective, scope, and context.[29] They will find that the Project's fourth component, learning tasks, has been redefined by Wyckoff as process and that he has developed two additional categories—timing and personnel. Although he had described all six categories earlier,[30] he first called for a redefinition of learning tasks in terms of process and the addition of timing and personnel in a review of the Cooperative Curriculum Project's comprehensive volume, *The Church's Educational Ministry: A Curriculum Plan.*

As this new design for Protestant curriculum is used and examined there is one suggestion that might be kept in mind. . . . The element of learning

27 "Toward a Definition of Religious Education as a Discipline," *Religious Education,* LXII (Sept.-Oct., 1967), 390.

28 *Ibid.,* 393.

29 *CCP,* 7-36. The Cooperative Curriculum Project speaks of "Components" of curriculum design which answer to the categories of inquiry. They identify the organizing principle as "a proper fifth component of the Design itself," *CCP,* 35, seeming to imply that it, too, answers to a distinct category of inquiry. I prefer to treat the organization of the curriculum as a "general curriculum concern" to distinguish it from the six categories of curriculum inquiry which it both resembles and differs from. See *infra,* pp. 50-51.

30 "An Organizing Principle for the Curriculum," an unpublished address delivered at the World Consultation on the Curriculum of Christian Education, Fürigen, Switzerland, June 13-July 4, 1964 (author's copy). (Xeroxed.) (Cited hereafter as "Fürigen address".) A report on the address, summarizing its main points and appearing under the author's byline but not written by him, may be found under the title, "Finding a Sound Design," in *World Christian Education,* XIX (4th Quarter, 1964), 118-19.

tasks might be recast in terms of the element of process (the category of process raises a whole question; the learning tasks provide one answer), and elements of timing and personnel might be added.[31]

With minor variations, my methodology adopts Wyckoff's six categories both because of the order they place among the myriad questions confronting curriculum design and because of their comprehensiveness in meeting the significant factors to be weighed. After developing the categories and the data sources of their replies, I shall also attempt to show how they meet the expectations of Goodlad's conceptual system, improve upon his "substantive" categories, allow for his levels of decision-making, and trace more exactly the movement from data sources to curriculum decisions.

Six Categories of Curriculum Inquiry Applied to Catholic Adult Christian Education

The contention of this chapter is—along lines already charted by Wyckoff—that the major questions of curriculum design for any age group are reducible to six: why? who? what? how? where? when? To each major question corresponds a category of inquiry: objective, personnel, scope, process, context, and timing.

The reader may notice that I have changed Dr. Wyckoff's ordering of the categories. Wyckoff's order is objective, scope, context, process, timing, and personnel. I did so only after using his order to analyze the four adult designs in the Dissertation.[32] I propose the different order both because it better indicates the logical dependency of the categories one upon another and because it proves a more fruitful chronological order of asking the questions in actual program design.

Objective remains the first category because it provides the orientation for the whole enterprise of adult Christian education and the practical focus of any given program. Personnel deserves to be considered next especially in adult education because the needs and competencies of learners and resource persons determine the scope (content, subject matter) to be learned. Scope belongs in third place because it comprises the meanings which satisfy the needs of learners. Those meanings, in turn, suggest the kinds and modes of process through which the meanings might best be appropriated. The context or settings, in turn, depend upon the learning processes employed. Timing (the frequency

[31] "Design in Protestant Curriculum," *Religious Education*, LXI (May-June, 1966), 173.
[32] See *Dissertation*, 40-80 and 448-50.

and duration of learning experiences) also depends upon the time required for the process to work.[33]

Usually this order is reversed when planning curriculum for the academic setting. Context and timing are givens. The context is school buildings, classrooms, lecture halls, laboratories, auditoriums, etc., and the timing is set by the academic calendar. Faculty and administration then fill this time and these settings with learning. Adult Christian education is bound by no prearranged settings or scholastic year. Consequently, it can deal with the questions why? who? what? and how? first; and the answers to these questions can determine the answers to where? and when?

I do not mean that there is no reciprocal influence between the answers given to later questions and those given to former ones. Availability of space and the practicality of scheduling will greatly influence objective, scope, and process but the former questions should at least be considered before the latter.

This sequence may become more apparent as each of the categories of inquiry is more fully developed and the questions relating to each category articulated. To that task, we now turn.

The Category of Objective

Since Protestant Christian education from 1872 has grown more consciously both educational and ecumenical,[34] no topic has received more attention than that of objectives. In dialogue with general educators Protestant educators have increasingly discussed age-level objectives, teaching unit goals, and expected learning outcomes. In dialogue with one another, they have discussed on the one hand the relationship between the objective of the church's educational ministry and the purpose of the church itself and on the other the specifically Christian character of goals, aims, and outcomes in Christian learning.[35] With the development of comprehensive curriculums they

33 For a fuller explanation, see Appendix B, QUESTIONS TO ASK IN PLANNING A PROGRAM, 207-16.

34 1872 marked the beginning of cooperative Protestant ventures in Christian education with the decision of the International Sunday School Convention to issue the Uniform Lesson Series. It was not the American Sunday School Union as reported by Marvin J. Taylor, "A Historical Introduction to Religious Education," in *Religious Education: A Comprehensive Survey*, ed. *eodem* (Nashville: Abingdon Press, 1960), 19. See also *infra*, 52.

35 For discussions on objectives in Protestant Christian education, see Lawrence C. Little, "The Objectives of Protestant Religious Education," in Taylor (ed.), *Religious Education. . .*, 66-77; Randolph C. Miller, "The Objective of Christian Education," in *An Introduction to Christian Education*, ed. by Marvin J. Taylor (Nashville: Abingdon Press, 1966), pp. 94-104; and Wyckoff, *The Gospel. . .*, 120-25.

have been further pressed to specify objectives. The Cooperative Curriculum Project has been especially effective in channeling the discussion and occasioning a sophistication of concepts and honing of terms which may eventually promise commonly held definitions, questions, and responses. Moreover, the discussion on objectives has been largely responsible for differentiating the other categories of inquiry that are distinct from it. Unfortunately, Roman Catholic educators have been strangers to the dialogue. Now that they are producing curriculums posthaste, they find themselves in a comparable position regarding objectives to that of Protestant educators prior to 1930.[36]

The year 1930 saw the beginnings of order brought out of the confusion which had been "objectives." Paul H. Vieth published his *Objectives in Religious Education*.[37] In it he made a distinction, the fruitfulness of which was not to be appreciated until the discussions of the 1950's, between comprehensive and specific objectives.

Comprehensive objectives are the more general statements of value to be achieved by religious education. Specific objectives are the desired outcomes in the experience of growing persons which are necessary steps in realizing the more comprehensive objectives, or which are, specific instances of the comprehensive objectives.[38]

Cautioning further that "there is actually no line of demarcation which can be drawn between comprehensive and specific objectives," [39] he framed seven comprehensive objectives [40] to which an eighth was added in 1940.[41]

[36] James Michael Lee, "Behavioral Objectives in Religious Education," *The Living Light*, VII, No. 4 (Winter, 1970), 12-19.
[37] (New York: Harper & Brothers, 1930).
[38] *Ibid.*, 32.
[39] *Ibid.*, 33.
[40] *Ibid.*, 80-88. Vieth's seven comprehensive objects were "I. To foster in growing persons a consciousness of God as a reality in human experience, and a sense of personal relationship to him. (p. 80) II. To lead growing persons into an understanding and appreciation of the personality, life, and teaching of Jesus Christ. (p. 82) III. To foster in growing persons a progressive and continuous development of Christlike character. (p. 82) IV. To develop in growing persons the ability and disposition to participate in and contribute constructively to the building of a social order embodying the ideal of the fatherhood of God and the brotherhood of man. (p. 85) V. To lead growing persons to build a life philosophy on the basis of a Christian interpretation of life and the universe. (p. 86) VI. To develop in growing persons the ability and disposition to participate in the organized society of Christians—the church. (p. 87) VII. To effect in growing persons the assimilation of the best religious experience of the race, as effective guidance to present experience. (p. 88)" Each comprehensive objective is followed by several specific objectives.
[41] The eighth was "to develop in growing persons an appreciation of the meaning and importance of the Christian family, and the ability and disposition to

Vieth's objectives guided much of Protestant Christian education until several committees were authorized in 1952 by the Commission on General Christian Education of the National Council of Churches to reevaluate general and age group objectives.[42] Although a special Committee on Christian Education Objectives studied general objectives over a period of five years,[43] it was the deliberations of another committee on objectives for senior high youth that proved most influential both in framing the objective(s) that eventually prevailed in the Cooperative Curriculum Project and in charting the category of objective as to itself and as distinguished from other categories of curriculum inquiry.

The latter committee's study paper, *The Objective of Christian Education for Senior High Young People*,[44] traces a variety of meanings that the word "objective(s)" had taken on. Its catalogue of meanings is valuable in clarifying the category itself and others that should be distinguished from it.

"Objectives" have sometimes been formulated in terms of the situation, the needs, the interests, and the duties of the pupil and the group. . . . But these matters might better be thought of as motivations.

"Objectives" have also at times been identified with the content of the curriculum, that is, with the realities of Christian faith and the concerns of Christian life. . . . [What] some have called objectives at this point might better be called by some such term as "themes."

Sometimes curriculum, designed in terms of these *themes* . . . has been organized around *topics* or *problems,* which in turn have been identified as "objectives" to be arrived at by a series of teacher-pupil *goals.* This seems a legitimate use of the term "goals" (or even "objectives") because in the learning process the teacher and pupil together make plans involving specific learning tasks, carry out the plans, review and evaluate and set new goals. It is, however, very deceptive to generalize these goals into "age-level" objectives. . . . Every theorist who uses "age-level objectives" decries their use even as he steps into the trap. They might better be recognized for what they are—points on a sequential scale of achievement, or levels of progress,

---

participate in and contribute constructively to the life of this primary social group." See Miller, "The Objective. . . ," in Taylor (ed.), *An Introduction to Christian Education,* 96.

42 *Ibid.,* 96-98.

43 See the study document produced by the committee, *The Objectives of Christian Education: A Study Document,* published for the Commission on General Christian Education National Council of the Churches of Christ in the U.S.A. (New York: By the Office of Publication and Distribution, n. d. [1958]).

44 Authorized for publication and distribution as a study paper by the Commission on General Christian Education of the National Council of Churches (New York: By the Office of Publication and Distribution, 1958).

to which the idea of "age-levels" may very well be irrelevant in many instances.[45]

In this study *motivations, themes, topics* or *problems,* and teacher-pupil *goals* are all recognized as fulfilling essential roles in Christian education but these roles are viewed in the nature of means and not ends. They seem to fall into a proper relationship when they are identified as possible avenues toward a single basic objective.

In this study, therefore, "objectives" of Christian education are conceived not as a list of tasks to be performed or relationships to be dealt with or areas of content to be covered, but as one end toward which the whole process is directed. Thus "objectives" become singular, that is, the *objective* of Christian education. The value of one purpose or one end in view, i.e., a single objective, is that it provides direction and perspective for the entire process. Its strength is its drawing power—its ability to give unity, direction, and selectivity to the entire educational plan. . . .

The one objective is, therefore, the objective for every learning task, every lesson, every unit, every meeting throughout the whole curriculum. . . .

Thus it can be seen that in curriculum design no attempt should be made to have the suggested teacher-pupil goals add up cumulatively to the achievement of the single objective, nor should they be derived by segmenting the objective. The sum of these *goals, themes, motivations, topics* or *problems* does not equal the objective. Rather, all are seen and examined in the light of the objective.[46]

The committee had improved upon Paul Vieth's distinction between comprehensive and specific objectives by discovering that there is but one comprehensive or basic objective in the light of which goals, themes, motivations, and topics or problems are to be examined.

Dr. Wyckoff, a member of the committee, elaborates upon the "typology of objectives" that the committee worked out. He does so both in *The Gospel and Christian Education* [47] and in *Theory and Design of Christian Education Curriculum.*[48] The latter provides the more mature and detailed typology.

The most complete typology of objectives available at present consists of the basic objective, personal ends, themes, topics and problems, group and individual goals, learning tasks, steps in developmental sequence, anticipated behavioral outcomes, and standards.

Basic objective. The basic objective is a statement of the purpose or basic

[45] It would be well for Catholic religious educators to note this fact, should they decide to develop "behavioral objectives" as called for by James Michael Lee in "Behavioral Objectives. . . ." See *infra,* 31.

[46] Pp. 11-13.

[47] Pp. 114-20, 125-27.

[48] Pp. 59-70.

function, the focus providing perspective, for the entire educational process.
. . .

Any satisfactory statement of a basic objective must necessarily be similar to the purpose of the church, since they must be in accord with each other. A statement of the church's purpose, however, will stress mission and ministry while a statement of the purpose of Christian education will stress the ways in which the person and the group are fundamentally introduced to and inducted into that mission and ministry. What will be stressed then are awareness and response.

The existence and use of a basic objective does not eliminate the necessity for other types of objectives such as those listed below. . . . By itself, the basic objective cannot act as a tool for complete curriculum construction. . . .

Personal ends. The situation, needs, interests, concerns, and duties of the pupil and the group shape or constitute objectives for them. . . . [They] are the only objectives that are really ever accomplished. In a sense, then, Christian education's task is that of the reconstruction and transformation of personal and group ends. . . .

Themes. . . . Such objectives, for all that they prefix such phrases as "to help pupils know," or "to develop in growing persons," actually constitute analyses of curriculum content or scope. . . .

Topics and problems. Topics and problems represent specific adaptations of themes for purposes of curriculum construction. . . . A problem is a topic encountered, which accounts for the educational power of a problem. . . .

Group and individual goals. Sometimes known as classroom goals, unit aims, or lesson aims, these group and individual goals come into existence when teacher and pupils make plans involving specific learning tasks (sometimes together, but often unfortunately in an un-co-ordinated way), carry out the plans, review, evaluate, and set new goals. . . .

. . . .

Group and individual goals are used to guide a lesson, a unit, a year's work, a cycle; they give hints on procedure, keep the process on the track, and provide standards for evaluation; they are specific, detailed, simple, unitary, and cumulative.

. . . .

Teaching-learning units will be much more valuable if they will suggest *a range of goals* (all possible avenues toward the objective) from which particular groups and individuals may choose the one or more that may be most appropriate to their situation.

. . . .

Learning tasks. Learning tasks are the great general activities engaged in the learning process. In many respects group and individual goals and learning tasks are the same thing. . . .

. . . .

Steps in developmental sequence. Steps in developmental sequence are calibrated levels of progress. The concept is intended to be substituted for that of "age-level objectives." . . .

. . . .

"Age-level objectives" almost invariably are built on the extremely dangerous assumption that an average is an end. The false assumption is that rates of progress are, or should be, uniform in sequences of experiences involved in coming to grips with the great themes of the Christian faith and the Christian life.

. . . .

How shall useful calibrations of steps in developmental sequence be set up? The suggestion is that this be done in terms of the five great learning tasks. . . .

Anticipated behavioral outcomes. Anticipated behavioral outcomes are specific knowledges, skills, and attitudes expected to result from the educational process. Much of the interest in anticipated behavioral outcomes stems from the fact that educators generally feel that they are indispensable in evaluation. . . .

This viewpoint needs to be seriously challenged at several points. Anticipated behavioral outcomes cannot be used systematically in constructing the program of Christian education and its curriculum. Although the outcomes of Christian education are behavioral, they cannot be anticipated in a standard way. Christian education is relational, not behavioristic; bringing man into encounter with God, his world, his fellow man, and himself will have behavioral results that may be anticipated in a general way (in terms of awareness and response for instance) but they cannot be nailed down specifically in advance. Theologically, the relation of law and grace, and works and faith, is most pertinent here.

Although anticipated behavioral outcomes cannot determine the curriculum, they may serve a useful purpose in suggesting (not determining) possible topics and problems and group and individual goals. Furthermore, they will be useful in evaluation, not as standards to be applied in a rigid way but as clues to what is taking place in the development of the individual and the group. Thus serious attention to knowledge and understandings, attitudes, and action patterns related to the great concerns in terms of the accomplishment of the Christian learning tasks is merited if used with proper caution.

Standards. Winchester was calling for standards when he asked for formulation of aims in terms of school management and in terms of "the larger aspects of organization." Although not of the most direct concern to curriculum theory and design, standards must be included in any typology of educational objectives.[49]

[49] *Theory and Design. . . ,* 61-70. Another very thorough "typology of objectives," which reveals Wyckoff's influence, may be found in *Educational Guide,* prepared for the Educational Plan of the Church of the Brethren (no facts of publication given [Elgin, Ill.: Christian Education Commission of the General Brotherhood Board, 1968]), pp. 2, 20-23.

So detailed a typology of objectives may seem an exercise in schoolmen's distinctions, yet the neglect of it leads to conceptual and linguistic chaos.[50] Furthermore, these pages have been quoted at some length because they reveal the beginnings not only of a careful delineation of the category of objective but also the emergence of other discrete categories that were formerly lumped under the category of objectives. Thus themes, topics, and problems are assigned to the category of scope. Group and individual goals, especially insofar as they correlate with learning tasks, become the specialized category of process in Wyckoff's system.[51] Steps in developmental sequence become eventually for Wyckoff the category of timing.[52]

All that remains distinctly to the category of objective is the basic objective itself, the end toward which the Christian educational enterprise is directed. This objective is to be "comprehensive, complete, ultimate. It must not be conceived as partial, fragmented, or intermediate." [53] It should also display the lifelong nature of Christian education. It should reflect "the conviction that the Christian faith and life can never be thought of as finally accomplished," yet it should be "valid at any given moment of time and at every level of maturity." [54] It should embody the paradox of the Christian life, "the already but not yet" dimension of living in the final age. So conceived, the single basic objective of a given curriculum is what classical philosophy would understand by the *finis operis,* the end or purpose of the enterprise itself.

The objective may be defined, then, as *the overall purpose which a curriculum plan seeks to help the learner achieve.* Accordingly, the *category of objective* comprises the *irreducible and unavoidable questions* [55] *which seek that purpose.* Briefly, the category of objective asks the "why" of curriculum.

The Major Question in the Category of Objective.—The major question may most briefly be put: Why adult Christian education? Since

50 See, for instance, the aimlessness and inconsequence of the panel discussion and two symposiums on objectives and goals for adult Christian education in *The Future Course of Christian Adult Education.* Selected Addresses and Papers Presented in a Workshop on the Christian Education of Adults, Pittsburgh, Pennsylvania, June 15-17, 1958, ed. by Lawrence C. Little (Pittsburgh: University of Pittsburgh Press, 1959), pp. 109-24, 176-85, 235-50.

51 *Infra,* 42-43.

52 *Infra,* 47-48.

53 *CCP,* 7.

54 *Ibid.,* 9.

55 Here as in the following categories of inquiry, irreducible and unavoidable questions mean that all the questions should be included to which commonly

the question asks the *finis operis,* the single, basic, comprehensive objective of adult Christian education, another way of phrasing it is: What is the purpose of adult Christian education?

In answering the question, the temptation is to write a book. However, if the statement of overall purpose is to act as the focus or orientation of the whole enterprise, it must be lean and succinct despite its generality. Designers need not be frustrated at its breadth, inasmuch as every answer to each succeeding question in all the categories is but a further specification of the objective itself.

As stated, the question asks the purpose of adult Christian education at its most theoretical level. The question must also be asked, however, at a more practical level regarding the purpose of any actual program. It may be put: What is the purpose of this particular adult Christian education program? Obviously, the answer given the theoretical question will influence the answer given the more practical one.

Subordinate Questions in the Category of Objective.—Following the methodology of the Cooperative Curriculum Project, we assign many questions which were formerly considered subordinate questions regarding objective(s) to other categories of inquiry. There remain, however, two questions which seem necessary to ask with respect to the objective once it is stated. The first regards the function of the objective, the second its relationship to the purpose of the Church.

The first subordinate question may be put: What is (are) the function(s) of the objective? According to Wyckoff, "by itself, the basic objective cannot act as a tool for complete curriculum construction." [56] What positive contribution, however, can a clear statement of objective make to curriculum planning? Of necessity it must be a general statement if it is to present the overall goal of a curriculum plan. It risks being so general that its influence upon curriculum planning becomes meaningless. The first subordinate question, then, tries to identify the contribution which a concise, though general, statement of objective should make to curriculum planning.

The second subordinate question deals with the relationship between the objective of adult Christian education and the purpose of the Church. It may be stated: What is the relationship between the objective and the purpose of the Church? The basic objective of Chris-

---

faced curriculum problems are reducible. On the one hand, the questions seek to be inclusive; on the other, they seek to reduce several concrete questions to a single one which searches out a curriculum principle in the light of which the others might be answered.

[56] *Supra,* 30.

tian education must obviously be in harmony with the purpose of the Church; but the question asks whether the objective is coextensive with, exhaustive of, or subordinate to the overall purpose of the Church. The answer whether explicit or implied, underlies every practical decision program designers make vis-a-vis liturgy, pastoral counseling, the lay apostolate, mission, and whatever other facets of the Church's life and work involve considerable Christian learning. The answer spells the difference between adult Christian education's exercising imperialism over or ministry to other aspects of adult faith and life in the Church.

These are the questions which would seem best retained under the category of objective, while other questions are assigned to the following categories of curriculum inquiry.

The Category of Personnel

Personnel was not identified as a separate component of curriculum by the Cooperative Curriculum Project, although much about the learner's role [57] and something of God's role [58] are treated under the component of learning tasks. Nothing is said about the teacher's role, an omission which Wyckoff sought to correct in his expanded paper, *Learning Tasks in the Curriculum.*[59]

Wyckoff's delineation of personnel as a separate category of curriculum inquiry was first presented, along with timing, at Fürigen in the Summer of 1964.

Who is involved in Christian education? Who are the persons who are partners to the educational transaction, and what are their roles? There are simple and narrow ways of answering this question: pupils and teachers, group members and leaders, and special educational institutions and agencies. Without going into the matter in detail, an observation or two may be made. First, Christian education genuinely carried on involves learners (who are learning in many different settings and in many different ways, most of them not connected with the church), teachers (who are themselves learners, but who in this connection also act as guides who invite learners into educational experiences), and God himself (whose Holy Spirit is the teacher, thus requiring that human learners and teachers conduct their enterprise in an atmosphere of prayer and of receptivity to his leading.) [60]

57 *CCP,* 24-34.
58 *Ibid.,* 31-34.
59 (Valley Forge, Pa.: American Baptist Board of Education and Publication, 1965), pp. 46-56.
60 "Fürigen address," 7.

He has since given his attention to the various roles of learners, teachers, and "outside curriculum planners" much after the fashion of John Goodlad's differentiating "levels of decision-making, specified according to remoteness from the learner." He announced the need for attention to these roles in his review of the Cooperative Curriculum Project's *The Church's Educational Ministry: A Curriculum Plan.*[61] He framed several questions pertaining to these roles in his article, "—Learning—Planning—Goals," in 1967.[62] Together with the Christian Education Commission of the Church of the Brethren he worked out in detail a denominational comprehensive curriculum plan which is quite revolutionary in respecting roles proper to learners, teachers, the local congregation's committee on Christian education, and the denominational Board of Christian Education in building curriculum.[63]

In program design, then, personnel means the persons who are involved in the educational enterprise and the roles they fill in relation to one another. More concisely, *personnel* may be defined as *the persons who learn from and teach one another in the educational process.* The *category of personnel* comprises *the irreducible and unavoidable questions which seek to discover the persons who learn from and teach one another in the educational process and the roles according to which they interrelate.* It asks the "who" of curriculum.

The Major Question in the Category of Personnel.—With respect to adult Christian education, the major question in the category of personnel would seem to be: Who interrelate as learners and teachers in adult Christian education? The question does not wish to give the impression that some exclusively teach while others exclusively learn. Among the human partners to the transaction those who are characterized rather arbitrarily as "learners" do, in fact, teach one another and their "teachers." Those who are designated "teachers" are, in fact, learners as well.

The question seeks not so much a listing of roles as an awareness of the persons involved in adult Christian education in terms of their needs and competencies. Consequently, the very asking of the question alerts program planners to begin with a knowledge of the persons for whom and hopefully with whom they are planning. To address the

---

61 "Design in Protestant Curriculum," 173.

62 *Church School Worker,* XVIII (Sept., 1967), 9-17, especially 13-15.

63 *Supra,* 31 n. 49: *Educational Guide.* The Church of the Brethren plan is revolutionary insofar as it trains the local congregation in the elements and dynamics of curriculum design and then supplies them with a key sorting card catalogue of resources which can be added to as new resources are developed by independent publishers and producers.

question, planners must learn the conscious needs persons have or help them to a conscious desire for the learnings which the planners design. While children's education may get by with needs determined by curriculum planners, adult education must deal with persons in terms of their conscious needs, demonstrated interests, and actual capabilities.[64]

The presence of "interrelate" in the question indicates that the persons should also be identified with respect to their roles. A partial identification of the persons who are commonly seen to be interacting in adult Christian education as it takes place in practice begets the series of subordinate questions.

Subordinate Questions in the Category of Personnel.—The presence of the first Person whose role is to be considered is believed, rather than observed, on the basis of the theological premise upon which adult Christian education rests. The first subordinate question to be asked, then, is: What is God's role in adult Christian education? The question will be as impossible of certain answer as the other questions regarding God that arise in the other categories, yet tentative answers to it will determine the theological direction that adult Christian education will take. They may also persuade program designers to pray prior to and during the planning process.

The second subordinate question has special reference to Roman Catholic program designs. What is the role of the College of Bishops in adult Christian education? The question is based upon the Catholic theological premise that the bishops of the Church in communion with the Bishop of Rome play a special part with respect to Christian education.[65] The Catholic curriculum planner who neglects this question, neglects as well the dynamics that have brought about and continue to influence the Catholic community's faith and life.

A third subordinate question regards the most obvious partner in the education transaction: What is the learner's role in a curriculum plan? The cast of the question has shifted from that of the first two.

---

[64] In my original methodology the category of personal following Wyckoff, was last (see *Dissertation*, 75-80). The consideration that adult education must begin with felt needs, with adults "where they are," with the questions they are actually asking, caused me to place it second, after objective. The study of Baltimore's planning approach influenced this major revision in methodology (see *Dissertation*, 380, 436-38).

[65] Vatican Council II. See *The Documents of Vatican II*, ed. Walter M. Abbott, Translations directed by Joseph Gallagher with an introduction by Lawrence Cardinal Shehan (New York: Herder and Herder, 1966). (Cited hereafter as *DV II*.) "Lumen Gentium," art. 25, pp. 47-50.

They were answerable in terms of theological "givens" that should be weighed in planning any curriculum. This question admits a variety of answers depending upon the answers which will be given to questions regarding the scope and process of the program. In a lecturing process the learner's role will be that of an attentive listener. In a discussion process the learner's role will be that of a contributor. In a seminar process the learner's role will be that of a questioner.

In correlation to the answer given the previous question will be that made to the following: What is the teacher's role in a curriculum plan? If, indeed, "teaching may be conceived as the guidance of learning," [66] the answer to this question will have to be as responsive to selections regarding scope and process as is the previous one.

The next subordinate question concerns the interaction of the foregoing persons at the most decisive level of their interaction, that of designing the program itself: What are the roles of learners, teachers, and others in designing a curriculum? This question asks who should build the curriculum. It cannot be presupposed that a central planning board should make all decisions regarding the provision of learning opportunities for adults. The extent to which learners and teachers can contribute to planning their own curriculum should be considered. Here Dr. Goodlad's differentiation of "levels of decision-making, specified according to remoteness from the learner" is especially pertinent.[67]

A final subordinate question concerns administering the curriculum: What is the role of administrators with respect to a curriculum plan? This question asks that the functions of supervisors, registrars, evaluators, secretaries, and others be detailed insofar as they are essential to the execution of a particular program. Many administrative decisions belong properly to administration and not to curriculum planning.[68] Others are so intricately connected with the curriculum's achieving its objective that they belong to curriculum planning. These latter are the concern of this question. The question only applies to the situation where the program planners are different from the program administrators. When curriculum is planned at the grassroots, usually the planning team also administers the program.

[66] Wyckoff, "—Learning—Planning—Goals," 9.

[67] So also is the argumentation of Bergevin and McKinley, *Design for Adult Education in the Church,* that adults will only learn to the extent that they have set their own learning goals and have had a voice in planning the program themselves. See especially, pp. xv-xxviii.

[68] *Infra,* 57-58.

The Category of Scope

As reported above, a distinct category of scope [69] grew out of the discussions on objectives sponsored by the Commission on General Christian Education of the National Council of Churches. Themes, topics, and problems which had formerly been called objectives were identified more precisely as the content or substance of the curriculum.

Thus, Paul Vieth's seven "objectives" which had guided Protestant Christian education for twenty-five years were now considered more properly to be seven great themes which Christian education was to help growing persons experience and appreciate. So too, the highly detailed "age-group objectives" which were simultaneously but independently being calibrated by curriculum planners of the Lutheran Church in America,[70] were seen to be statements of themes divided into topics and problems and to pertain, therefore, to the content rather than to the objective of the curriculum.

The category of scope, then, deals directly with the content or subject matter of the curriculum. Essentially the content of curriculum is an educative community's experience insofar as it is communicable.[71] It comprises the tradition of concepts, understandings, consensuses, attitudes, values, skills, habits, and all that contribute to the community's culture, its way of life. "Experience," therefore, does not wish to connote an anti-intellectual bias. It is chosen because it is an all-embracing word. It includes ideas and action, concepts and attitudes, judgments and dispositions, the cognitive and the affective, the intellec-

[69] The Cooperative Curriculum Project under Wyckoff's influence borrowed the term, scope, from general education curriculum theory (cf. Stratemeyer *et al.*, *Developing a Curriculum.* . . , 9-11). It was found especially expressive of the concept that the content of Christian education is a perspective or several perspectives upon the whole field of human relationships in the light of the Gospel. See Wyckoff *Theory and Design.* . . , 121-29.

[70] *The Age Group Objectives of Christian Education*, prepared in connection with the Long-Range Program of Lutheran Boards of Parish Education ([Philadelphia:] The Boards of Parish Education of The American Evangelical Lutheran Church, The Augustana Lutheran Church, The Suomi Synod, The United Lutheran Church in America, 1958).

[71] I prefer to consider scope the communicable content of an educative community's experience rather than "the content and experience of curriculum" as Dr. Wyckoff does. The difference may be only semantic. The experience of an educative community, i.e., its concepts, judgments, values, attitudes, commitments, action patterns etc., is that which becomes the very content of curriculum insofar as it is communicable (see immediately *infra*). On the content of curriculum being the culture (experience) of the educative community, see Smith, Stanley, Shores, *Fundamentals of Curriculum Development*, 3-22. I have lately come to consider "meaning" a more adequate expression than "communicable content." See *infra*, 109-13.

tual and the emotional, thought patterns and behavioral patterns. Furthermore, the scope of curriculum is the content of that experience insofar as it is communicable, that is, insofar as its concepts can be conveyed by words, its judgments by propositions, its attitudes by symbols, its values by participation, its ideals by identification, its skills and habits by practice.

Moreover, an evolving educative community is not satisfied with transmitting its culture. It wishes to initiate learners into the dynamics that have been creative of that culture itself so that learners in turn may contribute creatively to the evolution and even transposition of that culture.[72] Exploration, new insights, breakthroughs of thought and behavior also belong to the scope of curriculum. In short, scope deals with what is to be learned and taught, experienced and appreciated, explored and understood, grasped and lived through the curriculum.

The Church is an educative community with a rich experience to communicate creatively. She believes that she has heard the Word of God and shared His life. Her experience consists in hearing and believing the Word, in living with God through Christ, in worshiping Him, in witnessing to His acts, in obeying His commands, in suffering correction under His judgment. She communicates her experience in a variety of ways: through sacramental celebration, through living example, through corporate fellowship, through propositions of faith, through involvement in mission. The scope of Christian education curriculum tries to embrace the whole of this experience.

As soon as the breadth of the Church's experience is considered the question of sequence and balance in planned learnings arises. The possibility and necessity of learnings building upon one another deserve attention.

Briefly, *scope* may be defined as *the meanings which curriculum intends to explore and/or communicate. The category of scope* comprises *the irreducible and unavoidable questions which search out those meanings.* In a word, the category of scope asks the "what" of curriculum.

The Major Question in the Category of Scope.—With respect to adult Christian education curriculum, the major question in the category of

[72] This statement broaches the question—to what extent should education be transmissive and to what extent creative. It accepts Wyckoff's resolution: "In the past it has been most effectively transmissive when it has been recreative." See "Christian Education Redefined," 212; see also *The Task. . .* , 34-36. George Albert Coe posed the tension between the transmissive and creative aspects of Christian education in his classic *What is Christian Education?* (New York: Charles Scribner's Sons, 1929).

scope is as obvious to ask as it is difficult to answer. The question is: What is appropriate scope for adult Christian education? "What is appropriate" seeks a criterion for differentiating what is germane to specifically Christian education from what is germane to general and religious education.[73] In other words, what is Christian education's "own thing"? What meanings does it explore and communicate that are distinctively its own? The major question is obviously a large one. Its very magnitude necessitates subordinate questions.

Subordinate Questions in the Category of Scope.—The subordinate questions in the category of scope address the communicability of the Church's experience. The first is: How comprehensive should the scope of a curriculum plan be? Because of its magnitude, the Church's experience cannot be communicated or explored in its entirety. Yet, because of the Lord's commission from which Christian education traditionally derives its charter, "teach them to observe all the commands I gave you" (Mt. 18:20), there seems a demand at least to ask the question of comprehensiveness. It warns the curriculum planner against selecting the first themes that interest learners and himself without considering more significant learning opportunities from a field as vast and rich as the Church's experience. The question of comprehensiveness, then, leads unavoidably to two other questions one of manageability, the other of selectivity.[74]

The question of manageability might be put: What distinct dimensions of scope lend themselves to different kinds of learning? The thrust of the question is important. It does not ask, as curriculum planners frequently do,[75] "How might the content be divided into manageable learnings?

This latter putting of the question implies that program designers are to divide the content to render it manageable. The former implies that the scope may have dimensions of its own which render it manageably communicable and that it is the curriculum planners' task to discover rather than create these dimensions. Thus, when asked in Christian education, the question closely parallels the theologians' search for an adequate organization of the field of theology. For some,

---

[73] *Supra,* 8.

[74] "The basic problem of scope is that of being comprehensive (omitting no important element or experience) and at the same time producing a picture that is unified, manageable and reduced to the absolute minimum." Wyckoff, *Theory and Design. . . ,* 122. "May Christian education do its job adequately by selecting certain key elements (like the Bible, Christian ethics, etc.), and by limiting its scope to these elements?" *Ibid.,* 124.

[75] *Ibid.,* 122-23. Cf. Saylor and Alexander, *Curriculum Planning. . . ,* 245-304 and Stratemeyer *et al., Developing a Curriculum. . . ,* 86-112.

salvation history is the key to the organization of theology and correspondingly to the scope of Christian education.[76] For others, the inner logic which binds together the mysteries of divine intervention is the key.[77] For still others, the relevance of God's self-disclosure to man's existential needs is the key.[78] Presently, other theologians are searching for a key to the organization of theology in functional specialization.[79] Whichever organization of theology is chosen will have corresponding implications for managing the scope of Christian education.[80] With the discovery of a key to the organization of Christian experience should come as well a recognition of related themes, or clusters of themes, which lend themselves to related learning experiences.

Akin to the question of the manageability of scope is that of selectivity. It can be expressed: How shall dimensions of scope be selected for inclusion in a curriculum plan? This question presupposes the foregoing, that is, it asks which of the dimensions of the Church's experience or themes thereof will actually be selected for

[76] For example, see Josef A. Jungmann, *The Good News Yesterday and Today*, Trans. and ed. by Wm. A. Huesman (New York: W. H. Sadlier, Inc., 1962). Emile Mersch, *The Theology of the Mystical Body*, trans. by Cyril Vollert (St. Louis: B. Herder Book Co., 1951) organizes theology through a central theme, the whole Christ, worked out as the historical unfolding of a divine plan.

[77] This approach to theology claims St. Thomas Aquinas' *Summa Theologiae* as its origin and the teaching of the first Vatican Council (1869-70) as its charter. See *Enchiridion Symbolorum: Definitionum et Declarationum de Rebus Fidei et Morum*, ed. by Adolphus Schonmetzer (orig. ed. by Henricus Denziger) (32nd ed.; Freiburg im Breisgau: Herder, 1963), 3016 (1796). (Cited hereafter as *DS*.) An early but excellent example of organizing theology by the inner logic which binds together the mysteries is that of Matthias J. Scheeben, *The Mysteries of Christianity*, trans. by Cyril Vollert (St. Louis: B. Herder Book Co., 1947).

[78] This is the approach suggested by Karl Rahner in *Theological Investigations*, Vol. I: *God, Christ, Mary and Grace*, tr. with an introduction by Cornelius Ernst (new ed. with indexes; London: Darton, Longman & Todd, 1965), pp. 1-37.

[79] As, for instance, Bernard J. F. Lonergan. See "Functional Specialties in Theology," *Gregorianum*, L, No. 3-4 (1969), 485-505. See also David Tracy, *The Achievement of Bernard Lonergan* (New York: Herder and Herder, 1970), pp. 232-66. Functional specialization is more properly a methodology of doing theology rather than an organization of theology in subject specialties and field specialties.

[80] It is interesting to note that the recent *A New Catechism: Catholic Faith for Adults*, (trans. by Kevin Smyth from *De Nieuwe Katechismus* produced by the Higher Catechetical Institute at Nijmegen [New York: Herder and Herder, 1967]). (Cited hereafter as *Dutch Catechism*.) draws somewhat eclectically from three of the above approaches to the organization of theology. It begins with an exploration of man's perennial existential concerns and answers in historical religions (pp. 3-33); finds answers to these same concerns in the events of salvation history (pp. 34-236); and explores man's present vocation in terms of involvement in the mysteries through which the events of salvation history continue (pp. 236-502). The approaches are more intricately intertwined than such a division suggests but the predominant approach of each section seems to be as stated.

inclusion in the curriculum and why. In other words, whereas the question of manageability deals with possible constellations of content, that of selectivity deals with actual choices of content.[81] The question of selectivity is greatly compounded by having to weigh not only the key to the organization of Christian experience and its clusters of themes but also the learner's readiness, needs, and goals. As soon as this last consideration is introduced, the question of selectivity of scope becomes an indispensable aspect of the problem of organizing the curriculum which will be treated at length below.[82]

An additional subordinate question related to scope is: In what sequence will dimensions of scope be offered in a curriculum plan? [83] The question does not wish to preclude the possibility that no particular sequence of learnings will be offered. It is just as legitimate to offer participants a smorgasbord of themes with the expectation that they will build a sequence of learning themselves through their own integrative capacity. The question does ask, however, that program planners decide positively whether the sequence of learnings shall be built into the organization of scope, based upon the readiness levels of the participants, left to the participants' powers of integration, or dealt within a combination of all three.

The Category of Process

As the category of scope, so the category of process owes its origin as a distinct category to the discussions of the National Council of Churches' committees on "objectives." Many kinds of learning experiences and teaching-learning goals, formerly considered "objectives," were identified in the Cooperative Curriculum Project as "learning tasks," and more precisely by Dr. Wyckoff as process.

The category of process deals with the nature of learning, with the complexity of human becoming. Consequently, it is the most difficult

81 The Cooperative Curriculum Project planners put the matter differently. They distinguish the scope from the content of the curriculum. "The term 'scope of curriculum' is used to describe what is appropriate to be dealt with in the curriculum. It is distinctive from the term 'content of curriculum' in that this latter term has to do with what is in fact dealt with in the curriculum." *CCP*, 12. What underlies their distinction seems to be the question of manageability vis-a-vis selectivity.

82 *Infra*, 51-55.

83 In the *Dissertation*, 71, 72, 74, I treated the question of sequence under the category of timing. In the course of the work (see *Dissertation*, 459, 526-27), I began to think that sequence should be more properly related to scope. From experience in designing programs since the *Dissertation*, I am more convinced that sequence belongs to the category of scope.

category in which to ask questions without prejudicing the answers. The very cast of the questions reveals decisions the questioner has already taken regarding how learning happens. On the one hand, the questions must be broad enough to admit any kind of learning theory in their response. On the other, they must be pointed enough to require positive judgments as to what learning theory program planners will adopt.

Furthermore, process is the interaction of all the factors involved in Christian education curriculum. It is the catalysis of the Holy Spirit's influence, the learner's involvement, the teacher's guidance, and the stimulation of the curriculum materials reacting to one another in the Christian's becoming.[84] Thus, process is very similar to what shall presently be described as the organization of the curriculum [85] yet distinct from it. Process is the meeting of all the factors of curriculum in the act of learning. Organization is planning for the convergence of those factors so that learning will give promise of occurring. To oversimplify, organization plans what should happen in education; process is what happens in education. Accordingly, it is important when framing questions within the category of process not to ask those which more properly belong to the problem of organizing the curriculum.

Briefly, process deals with the dynamics of education, with methods through which the teaching-learning transaction takes place, with the ways and means by which dimensions of scope become internalized.

In curriculum, *process* might, then, be defined, as *the dynamics by which the learning-teaching experience happens.* The category of process comprises *the irreducible and unavoidable questions which seek the dynamics that will best ensure the desired teaching-learning experiences.* The category of process asks the "how" of curriculum.

The Major Question in the Category of Process.—With respect to adult Christian education curriculum the major question within the category of process is: How does adult Christian learning happen? This question admits of no sure answer. Yet curriculum planners answer it either consciously or implicitly in the very act of providing learning opportunities for others. The question pointedly insists that curriculum planners make explicit their judgments on learning theory.

[84] See Wyckoff, "Fürigen address," 4-5.
[85] *Infra,* 51-55.

Given the present lack of consensus on learning theory,[86] making such judgments will be difficult enough regarding the nature of learning in general. Given the added complexity of specifically Christian learning which normative Catholic doctrine insists is under the influence of God's grace,[87] the difficulty of such judgments increases. The question may, indeed, be somewhat narrowed by considering first, as Robert Boelke has, what proposed learning theories are in fact compatible with normative Christian theology and by eliminating those which are not.[88]

Moreover, it cannot be assumed that learning is of a single kind. Even with the unique characteristics of individual learners aside, there appear to be a variety of common learnings corresponding to the various ways of human knowing.[89] For decades, educators have recognized this fact by distinguishing between the learning of understandings, attitudes, and skills. The multiplicity of human learning gives rise to subordinate questions in the category of process.

Subordinate Questions in the Category of Process.—The first subordinate question is: What kinds of adult Christian learning are to be sought? The kinds of Christian learning are many.[90] They include learning the historical facts of God's intervening in human history; learning to understand the import of the doctrinal formulations through which the community of believers in Christ have witnessed to the deed of God; learning attitudes of piety, repentance, love, trust; learning appreciation for God's works and grace; learning the practice of worship, of ethical behavior, of witness. The kinds of Christian

---

[86] For a review of the more prominent learning theories see Ernest R. Hilgard, *Theories of Learning* (2d ed.) The Century Psychology Series, ed. by Richard M. Elliott and Kenneth MacCorquodale (New York: Appleton, Century, Crofts, Inc., 1956). For a recent survey of the debates about learning theory, see *Theories of Learning and Instruction*, The Sixty-third Yearbook of the National Society for the Study of Education, Part I, ed. by Ernest R. Hilgard (Chicago: The University of Chicago Press, 1964).

[87] Vatican Council I. *DS*, 3010(1791); 3032(1811); 3035(1814).

[88] *Theories of Learning in Christian Education* (Philadelphia: The Westminster Press, 1962).

[89] For an excellent study of the relationship between various kinds of knowing and learning see Philip H. Phenix, *Realms of Meaning: A Philosophy of the Curriculum for General Education* (New York: McGraw-Hill Book Company, 1964). On the analogous concept of knowing see Lonergan, "Cognitional Structure" in *Collection: Papers by Bernard Lonergan, S.J.*, ed. by F. E. Crowe (New York: Herder and Herder, 1967), pp. 221-39.

[90] See Boelke, *Theories of Learning. . .* , 31-58. Boelke further specifies the usual understandings, attitudes, skills into seven "concerns": knowledge, understandings, attitudes, values, skill-habits, motives, and changes in the self.

learning decided upon will greatly determine answers to the next subordinate question.

The second subordinate question is: How is the learner's motivation to be approached in pursuing the kinds of learning desired? The question asks that the relationship be seriously considered between teachers' and learners' motivations, aims, and needs on the one hand and on the other the kinds of Christian learning desired. It seeks to know how the search for meaning relates to learning Christian faith, how the drive for freedom relates to learning moral responsibility, how the desire for security relates to learning an appreciation for redemption, how the need to escape loneliness relates to learning Christian community. The question wishes to weigh the motivations, needs, and aims of learners and teachers in order to find out which are conducive to Christian learnings.

The last subordinate question follows upon the answers to the first two: What dominant teaching-learning modes give promise of achieving certain kinds of learning? Here, finally, the precise question of the selection of processes is asked. Robert Boelke's classification of various processes as they issue from different learning theories represents a wide consensus among Christian educators.

Persons learn through four processes: perception, practice, problem-solving, and identification. Perception suggests the theoretical foundation of gestalt psychology with its emphasis on relating parts and wholes. Practice is related to connectionism and reinforcement theory. It has usually made use of the laws of readiness, exercise, and effect. Learning as a result of problem-solving is associated with the theory of John Dewey. Persons confronted with a baffling problem adopt and test hypotheses until a solution is achieved. This in turn may lead to other problems and the process continues. Depth psychology has contributed to an understanding of identification. As the learner identifies himself with admired persons, he takes the qualities of the latter to himself.[91]

Let us note that the question asks us to identify only learning modes, not learning methods. By learning modes I mean the generic ways by which a kind of learning can be achieved.[92] Methods on the other hand refer to the practical dynamics of teaching-learning. Methods are related to modes as tactics to strategy. For example, problem-

[91] *Ibid.*, 24. Cf. Wyckoff, *The Gospel. . .* , 134-35 and *Theory and Design. . .* , 102-05.

[92] In this sense the *CCP* learning tasks are modes. They suggest the general dynamics of teaching-learning by which a certain kind of learning may be achieved. See Wyckoff, *Learning Tasks. . .* , 19, 23.

solving is a learning mode. Struggling with a moral case in a buzz group is a learning method which employs the mode of problem-solving.

If Wyckoff is correct that learning modes correspond to various kinds of learning,[93] then this last subordinate question also asks the aptitude between a given mode and a desired learning, e.g., between perception and theological insight; between problem-solving and ethical decision; between practice and attitudes of worship; between identification and discipleship.

The Category of Context

Unlike the categories of scope and process, the category of context was not isolated as a discrete category of curriculum inquiry as a result of the discussions on objectives by the National Council of Churches committees. Rather it grew from the necessity of Protestant Christian education to consider more broadly the total Christian learning situation which had been narrowly and uncritically limited to the Sunday School.[94] When curriculums which had originally begun as educational plans for the Sunday School became more inclusive, they sought increasingly to provide for coordinated learning experiences in a variety of settings: Sunday schools; youth fellowship; vacation Bible schools; weekday church schools, and others.[95] Thus, the distinction grew between the overall milieu or context of Christian education and the structured groupings or settings where Christian education takes place.[96]

More precisely, the *context* of curriculum can be defined as *the social and spatial environment of learning*. A *setting* within the context is a *specifically structured and situated grouping for learning*. The *category of context,* then, *comprises the irreducible and unavoidable questions which seek the overall and particular social and spatial environment for learning*. Concisely, the category of context wishes to know the "where" of curriculum.

The Major Question in the Category of Context.—With respect to adult Christian education curriculum, the major question within the category of context is: Where does adult Christian learning take place? The question hints at more or less favorable places for adult Christian learning. To offer a criterion by which the more favorable environment for Christian education can be identified is the point of the question.

93 *Theory and Design.* . . , 104-05.
94 See Taylor in Taylor (ed.), *Religious Education.* . . , 17-19.
95 Taylor (ed.), *Religious Education.* . . , 101-02.
96 *CCP*, 816, 820.

Subordinate Questions in the Category of Context.—The subordinate questions in the category of context meet the requirements of setting.

The first is: How shall persons be grouped for adult Christian learning? This question has to do with the social environment of adult Christian education. It seeks criteria according to which persons can best be grouped or group themselves to capitalize upon certain learning opportunities. The question takes on greater importance as studies in group dynamics reveal how much learners learn from one another.[97] The question of grouping asks what kinds of persons in what kinds of relationships help one another learn.

The second subordinate question is: How should the selected groupings be structured? "Structures" refer to determined patterns of relationships between persons in the learning situation. For instance, the structure of a lecture differs from the structure of a discussion group insofar as the persons involved, such as the lecturer and members of the audience or the discussion group leader and members, each have different recognized and accepted patterns of relationship one to another.

The third subordinate question is: Where shall the structured group meet? This question seeks the criteria that will determine the place where the learners, grouped and structured as they have been, can best take advantage of certain learning opportunities. The place can be a classroom, a church, a picnic area, a slum, a political convention, a home, a movie theatre depending upon the learning experience the group wishes to undertake.

Grouping, structure, and place make up the setting. Examples of the variety of ways in which they can be combined for adult education are presented in the work by Paul Bergevin, Dwight Morris, and Robert Smith, *Adult Education Procedures: A Handbook of Tested Patterns for Effective Participation.*[98]

The Category of Timing

Closely related both to process and context is timing. The Cooperative Curriculum Project did not consider timing a separate component of curriculum, but it did consider the "optimal time for learning" under the component of learning tasks.[99] Although it was not his origi-

---

[97] Besides Kidd, *How Adults Learn,* see *Group Dynamics: Research and Theory,* ed. by Dorwin Cartwright and Alvin Zander, (2nd ed.; New York: Harper & Row, Publishers, 1960), and *Spiritual Renewal through Personal Groups,* ed. by John L. Casteel (New York: Association Press, 1957).

[98] (Greenwich, Conn.: The Seabury Press, 1963).

[99] *CCP,* 29 and 24-34, *passim.* Cf. Wyckoff, *Theory and Design. . . ,* 163-77.

nal intention to do so,[100] Wyckoff's isolation of timing as a discrete category, seems to have evolved from his grappling with varying aspects of process vis-a-vis scope and context.[101] He expressly delineated the category for the first time at the World Consultation of Curriculum, Fürigen, Switzerland, June 13-July 4, 1964.

> When does Christian education take place? The matter of timing has several aspects. There is the learner's time: his readiness, and the schedule that is determined by his motivations and plans. There is God's time: the movement of his will and acts, sensitivity to which is the key to faithful response. There is "occasional" time: that of nature and human history, significant emergent events and trends in our environment and in our social and community life and culture. There is the church's time: by which it uses the past (tradition) and the future (its anticipation of God's will, emergent environmental factors, and emergent human needs) to determine the steps to be taken now and in the future in order that its response may be faithful.[102]

The category of timing, then, addresses the large question of what theologians prefer to call the *kairos,* the opportune moment of revelation and response. It seeks to weigh and balance the ongoing events of history through which God continues to reveal Himself and His will; the burning issues of the day in neighborhood, nation, and world; the seasons of liturgical celebration; the crises in the Church's life; the developmental pattern of the person's growth; and the unexpected experiences of this unique person's life—all with an eye to seizing upon the "teachable moment." Within the category of timing are met the questions which try to prevent the "too much, too soon," and "too little, too late" for which Christian education is roundly criticized.

From the intricacies of "God's time" and the "teachable moment," the category of timing descends to the practicalities of scheduling. It must consider the days and hours during which learning can occur, the dates and minutes that participants and resource persons can afford.

In curriculum, then, *timing* may be defined as *the succession of events and expressions during which learning occurs.* I prefer "succession" to "sequence," a less neutral word, because it does not prejudice the question as to whether sequence should be planned for in the design or built interiorly by the learner. Correspondingly, the

---

100 Interview with Dr. Wyckoff, July 3, 1968.

101 *Theory and Design. . . ,* 171, 176. *In Learning Tasks in the Curriculum* (Valley Forge, Pa.: American Baptist Board of Education and Publication, 1965), Wyckoff discusses one aspect of timing, the learner's readiness, when considering process in the light of scope, 24-29, and another aspect, occasional time, when considering process in the light of context.

102 "Fürigen address," 7-8.

category of timing comprises *the irreducible and unavoidable questions which seek the succession of events and experiences that will best promise the occurrence of learning.* It wishes to know the "when" of curriculum.

The Major Question in the Category of Timing.—With respect to adult Christian education curriculum, the major question in the category of timing is: When does adult Christian learning occur? As in the case of the major question within the category of process, this is a question which yields no sure answer prior to the occurrence of adult Christian learning. Yet the curriculum planner must address the question if for no better reason than to be aware of the "signs of the times" through which learning is continually occurring in the lives of adult Christians. The question also requires him to take a stand on the various levels of readiness of adults occasioned by age and experience for certain Christian learnings. It requires further that he decide upon the role of developmental tasks, if any, in the ongoing Christian learning of adults. The subordinate questions spell out these implications more exactly.

Subordinate Questions in the Category of Timing.—The first subordinate question in the category of timing is: What principle governs the responsiveness of a curriculum plan to God's present activity? The answer can be only tentative. The Old Testament prophets were called to interpret God's purposes for their day. Christian educators are rash to consider themselves similarly called and inspired. Yet they must seek a criterion which will render their planning somewhat sensitive to God's activity. For what God is presently doing in this age is both the occasion and the content of much important adult learning.

The second subordinate question is: What principle governs the responsiveness of a curriculum plan to current events in the Church and in the world? Here "Church" embraces the universal Christian fellowship and the local Eucharistic community. "World" includes neighborhood, work, city, nation, planet, and universe. The two are not considered exclusive of one another. The question asks that conflicts and experiences of solidarity, of depression and affluence, of war and peace, of crime and security, of violence and concord which play so large a part in the "live curriculum" of adults be explored for their contribution to planned adult Christian learning.

A third subordinate question is: How shall the readiness which is conditioned by age, experience, and responsibility influence a curriculum plan? This question places more pointedly the necessity of identifying stages that are fairly common to adults of various ages in a given culture. Such stages are, for example, described in Erik Erikson's *Childhood and Society* and Josef Goldbrunner's *Realization: The Anthropology of Pastoral Care*.[103] It also requires that curriculum planners weigh commonly shared adult experiences such as marriage, parenthood, employment or loss thereof, homemaking, loss of health, recreational and social involvements, for the readiness these experiences can provide an adult for certain Christian learning. Parental preparation of children for the sacraments, an increasing potential of adult education, pertains too, to the readiness question.

A last subordinate question is: What determines the frequency and duration with which related adult learning opportunities will be offered? This question asks the factors which determine how long a course will run and how many sessions will be held for how many hours each. The question is phrased rather generally so that it will meet questions of frequency and duration for settings quite differently structured from courses in an academic curriculum.

It may be noted that in all the foregoing categories, the major questions require broadly theoretical answers and the subordinate questions increasingly practical answers. I suggest this order because our theoretical positions greatly influence our practical decisions. Moreover, it seems that programs will be designed not only more soundly but also more creatively if the theoretical principles are brought to the fore first and critically assessed before making the practical decisions which constitute the finished curriculum plan.

*General Curriculum Concerns Related
to the Categories of Inquiry*

There are at least three general curriculum concerns that are not infrequently treated by curriculum theorists as discrete categories of inquiry similar to the six named above. The first concern is that of the organization, the second the evaluation, and the third the administration of the curriculum.[104] Each concern plays its part in the planning

---

[103] Erikson, *Childhood and Society*, *passim;* Josef Goldbrunner, *Realization: Anthropology of Pastoral Care*, Liturgical Studies, No. 10, trans. by Paul C. Bailey and Elisabeth Reinecke (Notre Dame, Ind.: University of Notre Dame Press, 1966), pp. 163-90.

[104] Thus, the Cooperative Curriculum Project planners explicitly identify the organizing principle as "a proper fifth component of the Design itself." *CCP*, 35. Similarly, Anderson, *Principles and Procedures. . .* , 218-47, Saylor and Alexander, *Curriculum Planning. . .* , 579-609, and Stratemeyer *et al., Developing a Curricu-*

of curriculum; but, the first, the organization of the curriculum, plays a more direct and decisive part in the design of a given program than the other two.

Although organization, evaluation, and administration can be called "categories of inquiry" insofar as each comprises questions which program designers must ask and try to answer, I prefer to consider them general concerns related to the six categories already delineated. The difference of organization, evaluation, and administration from objective, personnel, scope, process, context and timing consists principally in that the latter deal each with its own discrete curricular problem while the former deal simultaneously with the interrelation of all six problems.

There are also major differences between the manners by which organization, evaluation, and administration deal with all six problems. The organization of the curriculum seeks to integrate the answers to each question within all six categories so that each will bring its proper influence to bear upon the total program design. The evaluation of curriculum seeks at every stage of the planning and implementation processes to judge critically the statement of the problems and their solutions. The administration of curriculum looks to the practical application of the solutions to the problems worked out at the planning level.

How organization, evaluation, and administration are similar to yet different from the six categories of curriculum inquiry and one another will be clarified through an analysis of each task.

The Organization of the Curriculum.—The organization of curriculum has been a problem of growing complexity both to general and to Christian education. At first it emerged during the last century with respect to organizing the content of curriculum, with selecting what Herbert Spencer called "what knowledge is of most worth." [105] The problem of organization became far more complex when John Dewey introduced questions about the integration of subject matter and method in the learner. He saw education as the mastering of a subject through the reorganization of the learner's experience. [106] Since

---

lum. . . , 476-518 and 661-704, would seem to treat evaluation as a category of the same kind as scope, process, and sequence. Much of what the Cooperative Curriculum Project, *CCP,* 793-801, and Saylor and Alexander, 348-87, consider administrative concerns, I assign to the category of context.

[105] Herbert Spencer, *Education* (New York: D. Appleton and Company, 1860), pp. 13-14, quoted by Little, "The Objectives . . ." in Taylor (ed.), *Religious Education. . . ,* 66.

[106] *Democracy and Education: An Introduction to the Philosophy of Education* (New York: The Macmillan Company, 1916), pp. 146-227.

Dewey, the increasing magnitude of subject matter from which to choose and multiplying insights into the learning process have made the organization of curriculum the most crucial problem of general education curriculum design.[107]

Dewey's highlighting the subject matter-method nexus also created far-reaching repercussions in Christian education. Heretofore, Protestant Christian education, especially as exemplified in the Uniform Lessons, concerned itself with dividing content, taken primarily from the Bible, so that all significant "matter" would be covered in a certain number of years. The Uniform Lessons prided themselves on the feature that all age groups of the church studied the same content on the same Sunday. Principally through George Herbert Betts' *The Curriculum of Religious Education* in 1924 [108] and William Clayton Bower's book of the same title in 1925,[109] awareness of the need for child-centered and experience-centered curriculums grew in Protestant Christian education. The problem of organization was compounded from that merely of dividing content into manageable portions to that of relating content to learners' readiness.

The problem continued to vex Protestant Christian education until reasonable accord was reached through discussions of the Committee on the Study of Christian Education sponsored by the International Council of Religious Education in 1946.[110] Paul Vieth, chairman of the Committee, synthesized both the problem and the accord.

The crucial question in curriculum theory may be stated as follows: What shall be the *organizing principle* of the curriculum? The answers which have been made to this question fall into two general groups. The first finds the organizing principle in acquainting the learner with and adjusting him to

[107] Both Saylor and Alexander, *Curriculum Planning. . . ,* 245-347, and Stratemeyer *et al., Developing a Curriculum. . . ,* 85-112, treat at length various proposals to organize the curriculum. Stratemeyer *et al.,* outline four current and common organizations: (1) separate subjects, (2) subject fields or groups of related subjects, (3) broad areas that cut across subject fields, and (4) needs or problems faced by the group. Jerome S. Bruner (*The Process of Education* [Cambridge, Mass.: Harvard University Press, 1963]) and Philip Phenix (*Realms of Meaning . . .*) have recently begun to call for an organization of curriculum based upon leading the learner to understand the basic structures of human understanding as it operates in various fields and sciences.

[108] (New York: The Abingdon Press, 1924).

[109] (New York: Charles Scribner's Sons, 1928).

[110] The International Council of Religious Education, formed in 1922 from the International Sunday School Association and the Sunday School Council of Evangelical Denominations, became in 1950 the Commission on General Christian Education of the National Council of Churches. See Taylor in Taylor (ed.), *Religious Education. . . ,* 20-21. On the 1946 meeting of the International Council, see *The Church and Christian Education,* ed. by Paul H. Vieth (St. Louis: The Bethany Press, 1947), pp. 7-15.

some part of the heritage and content of the Christian faith. This may be the Bible, the redemptive activity of God in Christ, the major doctrines of the Christian faith, the church year. The second finds it in the present life experience of the learner, as an individual and as a member of a group, such as the home, church, community, world.

The problem would not be so difficult if a simple choice of one of these would suffice. But the moment such a choice is contemplated, it is at once clear that the other holds so much of truth that it cannot be left out. . . . An exclusive use of the first runs into the danger of remoteness from life, fruitless intellectualism, and pedantic authoritarianism. An exclusive use of the second runs into the grave danger of trying to educate without content, in an intellectual and a cultural vacuum, cut off from the rich heritage of the past and the enriching contacts of the present.

We are forced to conclude that any satisfactory theory of curriculum must come out of a synthesis of these two opposing points of view. . . .

The purpose of the curriculum of Christian education is to confront individuals with the eternal gospel and to nurture within them a life of faith, hope, and love, in keeping with the gospel. The organizing principle of the curriculum, from the viewpoint of the Christian gospel, is to be found in the changing needs and experiences of the individual as these include his relation to (1) God, as revealed in Jesus Christ; (2) his fellow men and human society; (3) his place in the work of the world; (4) the Christian fellowship, the church; (5) the continuous process of history, viewed as a carrier of the divine purpose and revealer of the moral law; (6) the universe in all its wonder and complexity.[111]

Briefly, the problem prior to 1946 was seen as a choice between deriving the organization of the curriculum from the integrity of the Christian message or deriving it from the experiences of learners. The problem was one of relating scope to process-timing. A tenuous solution was found in relating levels of learners' readiness to perspectives upon the whole of Christian faith.[112]

During the intensive study sessions of the Cooperative Curriculum Project from 1960-64, it became ever clearer, that valid as the 1946 solution was to the problem it addressed, the problem itself of the organization of curriculum had larger dimensions. It was seen not simply as a problem of relating scope to learning tasks but of interrelating all the components of curriculum one to another.[113]

As a result of his participation in the Cooperative Curriculum

[111] Vieth (ed.), *The Church and Christian Education*, 144-46. For Vieth's earlier involvement in the debate over the organizing principle, see his *Objectives*. . . , 35-43

[112] For a fuller treatment of the history of the problem of organizing the curriculum and the solutions offered in various denominational curriculums, see Wyckoff, *Theory and Design*. . . , 138-46.

[113] *CCP*, 34-36.

Project, Wyckoff's writings evidence the same enlarging perception of the problem of organizing the curriculum. His treatment of the organizing principle in *Theory and Design of Christian Education Curriculum* (1961) views the underlying problem practically the same as Vieth had stated it in 1946.[114] His address at Fürigen in 1964 views it in greater complexity.

The function of the organizing principle of the curriculum is to provide the guidance that curriculum builders need to fit these six pieces together [objective, scope, context, process, timing, personnel] so as to know what they are about as they do curriculum planning. The organizing principle must show how the *persons* involved may, within the *context, time* their use of the *process* in order that the *scope* may be covered and the *purpose* fulfilled. Yet this must be done as clearly and manageably as possible. Complex as the matter is, it may thus be brought within manageable compass. Indeed it must be, if both soundness and practicality are to be maintained in curriculum construction.[115]

The problem of organizing the curriculum, then, is the problem of interrelating the six categories of inquiry so that the answers given to each major and subordinate question will exercise its proper influence in planning the entire curriculum. We have already seen in the very phrasing of several of the major and subordinate questions evidence of their relatedness to questions in other categories. This has been especially true of subordinate questions in scope, process, context, and timing.

What is necessary, however, is to frame a single question which will both focus the compexity of the problem of organizing the curriculum and demand by way of answer an evaluative judgment which will act as a practical policy decision in organizing the curriculum.

The question can be put in a number of ways depending upon which of the six categories of inquiry the questioner considers most important in organizing the curriculum. If scope is seen as the key to curriculum organization, the question may be put: What dimensions of *scope* shall *persons* master through a *process timed* and *situated* so as to achieve the *objective?* If process is seen as the key, the question can be put: How shall the *process* be *timed* and *situated* so as to involve the *persons* in mastering the *scope* in order to fulfill the *objective?* If timing is seen as the key, the question may be put: When shall

---

114 P. 134: "The organizing principle serves the essential function of bridging the gap between the scope of Christian education and the actual learning situation."
115 "Fürigen address," 8-9.

the *process* be *timed* in the *context* so that *persons* might master the *scope* and achieve the *objective?* If context is seen as the key, the question may be put: Where shall the *process* be *situated* at a *time* when *persons* can master the *scope* in order to achieve the *objective?*

If, however, one tries to cast the question of organizing the curriculum in terms of objective or personnel, he immediately finds it impossible. He can only ask anew the major questions in the two categories. Moreover, upon closer investigation, the questions which consider context and timing keys to curriculum organization must unavoidably select process as that which is to be timed and situated. The reason is that context, process, and timing form a closely interdependent circle of categories with process itself the key. In substance, then, the variety of questions which might articulate the problem of organizing the curriculum are reducible to two, one which considers scope the key to organization and the other which considers process. Thus, despite the greater complexity the problem of organizing the curriculum has taken on by seeking to correlate all six categories, its final resolution continues to look to a choice between or synthesis of the demands of scope and process. I am increasingly convinced that the choice should fall upon scope, principally because it is the scope (content) of a program more than its process that characterizes a learning program as distinctively Christian.

The exercise of framing these questions also reveals some characteristics of the interrelations between the categories. First, it will have been noticed that no matter how the question of organization is put, the objective acts as the focus for the categories. Secondly, in every casting of the question, scope stands in a bipolar relationship to process-context-timing. Finally, scope and process-context-timing meet in the person of the learner. He it is who masters the scope through the process-context-timing to achieve the objective. These characteristics of the interrelations between the categories suggest the functions that the organizing principle will perform.

The problem of organizing the curriculum, then, although it constitutes a major curriculum concern and does indeed ask a curriculum question of the highest importance, were better not considered a category of curriculum inquiry itself similar and in addition to the other six categories. It does not deal with a problem distinct from the other six problems. It deals, rather, with the interrelation of the other six problems.

Evaluation of the Curriculum.—As Saylor and Alexander point out, evaluation refers to two types of procedures in relation to curriculum planning, "those which evaluate planning as a process, and those which evaluate planning through its results." [116] Stratemeyer *et al.* recognize the same distinction by isolating as topics of curriculum inquiry: "How shall pupil growth and progress be evaluated?" and "How shall curriculum improvement be assured?" [117] Although evaluation of the learner's growth through curriculum produces valuable judgment upon the program design and the categories of inquiry that initiated it, the evaluation of curriculum planning as a process pertains more directly to the major curriculum concern here treated. The former pertains to administration of the curriculum. The evaluation of curriculum planning as a process seeks to ensure the ongoing improvement of program design itself. It seeks to ensure that curriculum will not be static and fixed once for all.

The evaluation of curriculum planning as a process will operate on several levels and will concern each of the six categories of inquiry. On its most basic level it will question the adequacy of the categories themselves to deal with all the important questions that arise in curriculum planning. It will ask whether new categories must be added or old categories combined. It will search for different rearrangements of categories through a sharper identification of distinct problems. On the level of the present six categories, evaluation of curriculum planning as a process will continually rephrase questions so as to identify more clearly the choices that curriculum planners are to make. On the level of the questions as presently stated in the six categories of inquiry, evaluation will seek to answer them ever more pointedly, ever more responsive to changes in the data sources that require revised answers.

Thus, although the evaluation of curriculum planning as a process could be called a category of inquiry insofar as it asks crucial curricular questions, it might more accurately be denoted a major curriculum concern because its task is to scrutinize critically the delineation of the categories themselves, the casting of each question within each category, and the answers to the questions cast. This task it performs enroute, that is, as the delineation, the casting of questions, and their answering go on.[118] Evaluation is a continuing process of curricular self-criticism.

Put in the form of questions, the evaluation of curriculum planning as a process would have program designers continually ask themselves: Are these categories of curriculum inquiry necessary and sufficient to

[116] *Curriculum Planning. . . ,* 580.
[117] *Developing a Curriculum. . . ,* 18-19.
[118] Saylor and Alexander, *Curriculum Planning. . . ,* 579-80.

raise all the significant curricular questions? Are the questions within each category necessary and sufficient to deal with the distinct problem that the category faces? Are the answers to the questions in each category adequately reflective of the most reliable data sources. The very putting of these questions reveals that, rather than a systematic set of questions itself, evaluation is more a continual preoccupation with the validity of the categories, questions, and answers themselves.

Accordingly, evaluation of curriculum planning as a process were better not considered a category of curriculum inquiry, similar and additional to the other six. Unlike them, it deals not with one distinct curricular problem but with the positing and solving of all six problems. Evaluation, it might be said, presides over the six categories rather than resides among them.

The Administration of Curriculum.—Organization plays a decisive role in designing the curriculum. Evaluation criticizes the planning of curriculum enroute. Administration, too, although its execution follows upon the curriculum plan, nonetheless exercises a prior influence upon program design as it addresses each of the six curricular problems. It demands that the practicality of each of the answers given in each of the six categories be weighed. The objective must be able to be shared by supervisors, monitors, and teachers' aides. The selection of scope must be within the capacity of learners and teachers. The selection of process will be limited by the expertise of teachers. The choice of settings will be conditioned by the availability of persons and space. The determination of timing will depend upon the schedules of learners and teachers.

Yet, even if the practicalities of administration must be weighed in curriculum design, administration follows upon, rather than determines a curriculum plan. Therefore, many of the questions that the Cooperative Curriculum Project assigns to administration, I assign to the six categories themselves. For instance, I include questions of structure and setting for the learning situation within the category of context. The Cooperative Curriculum Project sees them as administrative questions.[119] I include the roles of administrative personnel within the category of personnel. The Cooperative Curriculum Project attributes to administration the description of these roles.[120] Were decisions regarding settings and personnel left to administration and not part of curriculum planning itself, it is strongly probable that such decisions would be opportunistic and pragmatic to the extent of

[119] *CCP,* 795, 806-13.
[120] *Ibid.,* 793-94.

blunting the effectiveness of the curriculum plan. This is a definite danger when a curriculum plan is centrally designed and locally administered. It is usually not a danger where programs are locally designed for then the team which designs the program is usually the same team which administers it.

There remain, however, to administration tasks peculiarly its own which can be foreseen by curriculum planning but the execution of which rests upon administrative decisions. Such are the recruitment of learners and teachers, the actual assignment of sites and their custodial care, the budgeting of the program, the secretarial services required by the program, and its supervision. Pertaining also to administration is the evaluation of the results of the curriculum in terms of learning outcomes.[121]

The decisions which belong immediately to administration are beyond the limits of this study. Again it deserves emphasis, however, that administrative decisions must be based upon the curriculum plan if it is the curriculum plan that will be administered and not a different curriculum created by the administrative decisions themselves. What does pertain to curriculum planning directly and therefore to this study is the concern for administrative practicality in answering all the questions in the six categories and in organizing the curriculum. The question might be put at the curriculum planning level: How administratively practical are the answers given to each question in objective, personnel, scope, process, context, and timing as organized by the organizing principle? As with the questions of evaluation, this is not a question to be asked systematically at regular intervals but a continual preoccupation for practicality that should temper the answers to all curricular questions.

Like the organization and evaluation of curriculum, then, administration is not so much a discrete category of curriculum inquiry as a general concern which affects all the categories simultaneously.

Answers to the Questions—Curriculum Principles

Having delineated six categories of curriculum inquiry and three general concerns which cut across the categories, we are now ready to consider the nature, function, and characteristics of the answers demanded by the questions in each of the categories and in the general concern of organizing the curriculum. Answers to the questions of evaluating and administering the curriculum are of a different kind.

121 For an overview of administrative tasks, see chapters xxiii-xxvi and xxix in Taylor (ed.), *Religious Education. . . ,* 247-93, 316-25.

As already explained, these latter will be answered to the degree that the answers to the former are valid and practical.

The Nature of the Answers.—The answers to the questions within the six categories and in the general concern of organizing the curriculum take the form of curriculum principles. Curriculum principles are guides to educational planning and practice. They consist of judgments which express the dependable relationship between two or more variables that interact in education. Such variables are persons, techniques, resources, and structures.[122]

As guides to curriculum planning and practice, principles, strictly speaking, are not the same as the concrete decisions which curriculum planners make in the actual construction of programs. They are rather the prior judgments in the light of which the concrete decisions are made. Unlike the concrete decisions, they are generalized guides able to govern several individual decisions. On the other hand, as practical guides, curriculum principles differ from the presuppositions upon which they in turn rest. These presuppositions may be implicit or explicit. They may be theological, educational, psychological, historical, or otherwise. Presuppositions, like curriculum principles, are judgments. They differ from principles, however, insofar as they are not immediately directed to practice. They provide theoretical justification for the principles. In brief, concrete program decisions are justified by principles which are in turn justified by presuppositions. Put another way, principles provide the "why" of concrete curriculum decisions; presuppositions provide the "why" of the principles. In practice, it is difficult to differentiate a decision from a principle and a principle from a presupposition; but, to distinguish one from the other theoretically is to clarify what kinds of answers the curriculum planner needs to the questions within the six categories and to the problem of organizing the curriculum.[123]

A *curriculum principle* may be defined, then, as a *judgment expressing the dependable relationship between two or more educational variables which guides curriculum planning and practice. Principles* will be *major* or *subordinate* depending on whether they respond to major or subordinate questions. The organizing principle will be single inasmuch as the question which it answers is single for the particular curriculum plan which it organizes.

It may be possible to delineate even more precisely the kinds of principles which are frequently found in curriculum designs. Some-

---

[122] Wyckoff, *Theory and Design. . .* , 83.

[123] So differentiated, principles and presuppositions are more sharply delineated than Stratemeyer's *et al.* "set of beliefs," *Developing a Curriculum. . .* , 23.

times a principle simply announces what the designers consider a "given." Usually theology or philosophy is enlisted by way of justification. These may be referred to as *declarative principles* and described as principles which *state a relationship of fact based upon a theological and/or philosophical interpretation of the variables and their interrelationship.* Declarative principles can frequently be expressed by the present tense of the copulative verb. Their similarity to presuppositions is close. They differ from presuppositions especially in their conciseness.

Other principles seem to arise from educational premises. They are *prescriptive* insofar as they can be neglected only at the risk of frustrating the normal function of an educational dynamic or technique. Usually *prescriptive principles* can be expressed by "should" or "must." They can be defined as principles which *rely upon an analysis of the functions of the educational variables between which they express the dependable relationship.* These are the statements which are most frequently considered principles in curriculum design for general education.

A third kind of principle may be referred to as *selective.* These are the principles which name one among several options which curriculum planners may, even arbitrarily, choose. More precisely, *selective principles* may be defined as those which *choose among the many relationships that may obtain between variables one that will govern a particular curriculum plan.* Usually selective principles are expressed by the future tense of the verb. They are similar to practical curriculum decisions.

Not infrequently, the principles which actually and consistently guide curriculum decisions remain unexpressed. Conversely, stated principles are not always followed in practice. Consequently, a distinction should be made between stated and operative principles. In this study an *operative principle* is understood as *one which, whether stated or implied, actually and effectively guides concrete curriculum decisions.*

From the nature and functions of curriculum principles, their characteristics follow. They should be succinct statements, brief single sentences if possible, nuanced in the light of their presuppositions but practical in their orientation. They should be clear and precise, sufficiently qualified to be flexible, yet direct enough to be realistic guides.

The function of the organizing principle deserves special attention. The organizing principle relates all the other principles of a curriculum one to another. It provides that no single principle will preclude the effectiveness of another. It sees that principles of objective, personnel, scope, process, context, and timing all bring their proper weight to bear upon the planning of curriculum. The organizing principle rests upon an evaluative judgment which considers the relative importance of all the curriculum principles and awards to each its rightful role. From its function, then, the *organizing principle* might be defined as *a statement embodying the evaluative judgment which relates the principles of objective, personnel, scope, process, context, and timing one to another in such a way that each exercises its proper guidance upon curriculum planning.*

Foundations for Principles—Data Sources

It has already been pointed out that curriculum principles rest upon theological, educational, psychological, historical, and other presuppositions which deserve to be made explicit and justified. Dr. Goodlad's injunction that these presuppositions should be informed by the "best knowledge available—that is, the data-source of funded knowledge" as contrasted to "conventional wisdom" has also been noted. Now it is necessary to identify these data sources or foundational disciplines, as Protestant Christian education is wont to call them, and to describe the manner by which curriculum principles are derived from them.

Foundational Disciplines.—Granted that Christian faith is an horizon upon the whole of reality, the scope of Christian education is literally as large as life. Accordingly, there are no sources of funded knowledge or conventional wisdom upon which Christian education cannot draw for curriculum principles. Yet certain established disciplines, because of their direct concern with Christian revelation or their systematic study of human meaning, value, and relatedness, contribute especially pertinent insights to the framing of curriculum principles for Christian education.

It is neither the need nor the intention of this section to define each of these disciplines in detail nor to give a lengthy bibliography for each. Extensive descriptions of the disciplines and their relevance to Christian education may be found in the two excellent surveys of current Christian education edited by Marvin J. Taylor in 1960 and 1966.[124] An annotated bibliography of works in each discipline was prepared by Dr. Wyckoff and the Joint Committee of Nine in 1960 with additions annually until the present.[125] This section follows

124 *Supra,* 26, nn. 34 and 35.
125 "Bibliography in Christian Education for Presbyterian College Libraries," submitted by the Joint Committee of Nine for use in the program for the preparation of Certified Church Educators (Assistants in Christian Education), ([Dis-

Wyckoff's identification of the foundational disciplines and his indication of their usefulness as data sources for Christian education curriculum principles.[126]

The most obvious data source is theology in all its several branches: biblical, systematic, moral, patristic, speculative, liturgical. Theology provides not only the scope of adult Christian education curriculum but also the normative and final critique of each principle in any curriculum category. Philosophy forms the next most obvious foundational discipline. Especially its branches of epistemology, metaphysics, ethics, and axiology investigating as they respectively do the fields of understanding, being, human responsibility, and personal value elucidate principles in all six categories but especially in scope, process, and personnel. The field of education is a third important foundational source for curriculum principles. Facing as it does similar problems in all six categories and mining from philosophy, history, sociology, psychology, and communications answers to its own curricular questions it offers Christian education both an heuristic structure and many tested answers to the latter's own questions. Especially with respect to process and the problem of organizing the curriculum, the foundational discipline of education assists Christian education. Secular, religious, and specifically Christian history offer an additional source of curricular answers in all categories but especially in the category of timing. With its organized understanding of past experience in the task of educating Christians, the history of catechetics suggests tested solutions to several curricular problems. The discipline of sociology also holds many implications for curriculum principles but no more decisively than in the category of context. The sociology of religion has been particularly fruitful in revealing the cultural dynamics of societal religion as a matrix for learning. The field of psychology is an invaluable data source especially for principles in the categories of process and timing. Its scientific study of human behavior and development must be weighed and incorporated in any principles governing human learning and learning situations. The marriage of sociology and psychology in the relatively recent discipline of social psychology studies the interrelation of society and the individual in human becoming and thereby offers Christian education a more complex but realistic view of contextual Christian becoming. (Social psychology seems to approximate the field of cultural anthropology which in-

tributed by D. Campbell Wyckoff, Princeton Theological Seminary, Princeton, N.J.], 1960). (Mimeographed.) (Addenda annually.)

[126] See Wyckoff, *The Task.* . . , 25-31; *The Gospel.* . . , 74-76; and *Theory and Design.* . . , 87-113.

creasingly preoccupies European catechetical theorists such as André Brien,[127] Pierre Liégé [128] and Marcel van Caster.[129]) The rapidly developing field of communications beginning with the semantics and symbolics of language and expanding into the realms of visual and dramatic forms is a necessary data source for Christian education in an era when most learning gives evidence of taking place through the influence of mass communications media. With Wyckoff, I agree, then, that theology, philosophy, education, history, social psychology, and communications deserve to exercise their influence upon the construction and sophistication of curriculum principles for adult Christian education.

The Derivation of Principles from Foundational Disciplines

The questions in all six categories and in the concern of organization are asked of persons. Persons involved in curriculum planning will invariably answer curricular questions in terms of their own Christian and educational experience, convictions, and expectations. But curriculum planners must be willing to have their experience, convictions, and expectations broadened, informed, criticized, and corrected by those larger, scientifically organized, and thoroughly thought-through bodies of experience, convictions, and expectations which are the foundational disciplines.

Since, however, the funded knowledge of the foundational disciplines is not usually oriented to solving curricular problems but rather to the formal objects of their own study, the first task of curriculum planners is to ask properly educational questions of the foundational disciplines.[130] This study has already attempted to do so in delineating its categories of inquiry and the general concerns related to them.

The second task of curriculum planners is to assess the insights which the foundational disciplines yield against their own experience in Christian education. Since Christian education is a practical undertaking, practical prudence, shaped by educational experience, will have to pass final judgment on the pertinence and application of insights from the foundational disciplines. Thus, a reciprocity between the experience of curriculum planners and the funded knowledge of the

---

127 *La cheminement de la foi* (Paris: Éditions du Seuil, 1964).

128 *Adults dan le Christ* (Brussels: La Pensée Catholique, 1958).

129 "Catechetical Renewal and the Renewal of Theology" in *Theology of Renewal*, Vol. II: *Renewal of Religious Structures*, Proceedings of the Congress on the Theology of the Renewal of the Church, Centenary of Canada, 1867-1967, ed. by L. K. Shook (New York: Herder and Herder, 1968), 222-41.

130 Wyckoff, *The Gospel. . .* , 78-81; *Theory and Design. . .* , 83-86.

data sources will beget curriculum principles which both incorporate the insights of the foundational disciplines and provide practical guidance for the enterprise of Christian education.

THE DISTILLATION OF INQUIRY AND RESPONSE—CURRICULUM DESIGN

The questions in the categories of inquiry seek answers in the form of curriculum principles. These principles, in turn, need an organizing principle to govern their coordinated influence in planning curriculum. Both the principles in each category and the organizing principle must be justified in the light of the experience of Christian education, informed, enlarged, and corrected by the foundational disciplines. In this study, the briefest possible statement of the body of these principles for a particular curriculum plan and their justification is the curriculum design.

This understanding of curriculum design is not universally shared by curriculum theorists, but it does enjoy wide currency. It closely approximates the understanding of the term in the Cooperative Curriculum Project and in the denominational curriculums based upon it. The Project's definition of curriculum design is "the basic principles, foundations, and framework which shape the Curriculum Plan, experienced in five interrelated components: Objective, Scope, Context, Learning Tasks, Organizing Principle." [131] The same understanding coincides with Stratemeyer's *et al.* less precise description: "The proposal that indicates the basis for the selection and organization of knowledge, concepts, and skills stressed in any given school system is its *curriculum design.*" [132]

For the purpose of this study curriculum design means *the systematic articulation, justification, and explanation of the principles which effectively guide curriculum planning and their correlation by an organizing principle.* So defined, there is a difference between a curriculum design and the design of a specific program. Several specific programs can be based upon a single curriculum design. The curric-

---

[131] *CCP,* 817-18. See also *The Design for the Curriculum of Education in the Ministry of Christian Churches (Disciples of Christ)* ([St. Louis:] Christian Board of Publication, 1966), pp. 2-3 (178-79), 38 (214) and *Design for Methodist Curriculum: A Statement of the Curriculum Committee, General Board of Education, The Methodist Church* (Nashville: Editorial Division, General Board of Education, 1965), pp. 7-8.

[132] *Developing a Curriculum. . . ,* 85. Saylor and Alexander, *Curriculum Planning. . . ,* 245, are even less precise: "By curriculum design we mean the pattern or framework or structural organization used in selecting, planning, and carrying forward educational experiences in the school. Design is thus the plan that teachers follow in providing learning activities."

ulum design articulates the basic principles, the program design incorporates varying practical decisions based upon those principles.

SUMMARY

This chapter sought to outline a conceptual system or methodological model or heuristic structure by which to deal with unavoidable curricular questions in adult Christian education. It sought to provide for adult Christian education what John Goodlad has asked for in general education curriculum research.

Goodlad asks for a rigorous formulation of curricular questions, differentiating major from subordinate ones and classifying the elements that tie the questions together in a system. He offers four "substantive" categories in which these questions arise—objectives, methods, organization, and evaluation. In addition, he asks that the data sources be identified from which the questions are to be answered and their relevance to the questions indicated. Finally, he requires that the levels of decision-making which these questions address be identified and their interaction demonstrated.

Following the work of the Cooperative Curriculum Project and D. Campbell Wyckoff, I have delineated six categories of curriculum inquiry and three general curriculum concerns in order to manage curricular questions. I have also attempted to differentiate major from subordinate questions in each category of inquiry. I distribute Goodlad's two "substantive" categories of objectives and methods over my own categories of objective, scope, process, context, and timing. I see aspects of his levels of decision-making as a sixth category—personnel. Furthermore, I have reinterpreted Goodlad's two other "substantive" categories, organization and evaluation, as general curriculum concerns which deal with the six categories of inquiry together. I have added a third concern, adminstration, to which other aspects of decision-making belong.

The six categories of curriculum inquiry are objective, personnel, scope, process, context, and timing. Following are their definitions and the major and subordinate questions in each.

The *objective* of the curriculum is *the overall purpose which a curriculum plan seeks to help the learner achieve*. It should be single, basic, comprehensive, complete, ultimate. The *category of objective* should comprise *the irreducible and unavoidable questions which seek that purpose*. It wishes to know the "why" of curriculum.

With respect to adult Christian education in general, the major question in the category of objective is: Why adult Christian education? With respect to a specific program the question is: What is the purpose of this adult Christian education program?

The subordinate questions are: What is (are) the function(s) of the objective? and What is the relationship between the objective and the purpose of the Church?

The *personnel* of curriculum are *the persons who learn from and teach one another in the educational process.* The *category of personnel* comprises *the irreducible and unavoidable questions needed to discover the persons who learn from and teach one another in the educational process and the roles according to which they interrelate.* It wishes to know the "who" of curriculum.

With respect to adult Christian education, the major question in the category of personnel is: Who interrelate as learners and teachers in adult Christian education?

The subordinate questions are: What is God's role in adult Christian education? What is the role of the College of Bishops in adult Christian education? What is the learner's role in a curriculum plan? What is the teacher's role in a curriculum plan? What are the roles of learners, teachers, and others in designing curriculum? What is the role of administrators with respect to a curriculum plan?

The *scope* of curriculum is *the meanings which curriculum intends to explore and/or communicate.* The *category of scope* comprises *the irreducible and unavoidable questions which search out those meanings.* It wishes to know the "what" of curriculum.

With respect to adult Christian education, the major question in the category of scope is: What is appropriate scope for adult Christian education?

The subordinate questions are: How comprehensive should the scope of a curriculum be? What distinct dimensions of scope lend themselves to different kinds of adult Christian learning? How shall dimensions of scope be selected for inclusion in a curriculum plan? In what sequence will dimensions of scope be offered in a curriculum plan?

The *process* of curriculum is *the dynamics by which the learning-teaching experience happens.* The *category of process* comprises *the irreducible and unavoidable questions which seek the dynamics that will best ensure the desired teaching-learning experience.* It wishes to know the "how" of curriculum.

With respect to adult Christian education, the major question in the category of process is: How does adult Christian learning happen?

The subordinate questions are: What kinds of adult Christian learning are to be sought? How is the learner's motivation to be approached in pursuing the kinds of learning desired? What dominant teaching-learning modes give promise of achieving certain kinds of learning?

The *context* of curriculum is *the social and spatial environment of learning*. A *setting* within the context is a *specifically structured and situated grouping for learning*. The *category of context* comprises *the irreducible and unavoidable questions needed to arrive at the over-all and particular social and spatial environment for learning*. It wishes to know the "where" of curriculum.

With respect to adult Christian education, the major question in the category of context is: Where does adult Christian learning take place?

The subordinate questions are: How shall persons be grouped for adult Christian learning? How should the selected groupings be structured? and Where shall the structured group meet?

The *timing* of *curriculum* is *the succession of events and experiences during which learning occurs*. The *category of timing* comprises *the irreducible and unavoidable questions needed to discover the succession of events and experiences that will best promise the occurrence of learning*. It wishes to know the "when" of curriculum?

With respect to adult Christian education, the major question in the category of timing is: When does adult Christian learning occur?

The subordinate questions are: What principle governs the responsiveness of a curriculum plan to God's present activity? What principle governs the responsiveness of a curriculum plan to current events in the Church and in the world? How shall the readiness which is conditioned by age, experience, and responsibility influence a curriculum plan? What determines the frequency and duration with which related adult learning opportunities will be offered?

In addition to the six categories of inquiry, this study has identified three general curriculum concerns which deal with all the categories together. The first is the organization, the second the evaluation, and the third the administration of the curriculum.

The concern of organizing the curriculum is the problem of interrelating the six categories of inquiry so that the answers given to each major and subordinate question will exercise its proper influence in planning an entire curriculum. Depending on whether scope or process is seen as the key to the organization of the curriculum, the question may be put in either of two ways: What dimensions of *scope* shall *persons* master through a *process timed* and *situated* so as to achieve the *objective?* or How shall the *process* be *timed* and *situated* so as to involve the *persons* in mastering the *scope* in order to achieve the *objective?* To either of the questions responds the organizing principle. The *organizing principle* is a *statement embodying the evaluative judgment which relates the principles of objective, personnel, scope, process, context, and timing one to another in such a way that each exercises its proper guidance upon curriculum planning.*

At the level of planning the curriculum, the general concern of evaluation deals with the validity of the planning process employed rather than with the results of the curriculum once planned. Evaluation continually asks: Are these categories of curriculum inquiry necessary and sufficient to raise all the significant curricular questions? Are the questions within each category necessary and sufficient to deal with the distinct problem that the category faces? and Are the answers to the questions in each category adequately reflective of the most reliable data sources?

Although administration follows upon curriculum planning, the general concern of administering the curriculum enters into curriculum planning insofar as it asks that all the answers given to the questions in each category and in the concern of organizing the curriculum be administratively practical. Administration continually asks the question: How administratively practical are the answers given to each question in objective, personnel, scope, process, context, and timing, as organized by the organizing principle?

The answers to the questions within the six categories and in the general concern of organizing the curriculum take the form of curriculum principles. A *curriculum principle* is a *judgment expressing the dependable relationship between two or more educational variables which guides curriculum planning and practice.* Principles are *major* or *subordinate* depending on whether they respond to major or subordinate questions.

Principles can further be distinguished as declarative, prescriptive, or selective. A principle is *declarative if it states a relationship of fact based upon a theological and/or philosophical interpretation of the variables and their interrelationship.* A principle is *prescriptive if it relies upon an analysis of the functions of the educational variables between which it expresses the dependable relationship.* A principle is *selective if it chooses among the many relationships that may obtain between variables one that will govern a particular curriculum plan.*

Furthermore, principles may be stated and/or operative. An *operative princple is one which, whether stated or implied, actually and effectively guides concrete curriculum decisions.*

Principles should be succinct statements, nuanced in the light of their presuppositions but practical in their orientation, sufficiently qualified to be flexible but direct enough to be realistic guides.

Curriculum planners frame curriculum principles in the light of their own Christian and educational experience, convictions, and expectations. This experience, however, should be broadened, informed, criticized, and corrected by those scientifically organized bodies of experience, convictions, and expectations which are the foundational disciplines of Christian education. These foundational disciplines include theology, philosophy, education, history, sociology, psychology, and communications. The task of curriculum planners is to ask properly educational questions of the foundational disciplines and to weigh the answers in the light of their own practical experience in Christian education.

The systematic articulation, justification, and explanation of principles which effectively guide curriculum planning and their correlation by an organizing principle is curriculum design. So defined, a curriculum design can be the basis for many specific programs.

This chapter has attempted to provide a methodology for "doing curriculum" analytically from its theoretical base to its practical product—the actual program design itself. The factors of curriculum have been identified (objective, personnel, scope, process, context, timing), major and subordinate questions have been organized around each factor, the kinds of principles the questions seek have been indicated, and the sources of these principles outlined. In the remaining chapters, we shall take each one of the factors and try to answer the questions by principles derived from the experience of adult Christian education and the foundational disciplines.

CHAPTER II

Objective–The Overall Purpose of Adult Christian Education

THREE QUESTIONS dominate this chapter: Why adult Christian education? What is (are) the function (s) of the objective? What is the relationship between the objective and the purpose of the Church? Let us work with each singly.

WHY ADULT CHRISTIAN EDUCATION?

This question seeks the single, basic, comprehensive, complete, ultimate purpose of adult Christian education at its most theoretical level. Practically the question must also be asked of any given program. In the latter case it can be phrased: What is the purpose of this adult Christian education program? In this chapter, I shall attempt to answer only the theoretical question. Answers to the practical question will differ from program to program but all of them should be consistent with one's basic answer to the theoretical question.

First, let us consider how two Protestant and two Catholics designs answer the question.

Since the American Baptist design uses the very methodology of the Cooperative Curriculum Project upon which my methodology is based, its statement of objective may prove especially illustrative. The American Baptist Board of Christian Education states an objective not just for adult Christian education but for all of Christian education. It is:

The objective of the church's educational ministry is that all persons be aware of God through his self-disclosure, especially his redeeming love as revealed in Jesus Christ, and enabled by the Holy Spirit respond in faith and love; that as new persons in Christ they may know who they are and what their human situation means, grow as sons of God rooted in the Christian community, live in obedience to the will of God in every relationship,

70

fulfill their common vocation in the world, and abide in the Christian hope.[1]

The statement is all embracing and thoroughly theological. It is evocative and challenging. What it says, it says well. However, in light of the very methodology which grounds it, the statement says too much. That methodology insists that the objective is "not a list of tasks to be performed or relationships to be dealt with or areas of content to be covered, but [is] one end toward which the whole process is directed." [2] The Baptist objective goes beyond that one end into the relationships to be dealt with and areas of content to be covered.

The first member of the objective would suffice: "that all persons be aware of God through his self-disclosure, especially his redeeming love as revealed in Jesus Christ, and enabled by the Holy Spirit respond in faith and love." What follows are subobjectives or themes which further specify the objective.[3]

The temptation to which the Baptist statement succumbs is easy to fall into. Whether stating an overall purpose for adult Christian education in general or for an actual program in particular, the temptation is to begin listing dimensions of scope or kinds of processes. The bare objective seems so vague and vacuous that one wants immediately to flesh it out. One must resist the temptation and leave further specification to the categories of personnel, scope, process, context, and timing. These categories will answer the questions of by whom, through what, how, where, and when the objective can be achieved.

Ferreting out an overall objective from the United Presbyterian curriculum materials is a more difficult matter. Not only do they fail to be based upon a consistent curriculum methodology but they also represent three, not one, distinct programs for adults.[4] More accurately they represent one approach to program planning and two developed programs.

The approach to program planning for adults is the "situational approach." Basically the approach is an invitation from the United Presbyterian Board of Christian Education to the local congregation to

[1] *Foundations for Curriculum,* American Baptist Approved Documents for Curriculum Building (Valley Forge, Pa.: American Baptist Board of Education and Publication, 1966), p. 13.

[2] *Supra,* 29.

[3] In the *CCP* design, which the Baptist design repeats with the addition of a few phrases, these sub-objectives become, in fact, the areas of scope. See *Dissertation,* 140-41.

[4] See *Dissertation,* 199-213, 220-21, 225-27.

design its own adult programs at the grassroots under the stimulus and with the resources of the Board. The approach is spelled out in *Lay Education in the Parish*.[5] Its rationale is set forth in *A New Venture in Church Education* [6] and in *A Dynamic Approach to Church Education*.[7] Monthly resources are supplied to congregations doing adult education "situationally" through *Trends: A Journal of Resources*.[8]

The Board of Christian Education also makes available two developed programs for adults. The first is a series of books for reading and discussion—The Decade Books.[9] The second is a guided study and discussion course which appears in a quarterly periodical *Enquiry: Studies for Christian Laity*.[10]

Our purpose here is not to analyze this planning approach or these two programs. In the notes, readers have been referred to the passages in my Dissertation where they can find this analysis. Rather our purpose here is to consider the various statements of overall purpose that are either articulated explicitly by the programs or can be discovered inductively from curriculum materials.

The "situational approach" projects several statements of overall purpose. The booklet which is considered the foundational document for the new approach, *A New Venture in Church Education*, states the overall purpose this way:

If church members are to participate meaningfully in worship and engage effectively in witness and service, they must be helped to develop the abilities to:

[5] Robert H. Kempes (Philadelphia: The Geneva Press, 1968). For an analysis of *Lay Education in the Parish*, see *Dissertation*, 221-32.

[6] Also known as *Christian Faith and Action: Designs for an Educational System* (distributed by the Board of Christian Education, the United Presbyterian Church U.S.A., Philadelphia, 1967). For an analysis, see *Dissertation*, 203-09.

[7] Gerald H. Slusser, ed. by Lindell Sawyers and Ray T. Woods (Philadelphia: The Geneva Press, 1968). For this book's development of objective, see *Dissertation*, 209-11.

[8] (Philadelphia: The Geneva Press, 1968+). For an analysis of *Trends*, see *Dissertation*, 233-40.

[9] Only eight of these books comprise the "Foundations of Christian Faith and Action." They are Robert J. Bull, *Tradition in the Making;* John Frederick Jansen, *Exercises in Interpreting Scripture;* Perry Le Fevre, *Man: Six Modern Interpretations;* Arthur C. McGill, *Suffering: A Test of Theological Method;* J. Robert Nelson, *Crisis in Unity and Witness;* Jack L. Stotts, *Believing, Deciding, Acting;* Stephen Szikszai, *The Covenants in Faith and History;* and O Z (sic) White, *Changing Society*. All are edited by Lindell Sawyers and Ray T. Woods and published in Philadelphia by the Geneva Press, 1968. For an analysis of the Decade Books, see *Dissertation*, 240-49.

[10] (Philadelphia: The Geneva Press, 1968+). For an analysis of *Enquiry*, see *Dissertation*, 249-58.

-interpret the Bible intelligently
-understand the beliefs of the church
-work for the unity and mission of the church
-grasp the implications of committing one's personal life to God
-deal with ethical issues
-solve contemporary problems.[11]

The six "abilities," later reduced to five,[12] become the advertised goals of the new venture. However, when one inspects the statement closely, one notices that the Presbyterian Board has done the same thing which the Baptist Board did. It states an overall objective and several sub-objectives. Despite the attention they receive in foundational and promotional materials, the "five abilities" are not the overall purpose but sub-objectives. "To participate meaningfully in worship and engage effectively in witness and service" is the overall objective.[13] The "five abilities" are means to that end.

Although commissioned as an explanatory booklet of "the new venture," [14] *A Dynamic Approach to Church Education* comes up with a different, in fact several different statements of overall purpose.

The goal is, rather, that an individual shall come to a self-conscious awareness of his own responsibility before God and that he shall commit himself to the whole of being and to making being whole, i.e. to the extension of the love of God and neighbor.[15]

And:

It is our goal, of course, that within the classroom context persons will come ever more self-consciously to understand themselves as responsible Christians in the world, and that they will see themselves as persons who can cooperate with that ever-present and continuing redemptive activity of God which is in every sector of the world.[16]

[11] *A New Venture. . . ,* 9.
[12] The last two were joined, *ibid.,* 10-13.
[13] This point is reinforced by other statements in *A New Venture. . . .* One is "only then can the church hope that its members will be able to participate responsibly in the life, worship, and mission to which they are called in Jesus Christ" (p. 7). Another is "the goal of such education in the church is to equip church members of all ages with the abilities required to live responsibly the Christian life" (p. 14).
[14] See "Outline for Lay Studies Book on Instruction in Church Education." An unpublished paper available in "Decade Books" file Division of Lay Education, Board of Christian Education, United Presbyterian Church in the U.S.A. Witherspoon Building, Philadelphia, Pa., October 24, 1966. (Spirit duplicated.)
[15] P. 38.
[16] P. 50.

And again:

The purpose in each case is to become agents of discernment, to discover in these events the present manner of God's activity which we have discerned in Jesus Christ.[17]

Though different in emphases, these statements of overall objective are obviously consistent with one another. They are, however, somewhat at variance with the statement of purpose in *A New Venture in Church Education* which they are meant to reflect. The statements favor almost exclusively the "engage effectively in witness and service" member of the "new venture" objective and the last two—the ethical —abilities of the "five abilities."

A still different, though not unrelated, statement of overall purpose is expressed in *Lay Education in the Parish.*

What is the purpose of Lay Education? . . . It is to *enable* the people of the church to *reflect* upon what faith in Jesus Christ means, and to *explore* its implications in everyday life.[18]

Like the "five abilities" and the first statement in *A Dynamic Approach to Church Education,* this is an "enabling" goal. "To *reflect* upon what faith in Jesus Christ means" relates it to the first two "abilities." "To *explore* its implications in everyday life" relates it to the fourth and fifth "abilities." More than any other, however, this statement approximates the second and third ones from *A Dynamic Approach to Church Education.*

These are various stated purposes in Presbyterian foundational or explanatory literature. Let us see how they compare with the purposes which emerge inductively from the materials based on them.

Trends is a thirty-two page periodical appearing monthly ten times a year. Its three sections seek to alert local planners to the many issues that beg for reflection ("Pinpointing the Issue"), the resources by which they might be explored ("Comment"), and the various methods that might be used in exploring them ("Venture"). As such, *Trends* tries to make the "situational approach" to planning adult programs operative and viable.

An investigation of its numbers through 1968 and 1969 seems to reveal this overall purpose: *that readers be aware of contemporary social and ethical issues and reflect on them from a Christian per-*

17 P. 120.
18 P. 38.

spective. Awareness seems the principle objective. Reflection from a Christian perspective is minor. Any purpose actively to change the situations observed and reflected upon is minimal. More than any other the purpose of *Trends* echoes that of *Lay Education in the Parish*.

The Decade Books, especially the eight referred to above as "The Foundations of Christian Faith and Action," comprise a developed adult program. To derive an objective inductively from all eight would be too lengthy a task. Fortunately there exist design papers of the Board of Christian Education which express many of the principles on which key decisions rest. An especially helpful one is "Description of Units for a Basic Course of Study for Teacher Education and Lay Study." [19] It states that "the overall purpose of this course of study, . . . is to help learners . . . to develop the five abilities that should be operative in communicant members of the church." Obviously this statement of purpose hues closely to the one expressed in *A New Venture in Church Education*.

Like the Decade Books, *Enquiry* also embodies a developed adult program. It is the successor to *Crossroads: Studies for Adults in Christian Faith and Life* which for eighteen years (1950-68) was the only adult program offered by the Presbyterian Board of Christian Education. Like *Crossroads* it is a quarterly publication. Like *Crossroads* it has three sections devoted to the same general areas but under different titles: Frontiers-The Human Scene; The Interpreter-The Lively Word (Biblical Studies); and Focus-Quest (Theological Studies). Nowhere does one find a statement of overall purpose in *Enquiry* but an inspection of numbers leads one to conclude that its purpose is *to encourage the development of informed and reflective Christians*.[20] The accent falls heavily upon intellectual development. As such the purpose does not reflect that of the "new venture" so much as the purpose which *Enquiry* inherited from *Crossroads*.

I have outlined these statements of purpose from the Presbyterian materials not as an exercise in tedium but for the valuable lessons they hold for thinking through an answer to the question: Why adult Christian education? If my methodology is correct, that question seeks the single, basic, comprehensive purpose for adult Christian education with which the purpose of any individual program will be in harmony. Because they are developed by members of the same team,

---

[19] Available in "Decade Books" file, Division of Lay Education, Board of Christian Education, United Presbyterian Church in the U.S.A., Witherspoon Building, Philadelphia, dated May 23, 1966.

[20] See *Dissertation*, 249-51.

the United Presbyterian Board of Christian Education and especially its Division of Lay Education, one might expect that all these materials would exhibit a unified purpose. They do not. The absence of unified purpose shows up in the programs and materials themselves—many of which overlap and compete with one another.[21]

The lesson is clear. If a team is to design and conduct a variety of programs, its members would be well advised to spend the necessary time to hammer out an agreed upon purpose. To the degree that they agree upon that purpose are they likely to complement rather than frustrate one another's efforts.

We are still looking, however, for examples of statements of overall purpose. We turn to those of the two Catholic diocesan religious education offices I have studied. I asked each office to answer the same questions about objective: What is the objective of your diocesan adult Christian education curriculum? and once answered: What is your justification for this statement?

Each of the diocesan offices, Lansing's and Baltimore's, plan, sponsor, and/or coordinate several programs in adult education. They range from CCD teacher formation courses to sacramental preparation programs, to lecture series, to small group discussions, to film seminars, to college level courses with academic credit. The answers of their diocesan staff personnel, then, are well grounded in wide experience.[22]

To the first question Lansing replied:

The objective of the Lansing diocesan adult Christian education curriculum is the mature adult Christian—knowledgeable in and committed to his faith, able to apply what he knows to daily life.[23]

In answer to the second question, Lansing quoted from articles 1 and 2 of Vatican II's "Declaration on Christian Education."

Baltimore answered the first question:

The objective of the diocesan adult Christian education curriculum is to assist adults to live a conscious and mature Christian life within themselves and with others through the action of the Spirit.[24]

21 *Ibid.*, 225-27 and 249-51.
22 Responding for Lansing was Dr. George A. Martin assisted by Rev. William Fitzgerald, Sister Angela La Branche, Rev. Robert Lunsford, Rev. William Meyers, and Mr. James Rauner. Responding for Baltimore as a team were Rev. Paul Asselin, recorder, and Rev. Robert A. Armstrong, Rev. Paul G. Cook, and Sister Teresa Mary Dolan.
23 *Dissertation*, 306.
24 *Dissertation*, 360.

In justification of its objective, Baltimore stated:

The justification for the objective is the theological and pastoral realization of what Christian life is and should be.[25]

We now have several Protestant and Catholic statements of overall purpose for adult Christian education to consider.

The dominant aspects of the various objectives seem to be the following. The American Baptist objective stresses awareness and response to God's revealing Himself. The Presbyterian objectives emphasize understanding of and involvement in God's activity in the present. Lansing seeks the development of a Christian person; Baltimore the encouragement of Christian living. The aspects are not mutually exclusive. Frequently, aspects which predominate in one objective are found explicitly or implicitly in the others.

In several of the objectives faith receives explicit attention but without agreement as to its meaning or function. The Baptist objective is to invite and increase faith (personal belief) in God's revealing Himself. For some Presbyterian designs the objective is to reflect upon faith (one's own or what Christians usually believe?) and to explore its implications in life. In Lansing's objective, faith seems to mean an objective body of truth which one should be knowledgeable in and committed to.

The Person of Christ plays an explicit role in only the Baptist and Presbyterian objectives. He is the Person through Whom especially God reveals Himself and His activity. He is the immediate object of the faith-response. Although the Person of Christ receives no direct mention in the Lansing or Baltimore objectives, a *Christian* person and *Christian* living are respectively the dominant intent of each. Apparently, both assume the meaning of the adjective to be sufficiently agreed upon not to require a clue as to their use of it.[26]

Both the Baptist and Baltimore objectives explicitly state the enabling role of the Holy Spirit. The Presbyterian and Lansing designs do not see the necessity of its being expressed in the objective.

Upon comparison, then, all the statements differ in emphasis, although they are not mutually exclusive. No one of them can be selected as representative of all. Only with distortion of one or another could they be combined into a single objective. Moreover, the justification of none is so persuasive as to favor its preference over the

25 *Ibid.*

26 The meaning of "Christian" is increasingly difficult to discern as the tendency grows to equate humanism with Christianity. See John B. Cobb, Jr., "The Intrapsychic Structure of Christian Existence" in *To Be a Man*, ed. George Devine (Englewood Cliffs, New Jersey: Prentice-Hall, Inc., 1969), 24-40.

others. Furthermore, none of the statements expresses learning as an aspect of the objective, despite the fact that it is an educational enterprise for which an objective is sought.

The field, then, lies quite open to fresh attempts to articulate a broad theoretical objective for adult Christian education. Every planning team should make the effort to frame or adopt its own. I shall offer mine shortly.

First, however, it may be helpful to suggest a few hints as to how a statement of objective may be more easily arrived at. I have discovered both from analyzing statements of objective and especially from drawing objectives inductively from program descriptions and materials that the objective should be but the briefest possible indication of the personnel, scope, and process of adult Christian education in general or of a given program in particular. Context and timing normally need not be indicated in the statement of objective though they can be. The more proper place for them to be expressed is in the organizing principle which, as will be later developed,[27] is usually an expansion of the objective. Consequently, simply to identify the target group (personnel), and succinctly to characterize the scope and process will suffice.

It takes much discipline to keep the objective as lean as possible. The temptation is always present to state in the objective what were better left for the major principles of personnel, scope, and process. However, remembering that these categories will continually amplify, and in the actual planning process change the objective, should keep one from feeling that the objective to too vague, too general, too vacuous. As a practical help, the planning team might restrict itself to ten words or less in stating the objective.

With these hints in mind let me offer a broad theoretical objective for adult Christian education.

It is *that mature persons learn the mystery of Christ*.

The statement is deceptively simple. It may also strike some as badly dated in light of Gabriel Moran's criticism of the catechetical principles of *Eichstätt* and *Lumen Vitae*.[28] It deserves, then, some justification.

Mature persons indicate the target group for adult Christian education. They are persons who are presumed to have already achieved a certain degree of self-acceptance, emotional balance, responsibility, intellectual development, and competence in coping with life. That maturity deserves to be presumed until proven otherwise. Adult Chris-

27 *Infra*, 196-97.
28 See especially *Catechesis of Revelation* (New York: Herder and Herder, 1966).

tian education programs that begin with the premise that persons have not yet learned to be personal, relational, human, or mature until enrolling in the program insult their participants. If it becomes clear that participants need to grow in these qualities before adult Christian education can begin, then program designers must adjust accordingly. But then the enterprise is more human or religious education, in my judgment, than, distinctively Christian education. In the language of recent catechetics it is pre-evangelization rather than evangelization. More accurately with respect to adult education, it might be termed pre-theologization rather than theologization. I do not mean that the task of pre-theologization may not be needed with respect to many adult Catholics. I only mean that pre-theologization ought to be presumed until proven otherwise and further that pre-theologization is not yet adult Christian education. In brief, *mature persons* identify the personnel of adult Christian education—that is, persons in whom a certain degree of emotional and intellectual growth has already been achieved.

Moreover, *learn* in the objective indicates in a word the process which is envisioned. The major and subordinate principles of process which will be stated and elaborated upon in Chapter V develop further what I mean by *learn*. Here it suffices to say that *learn* intends to describe a distinctively educational process. I have explained in the Introduction what I mean by education.[29] It is any continuous undertaking through which the participants intend consciously and primarily to learn. As such it differs from those other undertakings like worship, or changing the social structure, or rearing a family wherein much learning takes place but wherein the primary and conscious intention of persons is usually other than learning.

We are back then to the word *learn* itself. What does it mean? It means a process of reflexively conscious change, growth, transformation. By its nature, learning is or should be continual and on-going. More specifically with respect to Christian education, learning means for me "interpersonal appropriation by faith."

This phrase constitutes my major principle of process. It will be explained in Chapter V.

The mystery of Christ indicates the distinctive scope of Christian education. As such the meaning of the phrase will be enlarged upon in Chapter IV. However, some initial explanation and reason for its selection belong here, especially since there is no phrase in the overall objective which will more readily "turn off" religious educators than this one. Despite its hallowed history in Scripture and tradition, it

29 *Supra*, 7-8.

comes across as shopworn. It belongs to the salvation history catechetics of the 1960's more then to the social-psychological trend of the 1970's.

Yet, if we are to pinpoint the distinctive scope of Christian education, we need some term which evokes that scope in its breadth and also identifies its cohesive center. Contemporary scholarship offers several such terms. "The kingdom of God," [30] the *kerygma*[31] ,"the Gospel," [32] "the mystery of Christ" [33] are some prominent ones. Good reasons commend each. I find the last more acceptable than the others. While it is true that "the kingdom of God" describes the comprehensive category of Jesus' own preaching,[34] yet Christ himself as the prolepsis of that kingdom seems to have been the center of the teaching of the apostolic church.[35] Since Christian education continues the teaching task of the apostolic church, it seems that it should place the person of Christ at its center. To be true, the *kerygma* places the Christ event at its center; but, in itself, the *kerygma* is the verbal message about the central event not, save in the theology of Bultmann [36] and his followers, the event itself. So also "the Gospel," to the degree that it enlarges upon the *kerygma*, is a message about the event. I prefer a term that connotes directly the integrative event itself rather than the message about that event. Such a term is the mystery of Christ as coined in the Pauline corpus [37] and favored in the Second Vatican Council.

It is not necessary to reproduce here the excellent summaries of Paul's use of the mystery of Christ which can be found in biblical

[30] So Rudolph Schnackenburg, *God's Rule and Kingdom*, 2nd enlarged ed., trans. by John Murray (New York: Herder and Herder, 1968). For a survey of the meanings attached to "the kingdom of God" by various exegetes, over the last hundred years, see Gösta Lundström, *The Kingdom of God in the Teaching of Jesus*, trans. by Joan Bulman (Richmond, Va.: John Knox Press, 1963).

[31] So Rudolf Bultmann and his critics with different interpretations. See briefly, Rudolf Bultmann *et al.*, *Kerygma and Myth*, ed. H. W. Bartsch, rev. ed. and trans. by R. H. Fuller (New York: Harper and Row, Publishers, 1961).

[32] So Wyckoff, *The Gospel.* . . .

[33] So Josef A. Jungmann, *The Good News.* . . , esp. 17-23.

[34] See Wolfhart Pannenberg, *Theology and the Kingdom of God* (Philadelphia: The Westminster Press, 1969) esp. pp. 51-71.

[35] See Reginald H. Fuller, *The Foundations of New Testament Christology* (New York: Charles Scribner's Sons, 1965), p. 143: "This is why the proclamation of the church is not just an extension of Jesus' own proclamation of the kingdom of God. . . . [but] rather the proclamation of Jesus himself as the one in whom God began to act eschatologically . . ."

[36] Bultmann *et al.*, *Kerygma and Myth*, esp. 41-42.

[37] "Pauline corpus" here refers to those New Testament writings, except the Epistle to the Hebrews, traditionally attributed to St. Paul. It does not enter into the debate over whether Paul is the immediate author of the captivity epistles or the pastorals. It is only necessary that these be considered canonical writings of the New Testament.

dictionaries and commentaries.[38] Sufficient for the purposes of this study is to repeat that "in the Pauline corpus the term *mystērion* is firmly connected with the kerygma of Christ";[39] that it is the formerly secret design of God revealed to the elect (I Cor. 2:7; Rom. 16:25-26; Eph. 3:5-9; Col. 1:26) which affects the whole of history (Eph. 1:9-11; 3:10-11)[40] and finds its orientation in the Person and work of Christ (*ibid.;* Col. 1:15-20, cf. 1:27) especially in His death and glorification (I Cor. 1:23; Col. 1:20; 3:1-4); that the mystery works itself out through an *oikonomia* (Eph. 3:9) involving all the disciples of Jesus in His death and glorification (Col. 1:27: *Christos en ymin;* cf. Rom. 6:1-11) and in the building up of His Body (Col. 1:18: cf. Eph. 4:1-16) until all is recapitulated (Eph. 3:10) in the Christ in Whom all began (Col. 1:15-17).

The mystery of Christ receives its fullest development in the Epistles to the Ephesians and to the Colossians. Especially in the opening hymns (Eph. 1:3-14 and Col. 1:15-20) is the content of the mystery in its historical breadth and Christic centrality expressed. Ephesians emphasizes the historical breadth; Colossians the Christic centrality.[41] It is because the mystery of Christ as used in the Pauline corpus both centers upon the Person and work of Christ and evokes the whole sweep of the salvific tradition effected by God that I use it to express succinctly the scope of Christian education.

Moreover, the Second Vatican Council uses the same term and its cognates [42] with a more developed depth and sweep. This usage will

---

[38] Readers are referred to Gunther Bornkamm, "mystērion" in *Theological Dictionary of the New Testament,* Vol. IV, ed. Gerhard Kittel, trans. and ed. Geoffrey W. Bromily (Grand Rapids, Michigan: Wm. B. Eerdman Publishing Company, 1967), 817-28; C. F. D. Moule, "Mystery" in *The Interpreter's Dictionary of the Bible,* Vol. III, ed. G. A. Buttrick (New York: Abingdon Press, 1962), 479-81; John L. McKenzie, *Dictionary of the Bible* (Milwaukee: The Bruce Publishing Company, 1965), pp. 595-98; *The Jerome Biblical Commentary,* II, *ad loc.* and 805-17 ("Pauline Soteriology"); and *Peake's Commentary on the Bible,* ed. Matthew Black and H. H. Rowley (London: Thomas Nelson and Sons, Ltd., 1962), *ad loc.*

[39] Bornkamm, *Theological Dictionary of the New Testament,* IV, 819; cf. I Cor. 1:23 with 2:1 (variant: *mystērion*) and 2:7; see also Rom. 16:25-26. The authenticity of the latter passage is disputed (see *The Jerusalem Bible,* n. *ad loc.*). Insofar as the mystery of Christ "is almost equivalent to the Christian Gospel" (Moule, *Interpreter's Dictionary,* III, 480), my use of it as determinative of scope does not differ appreciably from the CCP "in light of the Gospel." See *CCP,* 13-14 and Wyckoff, *The Gospel. . . ,* 179-80.

[40] See Bornkamm, *Theological Dictionary of the New Testament,* IV, 820.

[41] See *The Jerome Biblical Commentary,* II, Eph. 1:9, *ad loc.*

[42] For a resumé of some pivotal texts and their import, see M. D. Chenu, "The History of Salvation and the Historicity of Man in the Renewal of Theology" in L. K. Shook (ed.), *Theology for Renewal,* Vol. I, (New York: Herder and Herder, 1968), esp. pp. 156-63. For the occurrences of the mystery of Christ and more or

be explained in Chapter IV when treating the various meanings of the mystery of Christ. Those meanings will be seen to be historical, theological, liturgical, and ethical.[43] Anticipating their explication, I may here define the mystery of Christ as *God's deed in the Person and work of Christ which gives purpose to all history and meaning to all reality and which invites persons to mystic and ethical involvement in process.*

These, then, are the preliminary reasons why I offer *that mature persons learn the mystery of Christ* as a broad theoretical objective of adult Christian education. For me that statement satisfactorily answers the question: Why adult Christian education? Now we turn to the function of the objective.

WHAT IS (ARE) THE FUNCTION(S) OF THE OBJECTIVE?

What is the advantage of framing an objective for adult Christian education in general or of a given program in particular? What does a statement of objective contribute to the planning process or the actual learning process?

The Baptist Board of Christian Education and the diocesan religious education staffs of Lansing and Baltimore considered the questions expressly. The Presbyterian Board seems not to. At least, no answer to it survives in foundational or descriptive curriculum materials.

To the question: What is (are) the function(s) of the objective? the Baptist Board replies that the objective should provide the direction for all the educational experiences in the curriculum; act as a criterion for planning short-term goals, learning activities, and resources; and serve as a means of evaluating the curriculum.[44]

Lansing states that the function of the objective "is to operate as the ultimate goal—to serve as the end toward which programs are constructed as means." [45]

Baltimore replies that "the function of the objective is the focus of attention toward which the programs should be directed." [46]

Upon inspection, it is obvious that the Lansing and Baltimore principles substantially agree with one another and with the first function

---

less synonymous phrases (the mystery of salvation, the mystery of God's love, etc.), see *Index Verborum cum Documentis Concilii Vaticani Secundi*, compiled by Xaverius Ochoa (Rome: Commentarium pro Religiosis, 1967), pp. 320-21.

43 *Infra*, 120-41.
44 *Dissertation*, 126-29.
45 *Ibid.*, 306-07.
46 *Ibid.*, 360-61.

of the Baptist principle—to "provide the direction for all the educational experiences in the curriculum." The latter goes on to express other important and distinct functions of the objective. Not only because it embraces the other two but especially because it is founded upon the considerable experience of Protestant educators in planning curriculum (the Baptist principle is further based upon the Cooperative Curriculum Project), I accept the Cooperative/Baptist principle as the most satisfactory answer to the question.

As stated however, the Baptist principle envisions an objective which will guide the central planning of curriculum for many local congregations. It is insufficiently nuanced to guide grassroots planning of adult Christian education. If devised and used by a local planning team, the objective will do all that the Baptist principle says but it will do more. It will also act as the criterion for negotiating program changes in the actual learning situation when the needs or expectations of participants indicate the advisability of change.[47] Planning is fine but many times, especially with adults, participants want something different from what program designers have planned. These desires have to be negotiated on location or else there will be so much hostility that little positive learning can occur. In this case, the objective of the program directly and the overall objective of adult Christian education indirectly become the principle of negotiation. More than anything else the objective of the program is the basis on which the learning contract is forged. If the suggested change facilitates that objective it can be adopted. If it does not it can legitimately be rejected and the decision will probably be accepted by all concerned.

Consequently, I offer as an answer to the question: What is (are) the function(s) of the objective? the principle: *the objective should provide the direction for all the educational experiences in a program; act as a criterion for planning and negotiating with participants short-term goals, learning activities, and resources; and serve as a means of evaluating a program.*

WHAT IS THE RELATIONSHIP BETWEEN THE OBJECTIVE AND THE PURPOSE OF THE CHURCH?

The answer to this question is important if Christian education is to take its proper place within the mission of the Church. Is the purpose

---

[47] For a treatment on this same use of the objective with respect to children's education, see D. Campbell Wyckoff, "Putting the Objective of Christian Education into Practice," *Children's Religion*, XXVIII (June, 1967), 3-5.

of Christian education coextensive with the mission of the Church? Is it one aspect of the mission of the Church? Can a particular program of adult Christian education be the be-all and end-all of the Church's mission. These are the kinds of questions that are reducible to the question itself.

In addressing the question: What is the relationship between the objective and the purpose of the Church? the Cooperative Curriculum Project speaks almost as if the mission of the Church and the purpose of Christian education are identical and coextensive.[48] Though based on the Cooperative statement, the Baptist Board qualifies its position:

The Objective for the church's educational ministry should not be different from the purpose guiding the total mission of the church. The Objective should reflect how education contributes to that basic purpose.[49]

The Presbyterian designs do not broach the question explicitly, but one of them sheds some light on the problem by observing that "lay education . . . concerns our conscious and deliberate effort in various settings, to increase our knowledge, to advance our understanding. . . ."[50]

Lansing states that "adult education in its broadest sense has elements of coextensiveness with the purpose of the Church, and hence there exists a very close relationship." Justification for the principle specifies more exactly that "there is only a formal and not a material difference between the objective of adult [Christian] education and the purpose of the Church."[51]

Baltimore sees "a direct relationship between the objective and the purpose of the Church, because the objective is within though not coextensive with the Church." The justification further explains that "the Church [is] a community of service witnessing to the risen Christ in the world, and the object of the curriculum is one of the functions to make this possible."[52]

Each design finds a close relationship between the objective of adult Christian education and the purpose of the Church. Neither Lansing nor Baltimore understand them to be identical. The Baptist Board hedges on the Cooperative Project's inclination to make them so. Baltimore's explanation of why the purposes are directly related but not coextensive is imprecise. Lansing provides a more fruitful suggestion

48 *CCP*, 8-10.
49 *Foundations for Curriculum*, 13.
50 Kempes, *Lay Education in the Parish*, 37.
51 *Dissertation*, 307-08.
52 *Ibid.*, 361.

that there is a formal but not a material difference between the objective of adult Christian education and the purpose of the Church.

Combining the insights of the foregoing principles and applying them to my own statement of objective, I propose that *the objective of adult Christian education agrees with the purpose of the Church materially but differs from it formally insofar as the objective of the former is that [mature] persons learn the mystery of Christ whereas the purpose of the latter is that persons live the mystery of Christ.* Learning is, of course, a kind of living; and, meaningful living involves continuous learning; but, learning, in the words of one Presbyterian design, formally "concerns our conscious and deliberate effort in various settings, to increase our knowledge, to advance our understanding . . ." whereas living formally concerns our effort to be, to become, to grow. This distinction may further clarify why I prefer to state the objective of adult Christian education in terms of learning and not living.

SUMMARY AND APPLICATION

In this chapter I have attempted to answer three questions: Why adult Christian education? What is (are) the function (s) of the objective? and What is the relationship between the objective and the purpose of the Church? I have attempted to do so only after analyzing several Protestant and Catholic responses to these same questions.

I offer answers to the questions in the form of curriculum principles —principles that can guide practical program planning for adults.

The first is a major and declarative principle: the objective of adult Christian education is that mature persons learn the mystery of Christ.

The second is a subordinate and prescriptive principle: the objective should provide the direction for all the educational experiences in a program; act as a criterion for planning and negotiating with participants short-term goals, learning activities, and resources; and serve as a means of evaluating a program.

The third is also a subordinate principle but declarative: the objective of adult Christian education agrees with the purpose of the Church materially but differs from it formally insofar as the objective of the former is that [mature] persons learn the mystery of Christ whereas the purpose of the latter is that persons live the mystery of Christ.

In practice a parochial or diocesan planning team should wrestle with these questions themselves. My principles are only illustrative of the kinds they may come up with. The planning team needs to work through to a broad theoretical purpose for adult Christian education before designing any individual program. If the team fails to do so at the beginning, some time or other during the planning process latent presuppositions, unexpressed goals, and hidden agendas will clog up the process itself. Laboring over an overall objective will force these presuppositions out into the open early when they can enrich the process rather than frustrate it. Once the team agrees on an overall purpose its planning of individual programs will go far more smoothly. Members will revise the overall objective from time to time in light of better theological and educational insights but usually a well thought through objective will stand for a long time and act as the broad theoretical purpose for several programs.

The team's effort to answer the subordinate question regarding the relationship of the overall objective to the purpose of the Church achieves much the same effect as the effort to state an overall objective and will be just as lasting. Grappling with the question gets many presuppositions about the mission of the Church vis-a-vis Christian education out in the open.

The planning team's statement of objective for an individual program is likely to have a more checkered history than the statement of broad theoretical objective. When beginning the process of designing a given program the team needs to identify its initiating objective. It will be imprecise and unformed at the outset, more a hunch or technically an heuristic of what the program will attempt. Vague as it is this objective is what gets the team started along the planning process. For that reason I call it the initiating objective. As the team proceeds to make decisions regarding personnel, scope, and process this initiating objective both influences those decisions and is influenced by them. Only after the major decisions are made regarding these other factors can the objective of the program be stated in a refined and nuanced way. I would advise that a planning team study carefully my answers to the question about the function of the objective before discarding it for another. Only if we have a thorough understanding of the function of the objective will we take the time to state the objective carefully and use it effectively.

CHAPTER III

Personnel—The Persons Who Learn from One Another in Adult Christian Education

 $\mathbf{T}$ HIS CHAPTER deals with persons—the persons who learn from and teach one another in adult Christian education. It will try to answer the questions that reveal those persons—their needs, their competencies, and the roles according to which they interrelate.

The major question is: Who interrelate as learners and teachers in adult Christian education? The subordinate questions are: What is God's role in adult Christian education? What is the role of the College of Bishops? What is the learner's role? What is the teacher's role? What are the roles of learners, teachers, and others in planning? and What is the role of administrators?

As with the principles regarding objective, I shall first survey the principles offered by Protestant and Catholic Christian educators before proposing my own.

WHO INTERRELATE AS LEARNERS AND TEACHERS IN ADULT CHRISTIAN EDUCATION?

Originally this question intended an identification of persons in terms of their roles.[1] That intention governed my application of the question when analyzing the Protestant designs. Diocesan responses, however, and further reflection upon the task of guiding local curriculum planning seem to require that the intent of the question be broadened. First, it will be instructive to review the answers to the question according to its original intent.

An identification of personnel in the Baptist Design names God,

[1] *Supra,* 36, n. 64.

learners, teachers, denominational officers, curriculum planners, and administrators as those who have different roles in adult Christian education.[2]

Understanding *"the heart of education* [to be] *the interaction between persons—especially between student and teacher,"* the Presbyterian designs consider in practice the roles also of the Board of Christian Education, local judicatories, and administrators.[3]

Lansing did not answer the question but described various relationships between learners and teachers determined by what the methodology of this study considers the structure of a setting and learning methods.[4]

Baltimore states that "those who attempt to live a conscious and mature Christian life within themselves and with others through the action of the Spirit are learners and teachers." [5]

Each of these responses offers some insight into the problem of personnel in program design. The Protestant designs offer an identification of the various roles that deserve specification if the interrelationship of persons in adult Christian education is to be appreciated. The roles have counterparts in Catholic adult education. These roles become the subject of subordinate principles. Although Lansing's reply misses the question at hand, it points out that roles will be determined largely by decisions as to process and context—a fact that will have to be weighed in articulating subordinate principles of personnel. Baltimore's principle offers a criterion by which those who interrelate in adult Christian education can be identified. In effect, they are those who jointly try to achieve the objective.

As stated, Baltimore's principle seems insufficiently pointed to direct curriculum planning; but, it offers a more useful approach to the major principle of personnel than the mere identification of persons or groups of persons by which I first intended the question to be answered. Moreover, the principle seems to be correct in considering the attempt to achieve the objective as the criterion which distinguishes persons as participants in adult Christian education. Since I propose a statement of objective different from Baltimore's, my major principle of personnel will also differ; but, it will incorporate the important insight that effort to achieve the objective characterizes persons as active participants. The principle I propose will, however, make explicit the fact that this effort is one of mutual assistance among the participants according to various roles.

[2] *Dissertation,* 181.
[3] *Ibid.,* 269-70.
[4] *Ibid.,* 325.
[5] *Ibid.,* 373.

Changing the intent of the question from a mere identification of roles to a criterion by which persons may be identified as participants is but one aspect of broadening the question. Further reflection upon the task of guiding the local planning of curriculum suggests broadening it in another direction.

In analyzing the Protestant and Catholic designs, it is obvious that felt needs or interests of learners and the competency of teachers are frequently specified as determinants of scope, process, context, and timing.[6] Consequently, the "who" of this major question might also intend that curriculum planners gain personal knowledge especially of teachers and learners in terms of their felt needs, interests, capacities for learning, and competencies. Here the question itself almost acts as a principle—a principle insisting that curriculum planners continually ask who, in their unique personalities, are those with whom and for whom they are planning programs. With these considerations in mind, I would answer the major question of personnel with the declarative principle that *those persons interrelate in teaching and learning adult Christian education who, through various roles, intend to assist one another in learning the mystery of Christ and whose needs, interests, capacities, and competencies largely determine the scope and process of a particular curriculum plan.*

Each planning team will state this principle differently in proportion as its statement of overall purpose differs from mine. But it is important to emphasize that willingness to pursue the objective, however stated, is that which places one in relationship to others in a program of adult Christian education. For instance, persons may be physically in a learning group who have little or no interest in the objective but who never miss a session because loneliness or gregariousness or political advantage or some other motivation occasions their presence. These persons do not relate to others as learners and/or teachers although they may do so as friends and companions. On the other hand, an administrator, or planner, or recruitor who may never be present in the learning group relates to the others as a real participant in the educational process because he works consciously for the objective. The principle, then, asks that all those who have some influence upon the achievement of the objective be identified, be known in terms of their needs and competencies, and be recognized for the relative importance of their roles vis-a-vis others. The subordinate principles which follow specify those roles and relationships more exactly.

---

[6] *Ibid.*, 400, 405, 409, 418, 429, and 433. These principles will be explained at length below in Chapters IV-VII.

What Is God's Role in Adult Christian Education?

This question is as presumptious to ask as it is impossible to answer. But the neglect of it renders program design for Christian education an exercise in pelagianism.

The Christian educator must recognize that he is involved in a species of religious education not religious studies. Religious studies, such as the history of religion, or psychology of religion, or sociology of religion analyze the beliefs, and behavior, and social constructs of believers from an "objective" viewpoint according to a more or less scientific method. The religious educator takes an active and involved role in the facilitation of the beliefs, and behavior, and social constructs which the scientist of religion studies. As a facilitator in the very process of inviting faith, the Christian educator cannot be neutral about God's role. He must try to discover what God's role properly is, respect it, and channel his own efforts accordingly.

The Baptist Design sees God's role as that of a "transforming power" in the learner's undertaking the learning tasks.[7]

The Presbyterian designs do not express a principle regarding God's role in adult Christian education.

Lansing understands "[God's] general role as creating Father, redeeming Son and life-giving Spirit [to be] shared by our curriculum with every other endeavor in the Church." [8] The statement appears too general to guide curriculum planning.

Baltimore states that "God's role in the curriculum is one of operation within the Christian Community, activating and sustaining a process of revelation which exists within the present continuing conscious experience of people, i.e., within the relationship of God and His people." [9]

The Baptist Design associates God's role in curriculum principally with process. Baltimore agrees but accentuates the context in which and by which the process happens. To put it another way, the Baptist principle emphasizes the power which God exercises upon the mind and heart of the individual learner enabling him to "listen with growing alertness to the gospel and respond in faith and love." Baltimore emphasizes God's initiative in continually disclosing Himself through the conscious experience of a community of persons.

I agree with both these emphases and see them as mutually complementary. Understanding the process of Christian education to be "in-

---

7 *Dissertation*, 160 and 181-82.
8 *Ibid.*, 326.
9 *Ibid.*, 374.

terpersonal appropriation by faith," I believe, for reasons that will be more fully developed in Chapter V that God's enabling grace is at work in the process of distinctively Christian learning. I also believe that this grace which moves the individual to appropriate personally the mystery of Christ is but an aspect of God's continuing availability to and through the community of believers who compose the context of Christian education.

However, I do not consider God's role in adult Christian education to concern only or mainly process and context. Insofar as the mystery of Christ is God's deed, God Himself is central to the scope of adult Christian education as well. Insofar as God continues to be active in human affairs now, He exercises a providential influence over the timing of adult Christian education. This statement will be more fully explained in Chapter VII. God's role, then, with respect to scope and timing deserves to be articulated along with His role with respect to process and context.

Consequently, I propose the declarative principle that *God's role in adult Christian education is to be the center of its scope, the enabling power of its process, the creator of its context, and the provider of its timing.* I hope that awareness of this principle will ensure that program design be undertaken in prayer and pursued without pretense.

WHAT IS THE ROLE OF THE COLLEGE OF BISHOPS IN ADULT CHRISTIAN EDUCATION?

The question obviously concerns only Catholic adult education directly. However, it is interesting to note that even though the American Baptist Convention is a "non creedal church organization," [10] the approval of the Board of Managers, American Baptist Board of Education and Publication, was obtained for all foundational curriculum documents.[11] Also the United Presbyterian Board of Christian Education sought and received the approval of the one hundred seventy-ninth General Assembly for its new curriculum plan.[12]

Nonetheless, the replies of Catholic diocesan teams will shed more light on efforts to frame a principle regarding the role of the College of Bishops.

Lansing states that "the role of the college of bishops and magis-

10 Glenn H. Asquith "Contemporizing Curriculum," *International Journal of Religious Education*, XLI (June, 1965), 16-17.
11 *Foundations for Curriculum*, 2, 7.
12 See *A New Venture. . . ,* 3.

terium in general, in our adult Christian education curriculum is a normative one as regards content." [13]

Baltimore replies by ascribing to the College of Bishops the prerogatives of educating which the Second Vatican Council seems to have affirmed of the Church as a whole. In practice, Baltimore operates "within the teaching authority of the local Ordinary." [14]

Lansing's principle is more directly addressed to program design than Baltimore's. It identifies scope as the component of curriculum which the College of Bishops most directly affects and understands the College to exercise a normative authority over scope. Lansing's application of the principle further states that that authority is both positive (proposing scope) as well as negative (ruling out heretical scope).[15] The principle does not receive detailed justification but simply expresses Catholic "conventional wisdom" on the role of episcopal magisterium.

Valid as the Lansing principle is, further reflection upon the role of the College of Bishops vis-a-vis the components of curriculum indicate that their influence extends beyond the scope of curriculum at least to context and perhaps to process. Moreover, their role with respect to scope deserves further precision. Consequently, let me first suggest and then justify at some length this principle regarding the role of the College of Bishops: *Being the persons upon whom the visible context of adult Christian education depends, the role of the College of Bishops is to pass final human judgment on the consistency of formulations of scope with the meaning of the Church's experience of the mystery of Christ and the fittingness of methods to convey that meaning.*

Since this principle touches upon the teaching authority which Catholics accord the College of Bishops, it can be explained and justified largely in light of the Second Vatican Council. It is not possible, of course, to do justice to all the considerations that impinge upon the principle, especially the infallible character of the teaching authority of the College of Bishops.[16] It is only possible to explain and

13 *Dissertation*, 326.

14 *Ibid.*, 374-75.

15 *Ibid.*, 326-27.

16 This is currently a highly vexed question after the appearance of Hans Küng's *Infallible? An Inquiry* (Garden City, N.Y.: Doubleday, 1971). For a brief survey of the ensuing debate see *Theology Digest*, XIX, No. 2 (Summer, 1971), 104-32. A preliminary bibliography on infallibility and the development of dogma which it guarantees might include Gregory Baum, "The Magisterium in a Changing Church," *Concilium*, I, No. 3 (January, 1967), 34-42; Herbert Hammans, "Recent Catholic Views on Development of Dogma," *ibid.*, 53-63; C. Larnicol, "Infallibilité de l'Eglise, du Corps episcopal, du Pape," *L'ami du clerge*, LXXVI (1966), 246-55, 257-59; Francis Lawlor, "Infallibility" in *New Catholic Encyclopedia*, VII, (New York: McGraw Hill, 1967), 496-98; Bernard Lonergan, "The Assumption and

justify the principle insofar as it is a practical guide to curriculum planning.

The principle is negatively cast. It says little about the positive teaching role of bishops with respect to adult Christian education. The negative cast does not wish to deny the valuable positive contributions which the teaching of the bishops provides the Church. The constructive teaching of the documents of the Second Vatican Council, of papal encyclicals, of the pastoral letters of the national conferences of bishops,[17] and of the pastoral letters and instructions of diocesan bishops stimulate and encourage significant adult Christian learnings. However, the principle is stated as it is because in practice Christian education is initiated and conducted for the most part by theologians, priests, religious, and laymen without the direct supervision of though ultimately accountable to the diocesan bishop.

The principle recognizes first that the diocesan bishop is the person in communion with whom Roman Catholic Christians build that community which largely provides their context of Christian education. The principle further intimates that his role as center of unity and officer of order in the community grounds the diocesan bishop's responsibility for teaching in his diocese.[18]

The Second Vatican Council is clear in affirming the diocesan bishop's role as center of unity in his diocese and personal link with the Church universal:

The Roman Pontiff, as the successor of Peter, is the perpetual and visible source and foundation of the unity of the bishops and of the multitude of

---

Theology" and "Theology and Understanding" in Crowe (ed.), *Collection. . . ,* 68-83 and 121-41; Daniel Maguire, "Moral Absolutes. . . ,"; John Henry Newman *An Essay on the Development of Christian Doctrine* (London: Sheed and Ward, 1960); Karl Rahner, "The Development of Dogma" in *Theological Investigations,* I, 39-77, "What is a Dogmatic Statement," V, 42-66, and "What is Heresy?" V, 468-512; Robert Richard, "Contribution to a Theory of Doctrinal Development," *Continuum,* II (1964), 505-27. For Protestant perspectives upon the problem, see Richard Drummond, "Authority in the Church: An Ecumenical Inquiry," *The Journal of Bible and Religion,* XXXIV (October, 1966), 329-45 and especially George Lindbeck, "The Problem of Doctrinal Development and Contemporary Protestant Theology," *Concilium,* I, No. 3 (January, 1967), 64-72.

[17] An especially positive pastoral of the bishops of the United States is *The Church in Our Day* (distributed by the United States Catholic Conference, 1312 Massachusetts Avenue, Washington, D.C. 1968). Somewhat more labored, but an incentive to education also, is *Human Life in Our Day* (distributed *eodem,* 1968).

[18] In fact, it seems that the bishop's role as center of unity and officer of order historically began the development which eventually saw the bishop become an authoritative teacher in a diocese. See Daniel Maguire, "Holy Spirit and Church Authority," *Commonweal,* LXXXIX, No. 6 (November 8, 1968) *(Holy Spirit: Commonweal Papers: 3),* 213-20.

the faithful. The individual bishop, however, is the visible principle and foundation of unity in his particular church, fashioned after the model of the universal Church. In and from such individual churches there comes into being the one and only Catholic Church. For this reason each individual bishop represents his own church, but all of them together in union with the Pope represent the entire Church joined in the bond of peace, love, and unity.[19]

The principle goes on to acknowledge that as a College together with their head, the Bishop of Rome, bishops can pass final human judgment upon the consistency of formulations of scope to the meaning of the Church's experience of the mystery of Christ. Traditional Catholic doctrine on the infallible teaching office of the College of Bishops provides both the explanation and justification of the statement.[20] "Formulations of scope" are specified because in all the Ecumenical Councils from Nicea (325 AD) through the Second Vatican (1962-65 AD) the College of Bishops has expressed itself in propositional statements of doctrine or rejected propositions which it considered erroneous.[21] "Pass final human judgment" is specified because over the centuries the College of Bishops has more frequently accepted or rejected formulations of doctrine which have originated among various teachers in the Church than proposed doctrine on its own initiative.[22] "Consistency . . . with the meaning of the Church's experience of the mystery of Christ" is suggested as a criterion of judgment because it makes positive agreement with the intent of the

[19] DVII, "Lumen Gentium," art. 23, p. 44.

[20] For a brief resumé of the history of teaching regarding infallibility from the New Testament until the present, see Walter Kasper, "The Relationship between Gospel and Dogma: An Historical Approach," Concilium, I, No. 3 (January, 1967), 73-79.

[21] See DS and DVII, passim. Especially early is the practice of episcopal councils to express their common faith in symbola fidei. (See DS, pp. 17-42.)

[22] This fact is especially evident in rejecting formulations of doctrine. Condemning propositions as erroneous and heretical begins with the Councils of Nicea (325 AD; DS, 126) and First Constantinople (381 AD; DS, 151). Eventually from the practice of provincial councils (Smyrna [351 AD; DS, 140] and First Toledo [400 AD; DS, 191-208] it takes on the classical formula, ei tis legei . . . anathema estō in the East (the "anathemata of Cyril" possibly approved by the Council of Ephesus [431 AD; DS, 252-63, see also p. 92] and Second Constantinople [553 AD; DS, 422-37 except 425]) and Si quis dixerit. . . , anathema sit in the West (Trent [1545-63 AD; DS, 1551-83, 1601-30, 1651-61, 1701-19, 1731-34, 1751-59, 1771-78, 1801-12] and First Vatican [1869-70 AD; DS, 3021-43]). The formula takes its origin from Paul's anathematizing anyone who should preach a Gospel other than the one he has preached (Gal. 1:8-9). At the suggestion of Pope John XXIII, the Second Vatican Council taught in positive propositions rather than condemned erroneous ones.

Scriptural witness and with the present consciousness of the Church [23] the practical norm of episcopal teaching authority with respect to Christian education rather than reference to truth in an "objective order." [24]

That the College of Bishops can exercise such teaching authority is amply expressed in the Second Vatican Council.

> Although the individual bishops do not enjoy [*sic*] the prerogative of infallibility, they can nevertheless proclaim Christ's doctrine infallibly. This is so, even when they are dispersed around the world, provided that while maintaining the bond of unity among themselves and with Peter's successor, and while teaching authentically on a matter of faith or morals, they concur in a single viewpoint as the one which must be held conclusively. This authority is even more clearly verified when, gathered together in an ecumenical council, they are teachers and judges of faith and morals for the universal Church. Their definitions must then be adhered to with the submission of faith.[25]

Nothing is directly stated in the documents of the Second Vatican Council which extends this authority to a judgment regarding methods (process) of Christian education. The prerogative is implicit, however, in all the statements which concern doctrinal teaching on the supposition that scope and process by their very nature intricately influence one another. Consequently, the principle also states that the role of the College of Bishops is to pass final judgment on the "fittingness of methods to convey that meaning." [26]

The teaching authority of the whole College of Bishops is not shared by diocesan bishops singly. However, *de facto*, the stimulus and

[23] Consistency with the present consciousness of the Church was the primary criterion employed in the definition of the dogmata of the Immaculate Conception (*DS*, 2800-04, see esp. 2802) and of the Assumption of Mary (*DS*, 3900-04). In both instances, the faith of the bishops of the universal Church was explored (*DS*, pp. 560-61 and 781).

[24] This is not to deny that authoritative church teaching states not only what is consistent with its present faith as informed by the Scriptures but also what is true in an objective sense. Rather, the principle wishes to stress that the primary concern of authoritative teaching with respect to Christian education should be to effect transcultural translations and transpositions of the faith of the Apostles and not to press theological development *per se*. For the sense in which these terms are meant, see Robert Richard, "Contribution to a Theory of Doctrinal Development."

[25] *DVII*, "Lumen Gentium," art. 25, p. 48. See the whole art., pp. 47-50.

[26] Most probably the case will not frequently arise when methods shall have to be judged unsuited to convey the meaning of the Church's experience of the mystery of Christ; but, in light of current learning experiments, *e.g.*, nude sensitivity sessions and hallucinogenic drug experiences, the necessity for such judgment is not beyond the realm of possibility.

approval of a diocesan bishop are often the most direct and practical way by which the prerogatives of the whole College affect programs of adult Christian education in a diocese. Especially through his encouragement or disapproval of programs and through his granting or withholding of an *imprimatur* to curriculum materials published in his diocese does a diocesan bishop exercise his role in planning curriculum.

The Second Vatican Council urges the diocesan bishop to go further and to concern himself more positively with the personnel, scope, and process of Christian education.

Catechetical training is intended to make men's faith become living, conscious, and active, through the light of instruction. Bishops should see to it that such training be painstakingly given to children, adolescents, young adults, and even grownups. In this instruction a proper sequence should be observed as well as a method appropriate to the matter that is being treated and to the natural disposition, ability, age, and circumstances of life of the listener. Finally, they should see to it that this instruction is based on sacred Scripture, tradition, the liturgy, the teaching authority, and life of the Church.

Moreover, they should take care that catechists be properly trained for their task, so that they will be thoroughly acquainted with the doctrine of the Church and will have both a theoretical and a pratical knowledge of the laws of psychology and of pedagogical methods.[27]

Granted the value of such active encouragement, the principle as stated means to guide the practical situation in catechetics where the diocesan bishop does well to respect and encourage the competence and initiative of Christian educators. They, in turn, should respect his local leadership to the degree that it reflects the final judgment of the whole College of Bishops regarding doctrine and methods.

WHAT IS THE LEARNER'S ROLE IN A CURRICULUM PLAN?

The major and first two subordinate questions were theoretical in their thrust. This and the remaining questions look more practically to actual programs.

In answering the question of the learner's role, the Baptist Design states the principle that the learner must actively undertake the learning tasks in pursuance of the objective. This principle rests on the centrality of "learning tasks" to the Baptist solutions regarding process.[28]

27 *DVII*, "Christus Dominus," art. 14, p. 406.
28 *Dissertation*, 155-62.

Insofar as they deal with the roles of learners, the Presbyterian designs understand these roles to be determined by decisions as to scope and process.[29]

Lansing's principle is that the learner's role "involves varying kinds of activites and passivities, depending upon the nature of the program with which he is involved." [30]

Baltimore states that "in the curriculum the learner's role should be such that he be called upon to share a responsibility to learn himself, Christ, and the Church, and to function as an adult mature Christian." In effect, Baltimore's principle is that the learner be actively involved in mastering scope.[31]

Thus each of the designs understands the role of the learner to be determined by decisions as to scope and process. Of the two, however, process exercises the more direct influence upon the learner's role since it is by involving himself in the process that the learner appropriates the scope. Within process itself, it seems that, in the methodology of this study, the teaching-learning mode is precisely what determines the learner's role since it is the mode which suggests the practical methods or dynamics of teaching-learning through which certain kinds of learning are achieved. Moreover, as Lansing's general principle of personnel pointed out, the structure of a setting also determines the learner's role.[32]

Accepting these statements from the four designs and adapting them to my methodology, I propose the prescriptive principle that *the learner's role should vary according to the characteristics of the teaching-learning mode(s) and the structure(s) of the setting in a curriculum plan.*

For example, if the learning mode is that of disclosure and the structure that of a lecture, the learner will be an attentive listener. If the mode is that of problem-solving and the structure is that of a buzz group, the learner will be an active participant in the collective effort to solve the problem. If the mode is that of inquiry and the structure that of a seminar, the role of the learner will be that of a questioner of the resource person. The role of the learner, in short, will differ from program to program depending upon the learning dynamics decided upon.

29 *Ibid.,* 269-71.
30 *Ibid.,* 327.
31 *Ibid.,* 375.
32 *Ibid.,* 435-36.

What Is the Teacher's Role in a Curriculum Plan?

I am uncomfortable with the word *teacher* in the question. It smacks too much of the classroom and of children's education. Would not leader, or resource person, or moderator, or facilitator, or almost anything else be preferable? Perhaps, but just as *teacher* gives the impression of classroom learning, so the other words carry with them specific role descriptions. *Teacher* at least has the advantage of being general. At any rate, it is used in the question so as to leave the role description as open as possible.

Let us see how Protestant and Catholic planning groups answer the question.

The Baptist principle is that the teacher provides the opportunity, challenge, resources, and guidance for the learner to undertake the learning tasks and to evaluate his progress toward the objective.[33]

The Presbyterian designs operate on the principle that the scope and process decided upon determine the role of the teacher or leader.[34]

Lansing's principle is that "the teacher's role, like the learner's role, depends upon the type of programs under consideration: different programs have different dynamics of teaching, and hence the definition—and role—of the teacher varies with each." [35]

Baltimore's principle is that "the teacher's role . . . is that he initiate the opportunity of Process and share the responsibility of the learner." [36]

As with principles for the learner's role, so the teacher's or leader's role follows upon decisions as to the process by which the scope will be learned.

Consequently, I propose a similar principle that *the teacher's role should vary according to the characteristics of the teaching-learning mode(s) and the structure(s) of the setting in a curriculum plan.*

For example, if the mode is that of initiation and the structure is that of a Eucharistic celebration, the teacher may well be the celebrant. If the mode is that of disclosure and the structure that of a cinema, the teacher's role may be that of a climate setter and explainer. If the mode is inquiry and the structure that of an encounter group, the teacher may be a facilitator.

---

33 *Ibid.*, 160-61.
34 *Ibid.*, 269-71.
35 *Ibid.*, 328.
36 *Ibid.*, 376.

These terms and the relationship of learning modes and structures of the setting to the roles of learners and teachers will become clearer in Chapters V and VI.

What Are the Roles of Learners, Teachers, and Others in Designing Curriculum?

The question forces us to face the relative merits of a program's being centrally or locally designed. If centrally designed, there is the advantage of its being professionally done but the disadvantage of its being irrelevant to the local scene. If locally designed there is the advantage of the program's arising out of grassroots needs but the disadvantage of its being parochial. Let us first see how various groups have handled the problem.

The Baptist Design operates on the principle that a denominational staff will usually plan curriculum for teachers and learners although it allows for some local planning.[37]

Of the Presbyterian designs, the "situational approach" insists that the decisive role in curriculum planning belongs to local leaders and learners and that the role of the Board of Christian Education is that of stimulating local creativity in curriculum planning. In practice, however, *Trends,* Decade Books, and *Enquiry* all present dimensions of scope and suggest processes by which they might be learned.[38]

Lansing's principle is that "participants help build curriculum through indicating in one way or another where their interests and potential for education lie; the teachers and curriculum planners strive to be sensitive to this." [39]

Baltimore responds that "the roles of the participants in building curriculum are expressed in the learners who are listened to . . . and the teachers who assist the learners to achieve the Objective." [40]

Both Lansing and Baltimore speak for programs which are planned by the diocesan office for learners, not for programs which are locally planned in each of the dioceses. The Presbyterian "situational approach" expresses the principle which seems to me to meet the present situation in Catholic dioceses most realistically and which enjoys persuasive justification both in terms of the learning characteristics of adults [41] and in terms of theological and sociological considerations.

[37] *Ibid.,* 182-83.
[38] *Ibid.,* 269-71.
[39] *Ibid.,* 328.
[40] *Ibid.,* 377.
[41] *Supra,* 6, n. 1.

The Presbyterian Division of Lay Education puts these considerations cogently in the paper "A Case for Resourceful Freedom in Lay Education." [42]

Theological justification rests upon two interrelated considerations. The first is that "theology is an activity as well as a subject."

> As an activity theology is critical exploration of the continuing, dynamic activity of the Word in history which causes faith to happen. Therefore, in theology we are not dealing with subject matter that has settled down and become fixed so that it can be neatly ordered and mastered. We are dealing with the Word which, in confronting us *today* and causing faith to happen, also confronts us with questions that we might otherwise be able to ignore. We discover that the subject matter of lay theological reflection cannot be closed to any of the concerns of human existence.[43]

The second consideration is that "the subject matter of theological reflection" is "faith as *an historical event.*" It is hoped that stating it so will "avoid either objective or subjective distortions," that is, that it will avoid isolating the "objective and autonomous activity of the Word . . . from the [subjective] response it calls forth." Accordingly, it means that

> Faith as an historical event is not so much defined as explored and that exploration is one of the tasks of lay theological reflection.
>
> In making such a statement, . . . it must be made clear that any plea for "teaching the faith" to the laity involves an objectification or rationalistic distortion of faith. There is great danger in preoccupation with sequenced content, simplified goals, and measurable consequences, since such may lead us inadvertently into the trap of fostering a set of right beliefs. . . .
>
> If theology is the attempt to understand faith as an historical event, then what precisely are its subject matter and its method and how do these interrelate? . . . The problematic of faith rather than system-building is the central concern. The very possibility and validity of "theology" are the urgent issues for clarification rather than the content.
>
> Lay education must help the laity do theology. That presently requires a curriculum of problematics, an evolving collage of inquiries. . . . How one expresses faith as one encounters in the world the continuing activity of the Word in human life and is confronted by the Giver of that Word—that is the focus for lay education in the Church.[44]

[42] An unpublished paper distributed among members of the Board of Christian Education, The United Presbyterian Church in the U.S.A., by members of the Division of Lay Education, Philadelphia, October 24, 1966. (Spirit duplicated.)

[43] *Ibid.,* 2.

[44] *Ibid.,* 2-3.

This is thorough justification indeed for the principle that learners themselves must choose what questions to explore. This principle, however, is reinforced by religio-sociological presuppositions.

Basic to this justification is the ecclesiological presupposition that *"the church is not to be viewed as mediator between God and the world, but as the community of secular men who have been drawn into faith and are called to worldly response."* [45] It follows, then, that

Out of the secular situation of the laity in all its varied, complex and fluid reality, the issues for theological reflection arise. The church's laity exist between two worlds: The world reconciled to God and the world subject to the spirit of this present age. The fact that Christian laity experience tension with the spirit of this age does not alter the fact that they are situated squarely and fully within it and are called to participate in activity that shapes the world's future. Such participation is their mission. The tension is the mark of the continuing activity of the Word. Exploration of this mission and this tension, which have been underscored by the developing theology of the laity, is the focused purpose of lay education.[46]

Therefore, "the subject matter of lay education should be organized around, and evolve in light of, what laymen find to be pertinent to their situation(s) as they pursue their life in the world." [47] Briefly, "the curriculum for lay education must take shape locally because the object of lay education is to help the laity wrestle with their own questions concerning their mission in the world." [48]

This reasoning persuades me to adopt the principle of the "situational approach." However, precautions need to be taken against an inadequacy of that approach, namely, the absence of principles according to which local programs might reliably be planned. It is also good for the principle to express the service which the Presbyterian Board of Christian Education tries to perform, that of broadening the perspectives of local planners by offering various curriculum resources.

I propose then as a prescriptive principle that *persons closest to the learning situation—learners, leaders, planners, administrators—should plan curriculum as much as possible for themselves guided by theologically and educationally sound principles and stimulated by broad*

45 *Ibid.*, 3.
46 *Ibid.*, 3-4.
47 *Ibid.*, 4.
48 *Ibid.*, 7. The passages show dependence upon Harvey Cox' *The Secular City: Secularization and Urbanization in Theological Perspective* (New York: The Macmillan Company, 1965) which was *au courant* at the time the paper was circulated.

possibilities as to scope, process, context, and timing which a central coordinating staff can make available.

The kinds of principles I refer to are those which are found throughout this book.[49] It has been written expressly to assist those who plan adult programs at any level.

WHAT IS THE ROLE OF ADMINISTRATORS WITH RESPECT TO A CURRICULUM PLAN?

The answer to this question frequently depends upon the answer given to the previous one. If a program is centrally planned and locally applied, administrators are those who apply the plan. If a program is designed at the grassroots, usually the planning team are the administrators.

The Baptist Design clearly assigns administrators the tasks of leadership development and evaluation of the results of a program and with some ambiguity charges them with the designation of settings as well.[50]

By implication, the role of administrators in the Presbyterian designs is to implement a curriculum plan.[51]

Lansing states that "the curriculum plan functions broadly as policy; the role of administrative personnel, (curriculum planners and teachers), both central and local level, is to implement it." [52] It is not clear whether curriculum planners and teachers are here considered to be administrative personnel.

Baltimore states that "the administrative personnel implement the curriculum by their acceptance of responsibility delegated by the bishop, and discharged through leadership in identifying the needs of the Community, and in offering service in response to these needs, all toward the Objective." Baltimore seems to equate administration with the overall task of curriculum planning.[53]

Baltimore and Lansing witness the fact that administration and curriculum planning are usually exercised in practice by the same persons in Catholic dioceses. The Baptist Design evidences a situation where curriculum is planned centrally but administered locally. The implication of the resources of the Presbyterian designs edited by the central Board of Christian Education is substantially the same. Despite

---

[49] See my article "Diocesan Coordination of Adult Christian Education," *The Living Light*, VII, No. 4 (Winter, 1970), 85-95.
[50] *Dissertation*, 183.
[51] *Ibid.*, 270-71.
[52] *Ibid.*, 329.
[53] *Ibid.*, 377-78.

diocesan practice, the Protestant designs point out that even though administration and curriculum planning may be performed by the same person, nonetheless the roles as such differ. Perhaps, then, it would be clearer to state the task of administration rather than the role of administrators. As Lansing well expresses, the relationship of curriculum planning to administration is that of policy to practice.

Consequently, I propose the principle that *the proper task of administration is to implement a curriculum plan.* It applies especially where the persons who plan a curriculum are not the same persons who administer it.

SUMMARY AND APPLICATION

I propose, then, a major and six subordinate principles regarding personnel.

The major principle is declarative: those persons interrelate in teaching and learning adult Christian education who, through various roles, intend to assist one another in learning the mystery of Christ and whose needs, interests, capacities, and competencies largely determine the scope and process of a particular curriculum plan.

The first subordinate principle is also declarative: God's role in adult Christian education is to be the center of its scope, the enabling power of its process, the creator of its context, and the provider of its timing.

The second subordinate principle is also declarative: Being the persons upon whom the visible context of adult Christian education depends, the role of the College of Bishops is to pass final judgment on the consistency of formulations of scope with the meaning of the Church's experience of the mystery of Christ and the fittingness of methods to convey that meaning.

The third subordinate principle is prescriptive: the learner's role should vary according to the characteristics of the teaching-learning mode(s) and the structure(s) of the setting in a curriculum plan.

The fourth subordinate principle is also prescriptive: the teacher's role should vary according to the characteristics of the teaching-learning mode(s) and the structure(s) of the setting in a curriculum plan.

The fifth subordinate principle is prescriptive too: persons closest to the learning situation—learners, leaders, planners, administrators—should plan curriculum as much as possible for themselves guided by theologically and educationally sound principles and stimulated by broad possibilities as to scope, process, context, and timing which a central coordinating staff can make available.

The last subordinate principle is prescriptive too: the proper task of administration is to implement a curriculum plan.

With respect to application, the key to applying all of them lies in identifying the needs of participants (major principle) and in involving them in the planning process (fifth subordinate principle).

The most convenient way to identify needs is through a survey or questionnaire. However, surveys are inadequate if they are designed to acquaint only the planning team with prospective participants' needs. Surveys must be designed so that they bring the participant to recognize these needs himself. Otherwise he will feel little inclination to pursue the learning programs planned by others around his needs.

How, then, can the participant practically be involved in the planning process? It is unrealistic to expect that a few hundred people will be able to design a program. The task is too complicated. However, hundreds and even thousands of participants can be involved in identifying their needs through surveys and then brought together in small groups to articulate both those needs and the learning goals that correspond to them. A smaller planning team can take those needs and goals and respond to them. This process has been worked out in detail and actually used in the GIFT (Growth In Faith Together) program.[54] Nine of the thirteen weeks of its concentrated stage are devoted to examining participants' needs and involving participants in articulating those needs and setting a priority among them. Once identified, these needs indicate the dimensions of scope and kinds of processes that can be planned. Accordingly, we now move to scope and process, the very nucleus of curriculum.

[54] See my article "GIFT—An Adult Program That Works."

CHAPTER IV

Scope—The Meanings Which Adult Christian Education Explores and Communicates

W E COME TO THE heart of program design—scope, process, and their mutual interrelationship. In working out an overall objective for adult Christian education (Chapter II), we noted that it should indicate in broad terms the scope and process of the undertaking. Practically all the principles of personnel (Chapter III) looked to decisions as to scope and process. We shall see in Chapters VI and VII that much of context and timing is determined by decisions as to scope and process. We have seen that the solution to the problem of organizing curriculum lies in the relationship between scope and process.[1] These next two chapters, then, are most crucial to successful program design.

Moreover, these chapters fit closely together. The questions of scope in this chapter are arranged with an eye to the questions of process in the next chapter. I shall attempt to answer them in such a way that the principles of scope and process may integrally complement one another.

As in the other chapters, I shall first review the replies given to the questions of scope and process by other Protestant and Catholic designs before proposing my own. However, since the justification for several of my principles rests upon theological and educational foundations different from those of the designs analyzed, it may be helpful at the outset to identify my sources.

The general approach to the scope-process interrelationship and the consequent effort to correlate the principles of scope and process rely upon Philip Phenix' philosophy of curriculum for general education developed in *Realms of Meaning*.[2] Suggested by Phenix' theory

[1] *Supra*, 51-55.
[2] *Supra*, 44, n. 89.

is my basic point of departure that meaning is the most appropriate category by which to deal with scope and that realms of meaning (dimension of scope),[3] each essentially distinct but interdependent, each with its own logical principles of construction, representative concepts, methods of inquiry, modes of understanding, and symbolical expression,[4] provide the clue to differentiating scope in such a way that each dimension thereof relates to a distinct (but interdependent) kind and mode of learning.

Phenix' theory of curriculum is in many respects parallel to, although independent of, Bernard Lonergan's interrelating a consistent theory of human understanding with a methodology of theology. Lonergan's theory of cognition is found succinctly and recently in "Cognitional Structure"[5] and earlier and more fully in *Insight*.[6] His methodology of theology has appeared recently in *Gregorianum*.[7] Phenix provides a model by which scope and process can be interrelated in education. Lonergan elaborates many of the specifics both regarding the manifold dimensions of theology and regarding the operations of understanding by which they may be appropriated. To a great extent, the justification for my principles of scope and process represent a cross-fertilization of Phenix' and Lonergan's contributions. Other sources, however, have been influential in arriving at individual principles.

With respect to scope, in addition to works of biblical theology and the teaching of the Second Vatican Council, the following authors have been especially influential. Oscar Cullmann's *Salvation in History*[8] when modified in the light of James Barr's *Old and New in Interpretation*[9] is a major source for elucidating the mystery of Christ as event. Cullmann's last chapter also proves germinally useful in developing the mystery of Christ as horizon, as celebration, and as moral imperative.[10] More pertinent to the mystery of Christ as horizon

3 My use of the term "dimensions of meaning" approximates Phenix' "realms of meaning." P. uses "dimensions of meaning" to indicate the four characteristics that set one realm of meaning off from another. See Phenix, *Realms of Meaning.* . . , 21-25.

4 *Ibid.*, 47-49.

5 *Supra*, 44, n. 89.

6 Bernard J. F. Lonergan, *Insight: A Study of Human Understanding* (London: Longmans, Green and Co., 1957).

7 *Idem*, "Functional Specialties. . . ." For an elucidating commentary, see David Tracy, *The Achievement.* . . , 232-66.

8 Trans. Sidney G. Sowers (New York: Harper & Row, Publishers, 1967).

9 *Old and New in Interpretation: A Study of the Two Testaments* (London: SCM Press Ltd., 1966).

10 Entitled "A Survey of Systematic Theology and the History of Dogma: Salvation History and the Post-Biblical Period," three sections address respectively

are David Tracy's "Horizon Analysis and Eschatology" [11] and the work of Gerhard Ebeling, Ernst Fuchs, and their American respondents in Robert Funk's *Language, Hermeneutic, and Word of God,*[12] and James Robinson's *The New Hermeneutic.*[13] The development of the mystery of Christ as celebration follows the rudiments of Odo Casel's *The Mystery of Christian Worship* [14] as refined by Louis Bouyer in *Liturgical Piety* [15] and further nuanced by Edward Schillebeeckx in *Christ the Sacrament of the Encounter with God.*[16] The mystery of Christ as moral imperative owes much of its elaboration to Bernard Häring's efforts to provide a Christological foundation and orientation for scholastic moral theology in *The Law of Christ* [17] and to James Gustafson's tracing the significance of Christ for the moral life through the work of several Protestant theologians in *Christ and the Moral Life.*[18]

With respect to process, Robert Boehlke's *Theories of Learning in Christian Education* [19] is an invaluable guide for assessing the pertinence of various learning theories to Christian education. Marcel van Caster's *The Structure of Catechetics* [20] presents several insights on kinds and modes of learning from which my justification of principles draws. However, it is Bernard Lonergan's analysis of human understanding which provides the learning theory out of which the justification fundamentally grows.

"Salvation History and Worship," 313-19, which coincides with my meaning of the mystery of Christ as celebration; "Salvation History, Faith and Exegesis," 319-28, which treats some of the same considerations as I consider under the mystery of Christ as horizon; and "Salvation History and Ethics," 328-38, which deals with the meaning of the mystery of Christ as moral imperative.

[11] *Continuum,* VI (Summer, 1968), 166-79.

[12] *Language, Hermeneutic, and Word of God: The Problem of Language in the New Testament and Contemporary Theology* (New York: Harper & Row, Publishers, 1966).

[13] *New Frontiers in Theology: Discussions among Continental and American Theologians,* Vol. II: *The New Hermeneutic,* ed. James M. Robinson and John B. Cobb, Jr. (New York: Harper & Row, Publishers, 1964).

[14] *The Mystery of Christian Worship and Other Writings,* ed. Burkhard Neunheuser (Westminster, Maryland: The Newman Press, 1962).

[15] Liturgical Studies (Notre Dame, Indiana: University of Notre Dame Press, 1955).

[16] Trans. Paul Barrett *et al.* (New York: Sheed and Ward, 1963).

[17] *The Law of Christ: Moral Theology for Priests and Laity,* Vol. I: *General Moral Theology,* Vol. II: *Special Moral Theology: Life in Fellowship with God and Fellow Man,* Vol. III: *Special Moral Theology: Man's Assent to the All-embracing Majesty of God's Love,* trans. Edwin G. Kaiser (Cork: The Mercier Press, 1963-67). Especially pertinent are the author's forewords and introductions to each volume, the "Prelude" of Vol. II, and the "Epilogue" of Vol. III.

[18] (New York: Harper & Row, Publishers, 1968).

[19] *Supra,* 44, n. 88.

[20] Trans. Edward J. Dirkswager, Jr., *et al.* (New York: Herder and Herder, 1965).

Other sources which are used to a lesser extent will be introduced in the notes.

The major question which occupies this chapter is: What is appropriate scope for adult Christian education? Subordinate questions are: How comprehensive should the scope of a curriculum plan be? What distinct dimensions of scope lend themselves to different kinds of adult Christian learning? How shall dimensions of scope be selected for inclusion in a curriculum plan? In what sequence will dimensions of scope be offered in a curriculum plan?

WHAT IS APPROPRIATE SCOPE FOR ADULT CHRISTIAN EDUCATION?

This question is one of germaneness. It seeks a principle broad enough to encompass all that adult Christian education may gainfully explore and yet pointed enough to differentiate the scope of Christian education from areas that can better be treated by secular education.

To the question: What is appropriate scope? the Baptist Design responds that "the scope for the curriculum is what God reveals to man and what this revelation implies for man in the whole field of relationships—God, man, the natural order, history." [21]

The Presbyterian designs understand the appropriate scope variously to be: "any question that seriously concerns [learners]"; "the questions and issues raised by the laity's struggle with the meaning of faith in their life in the world"; "social and ethical issues"; "contemporary issues; biblical meanings; and theological concerns." [22]

Lansing states as a general principle that "no authentic domain of human knowledge should be ruled out of the broadest potential scope for Christian adult education" but immediately distinguishes between this "broadest potential scope" and "operational scope" in justifying the principle.[23]

Baltimore replies that "the scope of the curriculum is to help adults learn themselves, Christ, and the Church, and [how] to function as adult, mature Christians." [24]

Neither the last two of the Presbyterian statements nor the Baltimore statement offer a criterion by which the scope of adult Christian education can be differentiated from that of general education. Rather,

---

21 *Foundations for Curriculum*, 17. See *Dissertation*, 132-38.
22 *Dissertation*, 261-63.
23 *Ibid.*, 309-10.
24 *Ibid.*, 362.

they suggest topics suitable for study. The first of the Presbyterian statements agrees with the Lansing principle; the second roughly corresponds to the Baptist principle. Consequently, the possibilities are reduced to two principles, the Baptist and Lansing's.

They seem at first glance to be contradictory. The Baptist principle sees "what God reveals to man" as appropriate scope for adult Christian education; Lansing wishes to exclude "no authentic domain of human knowledge." Upon closer study, more agreement becomes clear. The Baptist principle goes on to include "what this revelation implies for man in the whole field of relationships—God, man, the natural order, history." "The whole field of relationships" would seem to exclude "no authentic domain of human knowledge." Consequently, the two principles agree on the material object of the scope of adult Christian education. They do not agree on its formal object— or, at least, Lansing does not enunciate the positive formality in the light of which every domain of human knowledge can be considered appropriate scope. That formality is, in the words of the Baptist Design, "the light of the Gospel" or, as here expressed, "what this revelation implies. . . ."

Of the four statements under study, therefore, the Baptist one seems best to meet the demands of the question. However, valid as the statement is to express the Baptist understanding of scope against its own presuppositions,[25] I have a different understanding of scope and different presuppositions. Consequently, I propose a different major principle of scope, namely, that *the appropriate scope of adult Christian education is the meaning of the Church's experience of the mystery of Christ.*

Let me explain this principle and the presuppositions upon which it rests.

The principle takes *meaning* as its decisive category. The word is too rich in presuppositions and connotations to permit an immediate working definition. One can more feasibly emerge in explaining and justifying its selection.

One's meaning of "meaning" is rooted in one's understanding of man. I accept Philip Phenix' modification of the classic formula that man is a rational animal to "humans are beings that discover, create, and express meanings." [26] The reasons for modification contribute to the understanding of meaning.

---

25 *Ibid.*, 132-38.
26 *Realms of Meaning*, 21. So also Tracy, *The Achievement. . .* , 211, reporting Lonergan, ". . . Man is fundamentally a creature and creator of that aspect of being called meaning."

This philosophical answer [man is a rational animal] suffers from the limitation that such ideas as rationality, reason, and mind tend to be too narrowly construed as referring to the processes of logical thinking. The life of feeling, conscience, imagination, and other processes that are not rational in the strict sense are excluded by such a construction, and the idea of man as a rational animal in the traditional sense is accordingly rejected for being too one-sided.

This difficulty can be avoided by using a unifying concept that expresses the broader connotations of the idea of reason. The concept proposed is *meaning*. This term is intended to express the full range of connotations of reason or mind. Thus, there are different meanings contained in activities of organic adjustment, in perception, in logical thinking, in social organization, in speech, in artistic creation, in self-awareness, in purposive decision, in moral judgment, in the consciousness of time, and in the activity of worship. All these distinctive human functions are varieties of meaning, and all of them together—along with others that might be described—comprise the life of meaning, which is the essence of the life of man.[27]

This modification converges strikingly with Bernard Lonergan's reinterpretation of classical concepts of man.

Without denying human nature, it [an empirical approach] adds the quite distinctive categories of man as an historical being. Without repudiating the analysis of man into body and soul, it adds the richer and more concrete apprehension of man as incarnate subject.

. . . . Summarily, very summarily, I may perhaps say that such terms refer to a dimension of human reality that has always existed, that has always been lived and experienced, that classicist thought standardized yet tended to overlook, that modern studies have brought to light, thematized, elaborated, illustrated, documented. That dimension is the constitutive role of meaning in human living. It is the fact that acts of meaning inform human living, that such acts proceed from a free and responsible subject incarnate, that meanings differ from nation to nation, from culture to culture, and that, over time, they develop and go astray. Besides the meanings by which man apprehends nature and the meanings by which he transforms it, there are the meanings by which man thinks out the possibilities of his own living and makes his choice among them. In this realm of freedom and creativity, of solidarity and responsibility, of dazzling achievement and pitiable madness, there ever occurs man's making of man.[28]

Central to Phenix' and Lonergan's thought is the fact that man is

27 Phenix, *Realms of Meaning. . .* , 21.
28 "Theology in Its New Context" in *Theology of Renewal*, Vol. I: *Renewal of Religious Thought*, ed. L. K. Shook (New York: Herder and Herder, 1968), 39-40. More fully, see Tracy, *The Achievement. . .* , 206-31.

an incarnate subject who discovers, creates, and expresses meaning(s). Lonergan, however, goes on to explore aspects of meaning which Phenix intimates but does not develop.

With his profound interest in epistemology, Lonergan seeks to clarify the intentional aspect of meaning.[29] An incarnate subject *means* to affirm the true and the real in his judgments. He *means* to achieve the good and the valuable in his deciding and doing. He *means* to create the beautiful in his artistic activity. Briefly, an intentionality toward objectivity grounds all man's acts of meaning. It also grounds the possibility of sharing meaning. Even if objectivity is never reached by the incarnate subject it is intentionality toward the objectively true, good, and beautiful which enables one person to discover, create, and express meaning and another to find that meaning meaningful. The meaningful judgment, decision, or activity, then, is radically subjective but tendentially objective. The subjective intentionality of meaning toward objectivity not only must figure in a working definition of meaning but underlies the communication of meaning which is education. Moreover, it is because of their intentionality toward objectivity that meanings can be verified and consequently that education can be constructively criticized.

A still more complex aspect of meaning is developed by Lonergan. It is that acts of meaning are constitutive of the reality with which man deals. Phenix, too, appreciates the role of meanings in the evolution of cultural traditions;[30] but Lonergan makes of it a central question of inquiry.

At this point, permit me to resume what I have been trying to say. I have been meeting the objection that meaning is a merely secondary affair, that what counts is the reality that is meant, and not the mere meaning that refers to it. My answer has been that the functions of meaning are larger than the objection envisages. I would not dispute that for the child learning

[29] What follows draws upon Lonergan's treatment of intentionality and objectivity with respect to cognition. I apply that treatment to meaning in a way that L. may not have intended. See Bernard Lonergan's "Cognitional Structure," in Crowe (ed.), *Collection. . .* , esp. 227-39; "The Dehellenization of Dogma," *Theological Studies*, XXVIII (June, 1967), 336-51; and "Natural Knowledge of God" in *Proceedings of the Twenty-Third Annual Convention*, the Catholic Theological Society of America (Yonkers, New York: St. Joseph's Seminary, 1969), esp. pp. 58-67. Cf. Phenix, *Realms of Meaning. . .* , 22. In light of Tracy's *The Achievement. . .* , this interpretation of Lonergan remains uncertain. See p. 210, n. 6.

[30] "The types [of meaning] that are significant in actual human life are the ones that have an inherent power of growth and lead to the elaboration of the enduring traditions of civilization. These are the kinds of meaning that have proven fruitful in the development of the cultural heritage." *Realms of Meaning*, 23. However, Phenix is interested in this role of meanings especially insofar as they ground academic disciplines (see esp. 23-29).

to talk, his little world of immediacy comes first and that the words he uses are only an added grace. But as the child develops into a man, the world of immediacy shrinks into an inconspicuous and not too important corner of the real world, which is a world we know only through the mediation of meaning. Further, there is man's transformation of his environment, a transformation that is effected through the intentional acts that envisage ends, select means, secure collaborators, direct operations. Finally, besides the transformation of nature, there is man's transformation of man himself; and in this second transformation the role of meaning is not merely directive but also constitutive.

I might go on to enlarge upon the constitutive functions of meaning, and many profound themes might be touched upon. For it is in the field where meaning is constitutive, that man's freedom reaches its high point. There too his responsibility is greatest. There there occurs the emergence of the existential subject, finding out for himself that he has to decide for himself what he is to make of himself. It is there that individuals become alienated from community, that communities split into fractions, that cultures flower and decline, that historical causality exerts its sway.[31]

Now the ingredients of a working definition of meaning as I wish to use it are present: man is an incarnate subject who discovers, creates, and expresses meaning; meaning is radically subjective but intentionally objective; meaning is constitutive of culture. *Meaning, then, is that which subjects intend in their knowing, choosing, and doing, and which accumulatively constitutes culture.*[32] "Subject" and not "incarnate subject" has been used advisedly. On principle, God's activity as subject in creating and transforming the world mediated by meaning cannot be excluded.

Thus far, meaning in the singular has been considered—meaning as it may be used analogously of several kinds of meaning. Now we turn to those kinds of meaning which can be distinguished from one another. Phenix speaks of realms of meaning. I prefer rather to speak

31 "Dimensions of Meaning" in Crowe (ed.), *Collection. . . ,* 255. See the entire article, 252-67, which traces the breakdown of classical meanings and the emergence of contemporary ones. For the limitations and specifications of meaning as constitutive of human living, see Tracy, *The Achievement. . . ,* 217-21.

32 Nowhere, to my knowledge, does Lonergan supply a working definition of meaning. Phenix, *Realms of Meaning. . . ,* 5-6, cautions that "there is no single quality that may be designated as the one essence of meaning. Accordingly, we should speak not of meaning as such, but of meanings, or of the *realms of meaning.*" I understand meaning as a term that can be used analogously of several dimensions (or realms) of meaning. Tracy, reporting an even "later Lonergan" than I had access to, confirms that L. supplies no single definition of meaning and even warns against seeking "one universal, essential definition so beloved to the classical mind," *The Achievement. . . ,* 209.

of dimensions of meaning. For Phenix there are four aspects according
to which realms of meaning are differentiated: "the experience of reflective self-consciousness, the logical principles by which this experience is patterned, the selective elaboration of these patterns into
productive disciplines, and the expression of these patterns by means
of appropriate symbolic forms." [33] I understand dimensions of meaning to be differentiated according to the manner by which an experience is consciously apprehended and communicable.[34] Substantially I
agree with Phenix' four aspects but I find the expression "the logical
principles by which this experience is patterned" misleading and "the
selective elaboration of these patterns into productive disciplines"
too academically binding for adult Christian education. It is hoped
that these reasons may become clearer when the dimensions of that
special meaning with which the scope of adult Christian education
concerns itself are differentiated. I have already indicated that for me
it is the meaning of the mystery of Christ. I have also defined what that
term connotes for me.[35]

However, just as meaning is not definable save in terms of its constituents and of the dimensions of meaning to which it analogously applies, so the mystery of Christ is indefinable save in terms of its
constituents and dimensions.

To claim, however, that the mystery of Christ has meaning presupposes a faith option that God intends through Christ to exercise
an active role in the constitution of human meaning. I accept this
option as credible however undemonstrable. Accordingly, I agree with
Bernard Lonergan's understanding of divine revelation.

God becomes known to us in two ways: as the ground and end of the
material universe; and as the one who speaks to us through Scripture and
Tradition. The first manner might found a natural religion. The second
adds revealed religion. . . . But for the second, one must answer that, however trifling the uses to which words may be put, still they are the
vehicles of meaning, and meaning is the stuff of man's making of man. So
it is that a divine revelation is God's entry and his taking part in man's
making of man. It is God's claim to have a say in the aims and purposes,

---

[33] *Realms of Meaning.* . . , 25; for a fuller explanation, see pp. 21-25.
[34] My use, then, does not correspond to Lonergan's "dimensions and expressions"
of meaning recently publicized by Tracy, *The Achievement.* . . , 212-17. Fruitful,
indeed, would be a comparison of L.'s seven "expressions of meaning" and Phenix'
six "realms of meaning."
[35] *Supra,* 79-82.

the direction and development of human lives, human societies, human cultures, human history.[36]

The meaning of the mystery of Christ is from first to last, then, the meaning God's purpose gives it. Yet, that meaning is not immediately constitutive of the reality with which Christian education deals. God's meaning is mediated through the meaning of the Person and work of Christ which is, in turn, mediated through the community of persons who believe, worship, and witness in Him. The scope of Christian education, then, cannot be simply the meaning of the mystery of Christ but can only be the meaning of the Church's experience of the mystery of Christ.

By "experience" is meant not the first level of cognition, in Lonergan's sense,[37] but the full range of human response—cognitive, affective, deliberative, active—to the deed of God in Christ. Moreover, this experience is not that of the single believer but of the whole historical community of believers "from Abel, the just one, to the last of the elect." [38] When I speak of the "Church's experience," then, I mean to begin with the experience of the promised offspring of Abraham (Gen. 12:1-9; 15:1-21; 17:1-22; 22:1-18), gathered into the People of God at Sinai (Ex. 19:1-25; 24:1-8; 34:1-35; Dt. 4:9-20; 29:1-28), entrusted with the land of Canaan (Jos. 1:1-9; 24:1-28), ruled by the Davidic dynasty (II Sam. 7:1-17), chastened for their infidelity (Is. 5:1-7; Jer. 2:1-37; 11:1-14; 25:1-13; Ez. 20:1-44), restored to their homeland (Is. 43:1-7; 60:1-22; 62:1-12; Jer. 30:1-31; 31:40; Ez. 37:1-28; Ezra. 1:1-11), awaiting their new covenant (Jer. 31:31-34; Ez. 36:24-28) and new King (Is. 9:1-7; 11:1-9; Mic. 5:1-4; Ez. 34:23; Zech. 9:9-10) insofar as their experience tends toward and prepares for the deed of God in Christ.[39] I mean especially the historical and glorified Christ's experience of His Father's saving love which He continues to communicate to those who believe in Him.[40] I mean also the "global

---

[36] "Theology in Its New Context," 40.

[37] "Cognitional Structure," in Crowe (ed.), *Collection.* . . , *passim.*

[38] A patristic phrase, quoted in *DVII,* "Lumen Gentium," art. 2, p. 16.

[39] The relationship of the history of Israel to the Christ event (the Old Testament to the New) is, of course, a vexed question. For several conflicting views, see *The Old Testament and Christian Faith,* ed. Bernhard W. Anderson (New York: Harper & Row, Publishers, 1963). I find the relationship between the two testaments, as Barr, *Old and New.* . . , 149, cogently argues, "to depend on the belief that the One God who is the God of Israel is also the God and Father of Jesus Christ."

[40] See Gabriel Moran, *Theology of Revelation* (New York: Herder and Herder, 1966), pp. 57-76.

experience" of the eyewitnesses of Jesus and of the sharers in the apostolic experience of the risen Christ.[41] I mean the accumulative experience of the Christian Church, believing, worshiping, and witnessing through the centuries in various ecclesial manifestations down to the present and on into the future. It is the experience of this community of faith and life in Christ at its present moment in time, shaped by its past and drawn by its future,[42] that mediates the meaning of the mystery of Christ.

Justification for this assertion lies principally in the Pauline doctrine of the Church as the Body of Christ (I Cor. 12:1-30; Rom. 12:3-8; Col. 1:18; 2:9-13; Eph. 4:1-16). Its development in Scripture and Tradition has been thoroughly traced and systematically elaborated by Emile Mersch.[43] It has received magisterial emphasis, though with differences of detail, in Pius XII's *Mystici Corporis.*[44] The Second Vatican Council concisely and movingly presents the doctrine afresh.

In the human nature which He united to Himself, the Son of God redeemed man and transformed him into a new creation (cf. Gal. 6:15; 2 Cor. 5:17) by overcoming death through His own death and resurrection. By communicating His Spirit to His brothers, called together from all peoples, Christ made them mystically into His own body.

From Him, "the whole body, supplied and built up by joints and ligaments, attains a growth that is of God" (Col. 2:19). He continually distributes in His body, that is, in the Church, gifts of ministries through which, by His own power, we serve each other unto salvation so that, carrying out the truth in love, we may through all things grow up into Him who is our head (cf. Eph. 4:11-16, Greek text).

Christ, the one Mediator, established and ceaselessly sustains here on earth

41 See Rahner, *Theological Investigations,* I, 63-68.

42 To understand that the present experience of the Church, *shaped by the past and drawn by the future* is that which mediates the divine meaning of the mystery of Christ is fundamental to seeing the task of Christian education as both transmissive and creative. Christian education should try to transmit the past experience of the Church in such a way that the learner is freed positively to contribute to the experience of the Church here and now in order to co-create its future. See Wyckoff, "Christian Education Redefined," 211-18.

43 *The Whole Christ: The Historical Development of the Doctrine of the Mystical Body in Scripture and Tradition,* trans. John B. Kelly (London: Dennis Dobson Ltd., 1938), traces the historical development of the doctrine. *The Theology of the Mystical Body* (see *supra,* 40, n. 76) presents a systematic elaboration.

44 *Acta Apostolicae Sedis,* XXXV (1943), 193-248. The difference lies mainly in the fact that, whereas Mersch asserts that the Mystical Body is "not absolutely identified on this earth" with the visible Church (*The Theology. . . ,* 480; cf. *The Whole Christ,* 564), Pius XII teaches that it is (*AAS,* XXXV, 221ff; XLII, 571). The Second Vatican Council avoided the issue. See the third paragraph quoted from "Lumen Gentium," immediately *infra.*

His holy Church, the community of faith, hope, and charity, as a visible structure. Through her He communicates truth and grace to all. But the society furnished with hierarchical agencies and the Mystical Body of Christ are not to be considered as two realities. . . . Rather they form one interlocked reality which is comprised of a divine and human element.[45]

Because the Church is the extension of Christ, it is her present experience, shaped by the past and drawn by the future, that mediates God's meaning of the mystery of Christ here and now.[46] That experience provides the immediate scope of Christian education.

To identify the meaning of the Church's experience of the mystery of Christ as the appropriate scope of Christian education is to indicate its comprehensiveness. Indeed, it is impossible for the individual believer ever to appropriate it. So much the more necessary is it, then, for Christian educators to wrestle with the subordinate questions which bring the broad scope of Christian education within manageable and learnable proportions.

HOW COMPREHENSIVE SHOULD THE SCOPE
OF A CURRICULUM PLAN BE?

When the diocesan staffs of Lansing and Baltimore first faced this and the other subordinate questions of scope, they misunderstood the intent of the questions. This misunderstanding suggested that the questions themselves needed reexamination. They were adequate instruments for arriving at the Cooperative/Baptist principles of scope. They were useful for discovering the limitations of the Presbyterian principles. Why do they seem irrelevant to diocesan planning? The reason seems to be that the questions seek principles to guide the planning of an original, life-long curriculum and the materials to support it such as the Cooperative/Baptist Design undertakes. Neither of the dioceses under study tries to develop so ambitious a curriculum plan. The diocesan offices and local planners usually model adult programs upon religion courses in seminaries, colleges, and high schools, or construct them from curriculum materials not planned by themselves. Consequently, the questions do not correspond to the present experience of planning scope for diocesan programs. That is

<hr>

45 *DVII*, "Lumen Gentium," arts. 7-8, pp. 20-22. See both arts. in their entirety.
46 So also the Second Vatican Council: "This divine mystery of salvation is revealed to us and continued in the Church, which the Lord established as His own body." *DVII*, "Lumen Gentium," art. 52, p. 85.

not to say that the questions are irrelevant. In fact, until diocesan and parochial planners at all levels learn to ask themselves how comprehensive the scope of adult Christian education should be and what a variety of learning opportunities it lends itself to, there is little hope that the scope of diocesan or parochial programs will manifest a broad and creative response to concrete needs.

The first subordinate question is phrased: How comprehensive should the scope of a curriculum plan be? It is unclear whether "a curriculum plan" refers to a life-long curriculum plan, the plan of a short-term program, or the totality of curriculum plans of several short-term programs. The ambiguity is helpful because the question should be asked analogously of all these kinds of curriculum plans, just as the principle which answers it should be applied analogously to them.

Taking the question to apply to a life-long curriculum plan, the Cooperative/Baptist Design states that the content of the curriculum should be as comprehensive of the scope as persistent life issues permit it to be relevant to the learner. The principle rests upon the Design's distinction between content and scope of curriculum and its understanding of persistent life issues.

By scope of curriculum, the Cooperative/Baptist Design means all that "is appropriate to be dealt with in the curriculum" whereas the "content of curriculum has to do with what is in fact dealt with in the curriculum." [47] This content "is derived from the interaction between the gospel and the lifelong persistent concerns of the learner." [48] Themes of scope are identified in relation to these persistent life concerns.[49] However, the concerns themselves are not identified and grounded psychologically.[50]

With respect to the Presbyterian designs, the "situational approach" of set purpose does not address the question of comprehensiveness. Participants will select the themes in which they are interested. Only the Decade Books Design makes an effort to offer a comprehensive foundation in Christian faith and action. Its principle is that the "five abilities" describe a more or less comprehensive basis of Christian learning.

Lansing replies with a principle that answers the second subordinate question more directly than the present one. However, the concluding statement of the justification, responds negatively to the present question: "A Christian adult education curriculum should prescriptively

[47] *CCP,* 12; *Foundations for Curriculum,* 18-19.
[48] *CCP,* 18; *Foundations for Curriculum,* 21.
[49] *Ibid.*
[50] *Dissertation,* 145-47.

limit itself to those domains which have the most direct relevance for the Christian life." [51]

Baltimore states that "scope should be co-extensive with the objective, conditioned by the felt needs of the planning moment." [52]

Lansing's principle serves as a criterion for distinguishing "operational scope" from "broadest potential scope"—a distinction that is peculiar to Lansing's manner of dealing with scope. The criterion is not necessary when the general principle of scope, as in the case of the Cooperative/Baptist and Baltimore Designs, circumscribes what is positively appropriate to the scope of adult Christian education. Consequently, only the Cooperative/Baptist and Baltimore principles of comprehensiveness need be here considered. Both agree that the scope of a curriculum should be as comprehensive as relevance to the learners permits. Applying this criterion to my major principle of scope, I propose as a principle of comprehensiveness that: *the scope of adult Christian education should be as comprehensive of the meaning of the Church's experience of the mystery of Christ as relevance to adult learners permits.*

The principle is very general and is meant to be applied analogously. Applied to a life-long curriculum plan, it can stand as it is. Applied to either a single short-term program or a series of short-term programs, it will act as a reminder to program designers that the scope of Christian education is far broader than those themes to which immediate felt needs of participants point. The principle then acts as a stimulant to find ways to interest participants in the broader concerns of Christianity.

WHAT DISTINCT DIMENSIONS OF SCOPE LEND THEMSELVES TO DIFFERENT KINDS OF ADULT CHRISTIAN LEARNING?

This second subordinate question was originally put: What dimensions of scope lend themselves to manageable learning opportunities for adults? Both Lansing and Baltimore took the question to refer to administrative practicality.[53] The question meant to ask what aspects of scope serve as divisions of scope for cognate learnings.[54] The question can be more correctly put after the answers to its previous phrasing are considered.

[51] *Ibid.*, 310.
[52] *Ibid.*, 362.
[53] *Ibid.*, 311 and 363.
[54] *Ibid.*, 57-59.

The Cooperative and Baptist Designs state different principles in answering the question. The Cooperative Design states that the scope will be organized into five areas of equal significance which provide distinct perspectives upon the whole scope:

Life and Its Setting: The Meaning and Experience of Existence
Revelation: The Meaning and Experience of God's Self-Disclosure
Sonship: The Meaning and Experience of Redemption
Vocation: The Meaning and Experience of Discipleship
The Church: The Meaning and Experience of Christian Community [55]

The Baptist Design reorganizes the five areas into three annual perspectives—Knowing the Living God, God's Call to Live in Christ, and Being the Community of Christian Life.[56]

Of the Presbyterian designs only those of the Decade Books and *Enquiry* manifest operative principles which meet the present question. The Decade Books follow the principle that the "five abilities" (to interpret the Bible intelligently, to understand the beliefs of the church, to work for the unity and mission of the church, to grasp the implications of committing one's personal life to God, and to deal with ethical issues and solve contemporary problems) lend themselves to manageable learning opportunities for adults. *Enquiry* sees dimensions of scope as contemporary issues, biblical meanings, and theological concerns.[57]

Lansing indicates what may pass for dimensions of scope in response to the first subordinate question. They are "1) theology both speculative and applied; 2) those domains which have significant implications for moral decisions and Christian behavior; and 3) areas of immediate practical concern for the well functioning of the Church." [58]

Baltimore indicates dimensions of scope rather loosely in answer to the major question of scope. They are "[the learners] themselves, Christ, and the Church, and [functioning] as adult, mature Christians." [59]

It is immediately obvious that, however much topics like the Bible,

---

[55] *CCP*, 17. A brief description of each area is given, pp. 18-22, and a fuller description of each together with its themes, pp. 39-250.
[56] The arbitrary reorganization renders suspect the consistency of the Baptist Design's solution to problems of scope. See *Dissertation*, 142-43.
[57] *Ibid.*, 242-44 and 251-53.
[58] *Ibid.*, 310.
[59] *Ibid.*, 362.

the Church, and morality reoccur, there is no unanimity in identifying dimensions of scope. Each design seems to have arrived at its outline quite differently. Consequently, there is little point in collating the various dimensions of scope suggested by the designs.

Moreover, none of the designs seems to have identified dimensions of scope precisely with respect to kinds of learning (process). Only the design of Decade Books relates the two: to interpret (process) the Bible (scope); to understand (process) the beliefs of the church (scope); etc. This correlation gives little evidence of being intentional and even less of being worked out in a disciplined way.[60]

What seems needed, then, is an identification of disinct dimensions of scope which relates them immediately to different kinds of learning. Accordingly, the question should be more properly put: What distinct dimensions of scope lend themselves to different kinds of adult Christian learning?

In keeping with the major principle of scope, I propose the principle: *distinct dimensions of scope which lend themselves to different kinds of learning are the meaning of the Church's experience of the mystery of Christ as event, as horizon, as celebration, and as moral imperative.* This principle deserves very thorough explanation and justification. It is the pivotal principle of my curriculum design.

From the statement of the principle, it can be seen that these four dimensions are respectively historical, theological, liturgical, and ethical. Besides explaining each dimension, I hope to show how each is intimated in the New Testament, expressed in the documents of the Second Vatican Council, and developed in the thought of current theologians.

The Mystery of Christ as Event.—The meaning of the mystery of Christ as event is expressed in New Testament formulations. "Without any doubt, the mystery of our religion is very deep indeed: He was made visible in the flesh, attested by the spirit, seen by angels, proclaimed to the pagans, believed in by the world, taken up in glory" (I Tim. 3:16). Paul does not preach a speculative wisdom but "a crucified Christ" (I Cor. 1:23). In contradistinction to myths against which the later Epistles warn (I Tim. 1:4; 4:7; II Tim. 4:4; Tit. 1:14; II Pet. 1:16), the apostolic witness testifies "that Christ died for our sins, in accordance with the scriptures; that he was buried; and that he was raised to life on the third day, in accordance with the scriptures" (I Cor. 15:4).

---

[60] *Ibid.*, 203-09. Efforts to correlate scope and process do not seem to provide the reason for stating learning goals in terms of abilities nearly so much as efforts to obviate polarities in Christian faith and life. See Nelson's address, *ibid.*, 206-07.

Moreover, the death and glorification of Christ is the event which gives purpose to the whole of history. "He has let us know the mystery of his purpose, the hidden plan he so kindly made in Christ from the beginning to act upon when the times had run their course to the end: that he would bring everything together under Christ, as head, everything in the heavens and everything on earth" (Eph. 1:8-10; cf. Col. 1:15-20). This reconciliation is effected "by his death on the cross" (Col. 1:20).

The documents of the Second Vatican Council present substantially the same historical dimension of the mystery of Christ in a synthetic way. The mystery of Christ "affects the whole history of the human race" [61] and is the integrating factor of the whole sweep of salvation history.

In His goodness and wisdom, God chose to reveal Himself and to make known to us the hidden purpose of His will (cf. Eph. 1:9) by which through Christ, the Word made flesh, man has access to the Father in the Holy Spirit. . . . This plan of revelation is realized by deeds and words having an inner unity: the deeds wrought by God in the history of salvation manifest and confirm the teaching and realities signified by the words, while the words proclaim the deeds and clarify the mystery contained in them. By this revelation then, the deepest truth about God and the salvation of man is made clear to us in Christ, who is the Mediator and at the same time the fullness of all revelation.[62]

Here the mystery of Christ has the meaning of event.

That the mystery of Christ is historical event, indeed a sequence of saving events culminating in the death and resurrection of Christ and continuing to a temporal consummation, was a theological truism until challenged by Rudolf Bultmann.[63] Bultmann grants that the Old Testament presents salvation history but contends that the core of the New Testament, stripped of its mythical and historicizing aspects, does not. Rather, the *kerygma* of the New Testament is an ever contemporary call to existential decision to reassess oneself in the light of God's definitive forgiveness in the death of Jesus.[64]

In the face of Bultmann's contention, I am persuaded by the central thesis of Cullmann's *Salvation in History*:

61 *DVII.*, "Optatam Totius," art. 14, p. 450.
62 *Ibid.*, "Dei Verbum," art. 2, p. 112.
63 Bultmann *et al.*, *Kerygma and Myth, passim;* Cullmann, *Salvation in History,* 40-47. For a valuable insight in resolving the debate, see Tracy, *The Achievement. . . ,* 246-47, where he persuasively argues that Cullmann is preoccupied with judgment (history) and Bultmann with decision (dialectics).
64 Bultmann *et al.*, *Kerygma and Myth,* 36-38.

Certainly the whole New Testament contains the call for the decision of faith and implies a new understanding of existence. But does not this call rest on the faith that a divine history has occurred, is occurring, and will go on occurring, which, while envisaging this faith, is first of all independent of it and stands over against the believer? [65]

Not all of Cullmann's arguments are equally persuasive nor all his expressions felicitous. For instance, it seems deterministic to describe faith as "*aligning our existence with this series of events* hic et nunc." [66] Rather, the New Testament affirmation and acceptance of Jesus as Lord (Acts 2:36; I Cor. 12:3; Phil. 2:11) seems a more inviting and personal as well as a more accurate New Testament description of faith.[67] Moreover, despite Cullmann's often stressing the relationship between event and interpretation and the part of both in constituting salvation history,[68] the very polemics in which he is engaged cause him to accentuate the priority of events over interpretation.[69] Here Barr presents a telling corrective.

Contrary to much contemporary opinion, we shall not succeed if we try to formulate the centre of the tradition as an 'event' or series of events, which can then be spoken about as 'acts of God in history'. This will not work either descriptively or historically. It will not work descriptively because the 'acts' cannot be isolated as the supremely important content of the subject-matter as it stands, and the material other than the description of the 'acts' cannot be taken as subsidiary in nature. It will not work historically, for the material directly descriptive of the acts cannot be seen as an indication of a primitive datum from which the rest of the narratives and other materials has been derived.[70]

He suggests instead that the divine salvific activity is to be found especially in the production of a tradition, consisting of "acts, events, speeches, thoughts, conversations, and all sorts of information, in a highly varied complex." [71] The cohesiveness of this tradition is supplied by the narrative progression of the Scriptures which resembles history without satisfying contemporary concepts of history.[72] This

---

65 P. 12.
66 *Ibid;* cf. 69 and 117.
67 Cullmann, *Salvation in History,* 117, associates alignment with salvation history with personal acceptance of the risen Lord but the preferred expression for him remains the former.
68 Esp. 88-97.
69 Pp. 136-66.
70 Barr, *Old and New. . . ,* 16.
71 *Ibid.,* 81.
72 *Ibid.,* 19-21; cf. 65-102 at length.

tradition "provides the matrix for the coming divine acts and the impulse for their very occurrence." [73] It is in the context of this tradition that Jesus' life, preaching, and work can be apprehended as soteriological.[74] Perhaps it is not inaccurate to say that Barr would prefer "eventful tradition" to salvation history.

Were we to incorporate Barr's corrective adequately, we should be tempted to speak of the mystery of Christ as word-event rather than as event. However, that term has been preempted by the "new hermeneutic" represented by Ernst Fuchs and Gerhard Ebeling. If I understand them correctly, both try to posit the objective grounds for the existential self-understanding of faith, which in a pre-Bultmannian context are supplied by act(s) of God in history, in the givenness of the New Testament text which represents a singularly effective "language event." [75] The interpreter's task, then, is not to search for the "objective meaning" of the writers of the text, but to be interpreted by the text itself so that the word-event then may become word-event now.[76] Valuable as this insight is for faith [77] and for preaching, I remain persuaded, with Cullmann, that "the traditional *kerygma* has events as its object. It has as its aim the leading of the person to whom it is delivered to this object, that is, to the (interpreted) events." [78] I contend that it is what God has done in Christ as much as the language that proclaims and responds to that deed which demands the conversion of self-understanding which is an aspect of faith.

More precisely I am persuaded that the New Testament means to affirm the death, resurrection, and second coming of Christ as happenings which have occurred, are occurring, or will occur independently of their proclamation. The character of the happenings is differently affirmed. The death of Jesus is affirmed as a past occurrence. The resurrection is affirmed not so much as a past act but as a present fact, namely, that the risen Christ is alive in a transformed yet incarnate way.[79] The final coming of Christ is affirmed as a temporally

---

[73] *Ibid.*, 156.

[74] *Ibid.*, 157ff.

[75] Translating with Funk, *Language. . .* , 23-24, *Wortgeschehen* and *Sprachereignis*. For a resumé of the points that Fuchs and Ebeling hold in common, see pp. 47-71. For a resumé of each separately, see Robinson, *New Frontiers. . .* , II, 49-69. For representative articles by each, see pp. 78-145.

[76] Robinson, *New Frontiers. . .* , II, 52.

[77] Consequently, I incorporate several insights of Fuchs and Ebeling in my treatment of the mystery of Christ as horizon, rather than as event. See *infra*, 129-31.

[78] Cullmann, *Salvation in History*, 93.

[79] See Raymond E. Brown, "The Resurrection and Biblical Criticism," *Commonweal*, LXXXVII, No. 8 (November 24, 1967) (*Jesus: Commonweal Papers: 2*), 232-36.

future eventuality.[80] Whether one affirms these events today is, of course, a matter of what one is willing to believe on the word of the apostolic witness.

But I maintain that the New Testament invites persons today to affirm these events as past, present, or future happenings. Still more, it invites them to believe the salvific significance of these events, that is, that Jesus died "for our sins" (I Cor. 15:3) and was raised "for our justification" (Rom. 4:25).

Gathering these strands of the New Testament, the Second Vatican Council, and the thought of contemporary theologians together, the meaning of the mystery of Christ as event can be described as *the eventful tradition of human acts initiated by God, integrated by the death and resurrection of Christ, contributed to by all those who are moved by the Spirit of Christ, and purposed by God for a consummation that will be man's as well as His.*

The Mystery of Christ as Horizon.—In addition to an historical dimension, the mystery of Christ also has a theological one. It may be termed the mystery of Christ as horizon.

Horizon is here used in the technical sense developed by Bernard Lonergan and articulated by David Tracy.

With these basic presuppositions in mind, therefore, one may speak of Lonergan's definition and use of horizon. A horizon, for him, is defined as a maximum field of vision from a determinate viewpoint. It possesses both an objective and a subjective pole, each one of which is conditioned by and conditions the other. The subjective pole refers to the intentionality-meaning possibilities of the present stage of development of the subject. The objective pole refers to the "worlds" of meaning achieved by or open to the subject at his present stage of development.[81]

Once a person believes the mystery of Christ to be fact, and indeed salvific fact for him, that faith becomes the radical perspective from which he views himself and all reality. The mystery of Christ as horizon refers both to the perspective out of which one views with all its complex operations (subjective pole) and to the distinctively perceived reality (objective pole) which the Christian views. More cryptically, the mystery of Christ as horizon refers both to the act of faith and the object of faith. To lead persons to ever more consciously differentiated reflection upon themselves as believing subjects and

80 Cullmann, *Salvation in History,* 166-85.
81 Tracy, "Horizon Analysis. . . ," 172, more fully 167-76; *idem, The Achievement. . . ,* 7-21.

upon reality as God's ongoing and redeemed creation is the scope of the mystery of Christ as horizon.

Reflection by the consciously believing subject upon the relationship between God, himself, and the whole of reality is limitless in its learning potential. In a person of relatively undifferentiated consciousness [82] that reflection will be simply experienced and simply expressed. That simplicity does not prevent a person from being any less firm in faith or heroic in virtue.[83] For a person of relatively differentiated consciousness, reflection by and upon himself as a believer will bring him to analyze the complex cognitive and affective conversions [84] which contribute to his basic Christian horizon. Likewise, to the degree that a person's relative horizon [85] is developed, to that degree will his reflection upon the relationship between God and reality be simple or complex. A person whose relative horizon is quite limited will be likely to understand the relationship between God and the world as simplistically as the earlier Old Testament writings that see all events as the direct acts of God. A person whose relative horizon (psychological, sociological, cultural) is highly developed will wish to explore the most intricate direct and indirect relationship between God and the constantly changing process of reality. To the extent, then, that a person reflects as a believing Christian and questions the relationship of historical reality to God, to that extent does the mystery of Christ as horizon provide limitless potential for learning.

[82] For a brief statement of Lonergan's use of differentiated and undifferentiated consciousness, see Tracy, "Horizon Analysis. . . ," 171-74. Operations are conscious inasmuch as they render the subject immediately aware of himself and of his operations and mediately of objects. Through questioning the subject can learn to differentiate three pairs of antithetical "worlds," those of the profane and the sacred, of common sense and theory, of the interior and the exterior. Differentiated consciousness not only experiences but also understands the distinction between those "worlds" and can move back and forth among them.

[83] So also Bernard Lonergan: "It is the eye of faith that discerns God's hand in nature and his message in revelation. It is the efficacious reality that brings men to God *despite their lack of learning or learned errors*" (italics mine), "Natural Knowledge of God," 65.

[84] For Lonergan, the basic conversions are four: *intellectual*, i.e., "self-appropriation of one's rational self-consciousness"; *moral*, i.e., the transition from knowing to deciding in accord with one's knowledge; *religious*, i.e., an openness to transcendence; and *Christian*, i.e., transformation-in-faith into the death-resurrection of Christ. See Tracy, "Horizon Analysis. . . ," 175, and *The Achievement*. . . , 143-44, 164-82, and esp. 250, n. 29 which reports the incompleteness of L.'s analysis of Christian conversion.

[85] Tracy, "Horizon Analysis. . . ," 175: "Relative horizon is one's present horizon relative to one's psychological (education), sociological (society), and cultural (epoch) development." According to Tracy, *The Achievement*. . . , 254, n. 34, L.'s distinction between "relative" and "basic" horizon needs further clarification.

One's Christian horizon comes to articulation in affirmations of faith. When these affirmations are made by the whole Christian community of a given period they become doctrines of faith for that and succeeding generations of Christians. Consequently, it is necessary to learn the doctrinal tradition of Christians from the New Testament on as a prelude to articulating one's own faith horizon. Both tasks are equally important: learning the doctrinal tradition and, in light of the tradition, articulating one's faith horizon today.[86] However, it is the second task which more properly refers to learning the mystery of Christ as horizon. The first task pertains more to learning the mystery as event. The point is that once a faith horizon is formulated and passes over into the doctrinal tradition it becomes spoken event and part of the eventful tradition itself.[87]

Besides reflecting as a believer upon the relationship of the whole of reality to God, besides articulating that reflection for oneself and for others, the mystery of Christ as horizon encourages the Christian to develop an open and evolving synthesis of his reflection.[88] To relate his judgments one to another, to find the consistency between his own affirmations and those of the doctrinal tradition, to compare his synthesis with those of other epochs and to bring it under the judgment of eschatological promise is a further aspect of coping with the mystery of Christ as horizon.

In brief, reflecting upon one's basic Christian perspective with its subjective operations and objective terms, articulating those reflections, and synthesizing them pertain to the mystery of Christ as horizon. Preliminary justification for this meaning of the mystery of Christ in the New Testament, in the Second Vatican Council, and in current theology now deserves to be given.

Obviously, the New Testament does not employ the language of horizon analysis. However, to explore the subjective pole of the mystery of Christ as horizon is to render reflexively conscious Paul's intent:

---

[86] This movement, from learning the doctrinal tradition to articulating one's faith horizon today in the light of it, parallels Lonergan's two phases of theology *in oratione obliqua* and *in oratione recta* ("Functional Specialties. . . ," 492-95) or as he has come more lately to speak of "mediating" and "mediated" theology. See Tracy, *The Achievement*. . . , 240, 262-66.

[87] *Supra*, 122-23 and *infra*, 140.

[88] The development of one's faith horizon through articulation to synthesis corresponds to Lonergan's successive functional specialties of foundations to doctrines to systematics. See "Functional Specialties. . . ," 490-92; Tracy, *The Achievement*. . . , 251-57.

An unspiritual person is one who does not accept anything of the Spirit of God: he sees it all as nonsense; it is beyond his understanding because it can only be understood by means of the Spirit. A spiritual man, on the other hand, is able to judge the value of everything, and his own value is not to be judged by other men. As scripture says: *Who can know the mind of the Lord, so who can teach him?* But we are those who have the mind of Christ. (I Cor. 2:14-16; cf. II Cor. 5:16-17) [89]

John also insists upon the same phenomenon—that to accept Christ a person must understand from a radically different perspective, a perspective which is in a way God's own:

> No one can come to me
> unless he is drawn by the Father who sent me,
> and I will raise him up at the last day.
> It is written in the prophets:
> *They will all be taught by God,*
> and to hear the teaching of the Father,
> and learn from it,
> is to come to me. (Jn. 6:44-45) [90]

The objective pole of the mystery of Christ as horizon also draws its beginnings from John and Paul. The believer is to understand that the events and developments of every age—especially one's own—"were created through him [Christ] and for him" (Col. 1:16; cf. Jn. 1:1-3) and that "he holds all things in unity" (Col. 1:18) and that the Father will "bring everything together under Christ, as head, everything in the heavens and everything on earth" (Eph. 1:10). Moreover, Paul invites the Christian to unlock the process by which God's purpose is being accomplished. "From the beginning till now the entire creation, as we know, has been groaning in a great act of giving birth; and not only creation, but all of us who possess the first fruits of the Spirit, we too groan inwardly as we wait for our bodies to be set free" (Rom. 8:22-23). It is the Spirit who "will lead [the believer] to the complete truth" (Jn. 16:13).

In the statements of the Second Vatican Council, the mystery of Christ may also be interpreted as providing a basic horizon with subjective and objective poles fruitful for theological speculation. Subjectively, the mystery of Christ "reveals man to man himself":

[89] Note that this statement occurs in a context where Paul speaks of the mystery (I Cor. 2:7; 1:22, and possibly 2:1). See Bornkamm, *TDNT*, IV, 819.

[90] Cf. Jn. 1:9-13; 3:8, 21; 5:37-38; 6:37; 8:19, 31-32, 42-47; 9:39; 10:14-15, 25-27; 12:35-36, 44-46; 17:7-8; 18:37-38.

The truth is that only in the mystery of the incarnate Word does the mystery of man take on light. For Adam, the first man, was a figure of Him who was to come, namely, Christ the Lord. Christ, the final Adam, by the revelation of the mystery of the Father and His love, fully reveals man to man himself and makes his supreme calling clear. It is not surprising, then, that in Him all the aforementioned truths find their root and attain their crown.[91]

Christian faith also implies a change of perspective on all reality. "Faith in the mystery of Christ's death and resurrection" effects a "transition, which brings with it a progressive change of outlook." [92]

Moreover, the mystery of Christ contributes a cohesiveness to the theological elaboration of one's self-understanding and the faith perspective which it initiates.

Sacred theology rests on the written word of God, together with sacred tradition, as its primary and perpetual foundation. By scrutinizing in the light of faith all truth stored up [better: grounded (conditam)] in the mystery of Christ, theology is most powerfully strengthened and constantly rejuvenated by that word.[93]

And again:

In the revision of ecclesiastical studies, the first object in view must be a better integration of philosophy and theology. These subjects should work together harmoniously to unfold . . . the mystery of Christ. . . .[94]

These are some uses of the mystery of Christ by the Council documents which correspond to my conception of the mystery of Christ as horizon.

Current theology is only beginning to speak of horizon analysis as an "heuristic and schematic possibility" [95] for thinking through the mystery of Christ today.

In my explanation of the term I have drawn heavily upon Lonergan and Tracy. Yet the task they set for themselves parallels the efforts of several Christian educators and theologians.

When the United Presbyterian Division of Lay Education invites adults to "do theology" rather than learn a "set of right beliefs," [96]

[91] DVII., "Gaudium et Spes," art. 22, p. 220; cf. art. 38, pp. 235-36; art. 41, p. 240; "Gravissimum Educationis," Intr., p. 638.

[92] Ibid., "Ad Gentes," art. 13, p. 600.

[93] Ibid., "Dei Verbum," art. 24, p. 127.

[94] Ibid., "Optatam Totius," art. 14, pp. 449-50.

[95] Tracy, "Horizon Analysis. . . ," 167.

[96] Supra, 100-01.

it encourages them to learn the mystery of Christ as horizon. When Wyckoff states that "the scope of the curriculum is the whole field of relationships—God, man, nature, history—in light of the gospel, and in this sense the gospel completely redefines the meaning of the field," [97] he describes what I mean by the horizon which faith in the mystery of Christ provides. When Nels Ferré, in attempting a theology for Christian education, insists that "faith must serve as the heuristic, organizing center of knowledge without violating or encroaching in any way on any subject of knowledge," [98] he is concerned that the mystery of Christ provide a genuinely open basic horizon which respects the enlargement of one's relative horizon and is enriched by that enlargement.

Moreover, a theologian such as Wolfhart Pannenberg is not just semantically close to the mystery of Christ as horizon in saying:

> History is the most comprehensive horizon of Christian theology. All theological questions and answers are meaningful only within the framework of the history which God has with humanity and through humanity with his whole creation—the history moving toward a future still hidden from the world but already revealed in Jesus Christ.[99]

He points to the interdependency of the mystery of Christ as event and as horizon. It is especially the raising of meaningful questions [100] and working out answers *for the present* that pertain to analyzing the horizon provided by history (in our terms the eventful tradition).

Despite their differences from the Pannenberg circle in both presuppositions and method, the proponents of the "new hermeneutic," Ernst Fuchs and Gerhard Ebeling, seem involved in a task which closely resembles what I mean by learning the mystery of Christ as horizon. It is not possible to present here a summary of their work. That has ably been offered to American readers by Robert Funk and James Robinson.[101] It is possible only to suggest some points of approximation between the new hermeneutic and horizon development.

---

[97] "Instruction, the Person and the Group," *Religious Education*, LXI, 1 (Jan.-Feb., 1966), 12.

[98] Ferré, *A Theology for Christian Education*, 46.

[99] "Redemptive Event and History" in *Essays on Old Testament Hermeneutics*, ed. C. Westermann, trans. and ed. J. L. Mays (Richmond, Virginia: John Knox Press, 1963), p. 314. For an introduction to Pannenberg and his circle see *Revelation as History*, ed. W. Pannenberg, trans. by D. Granskow (New York: The Macmillan Company, 1968).

[100] Cf. Tracy, "Horizon Analysis. . . ," 169 and 171 for the "centrality of not new answers but new questions" to horizon analysis.

[101] *Supra*, 107.

Central to the new hermeneutic is that it understands "its task as translating meaning from one culture to the other, from one situation to the other." [102] It conceives this task as so embracing the whole theological enterprise that " 'hermeneutic' can become coterminous with Christian theology as the statement of the meaning of Scripture for our day." [103] Indeed for Ebeling "the new hermeneutic has become in fact a new understanding of theological scholarship as a whole." [104]

Especially in the summary of his position does Ebeling reveal how useful his understanding of the hermeneutical task is for what we have called learning the mystery of Christ as horizon.

The criticism to make against a theology that has become traditionalistic and positivistic is not that it abides by the given, the tradition. Quite the contrary. It is precisely under the appearance of especially loyal allegiance to the tradition that *de facto* it is given up. For it is 'presented' as *traditum* and thus as *praeteritum,* rather than by responding responsibly in pointing into the future with a word happening today, so that what is transmitted, the *traditum,* can take place as *traditio,* the act of transmitting. . . .[105] Dogmatic theology completes the task of interpretation not in the sense of a method competing with historical exegesis, but rather in the sense of a turn, called for by the subject matter itself, from the historical to the dogmatic way of understanding.[106] In dealings with the text *its* being interpreted by us turns into *our* being interpreted by the text. . . . For the text is not there for its own sake, but rather for the sake of the word event that is the origin and hence also the future of the text. Word event is the event of interpretation taking place through the word. Hence the text is there for the sake of the event of interpretation, which is the text's origin and future. For the word that once happened and in happening became the text must again become word with the help of the text and thus happen as interpreting word. . . .[107] The depths of such event of interpretation are of course only fully grasped when it is recognized that this bringing into truth is at the same time the exposure and the alteration of reality.[108] Thus the object of dogmatic theology is the word event itself, in which the reality of man comes true.[109]

This summary seems to express, if in a different way, the elements of learning the mystery of Christ as horizon. Because of the pre-

102 Robinson, *New Frontiers. . . ,* II, 4.

103 *Ibid.,* 6.

104 *Ibid.,* 63.

105 *Supra,* 126.

106 Note the similarity to Lonergan's movement from foundations to doctrine. See *supra,* 126, n. 86.

107 So the task of the mystery of Christ as horizon is to "do" theology oneself in light of the doctrinal tradition, not simply to appropriate the tradition.

108 Here the objective pole of the mystery of Christ as horizon is well expressed.

109 Robinson, *New Frontiers. . . ,* II, 67-69.

suppositions Ebeling has adopted from Heidegger and Bultmann, he makes the givenness of the biblical text and not historical event [110] his point of departure. But thereafter the invitation to understand oneself anew (subjective pole of basic Christian horizon) [111] through the text and to do so fully through an event which exposes and alters all reality (objective pole) in such a way that one participates in the very tradition from which one learns is substantially the task which learning the mystery of Christ as horizon hopes to describe.

For purposes of a working definition, then, the mystery of Christ as horizon may be stated as *a call to analyze the basic perspective from which one views himself and the whole of created and historical reality as changed by the deed of God in Christ, to articulate that analysis, and to relate those articulations to one another in a coherent synthesis.*

The Mystery of Christ as Celebration.—Besides an historical and a theological dimension, the mystery of Christ also has a liturgical dimension. It may be called celebration. Here celebration means a participation through sacramental worship in the salvific activity of Christ.[112]

It is quite true, as Odo Casel observes, that "when we are considering the meaning of the term *Mystērion* in Scripture, it is right to say that the word seldom has a direct relationship to ritual in the text." [113] Yet, as he further observes "the primitive meaning of the

110 This would seem to be the major difference between Ebeling's position and mine. Ebeling would, however, seem to leave the way open to historical event being the object of proclamation and consequently the foundation of the text: ". . . that results from the basic starting point in the process of the text becoming proclamation. The question as to the real nature of this event must therefore be at least one essential element in the doctrine of the word of God" (Robinson, *New Frontiers. . .* , II, 88).

111 It is not altogether clear that Ebeling, in speaking of "our being interpreted by the text," means what Lonergan and Tracy call the subjective pole of horizon. They mean the subject as subject and not as object, as reflecting and not as reflected upon, to be the subjective pole of horizon (Lonergan in Crowe [ed.], *Collection. . .* , 173-92, 227-30, and Tracy, "Horizon Analysis. . . ," 171). Ebeling does not distinguish. He may be speaking of the subject more as object than as subject.

112 Here, according to St. Augustine's classical distinction, celebration is contrasted with commemoration. Bouyer, *Liturgical Piety,* 205, quotes him as saying "Easter . . . is a *sacramentum,* because in it we not only *commemorate* the death and resurrection of Our Lord, but we also *celebrate* our own actual passage from death to life, from a mortal life to life everlasting. But the feast of Christmas, insofar as it *recalls* Christ's Nativity, is only a *commemoratio,* an anniversary." (Italics, Bouyer's.)

113 Casel, *The Mystery of Christian Worship. . .* , 97.

word lies in worship, and . . . this deepest layer never entirely disappears . . ." [114] Consequently, the adoption of Paul's term which denotes the deed of God in Christ (mystērion) to characterize the liturgical acts (mysteria-sacramenta) which actualize that deed in the life of believers is quite natural. Gunther Bornkamm traces both the movement and its theological import.

The original cultic concept of mystery found rejuvenation in the early Church when mystērion became a fixed term for the sacraments. Already Just. And Tert. can compare the pagan mysteries with the Christian sacraments. . . . The same basic idea is seen in both, though the content differs. As the pagan mysteries actualise the destinies and acts of their gods in sacred actions and thus give participants a share in them, so in the symbolical [n. symbolon always having the sense of signum efficax] ritual of the Christian sacraments there takes place a cultic repetition and re-presentation of the historically unrepeatable redeeming act of Christ. . . . Terminologically, this understanding comes to be fixed only in the 4th cent. Mystērion now becomes a term for baptism and the Lord's Supper. . . .

The nature of the relation between the saving acts and the cultic representation is brought out particularly well by the fact that both are called mystērion.[115]

Even if the mystery of Christ is not used by Paul with liturgical import, he does link the content of the mystery, that is, the historical death and resurrection of the Lord, with Baptism and the Eucharist. "You have been taught that when we were baptized in Christ Jesus we were baptized in his death; in other words, when we were baptized we went into the tomb with him and joined him in death, so that as Christ was raised from the dead by the Father's glory, we too might live a new life" (Rom. 6:3-4). And with respect to the Eucharist: "Until the Lord comes, therefore, everytime you eat this bread and drink this cup, you are proclaiming his death, and so anyone who eats the bread or drinks the cup of the Lord unworthily will be behaving unworthily towards the body and blood of the Lord" (I Cor. 11:26-27).

The association between the mystery of Christ and the mystēria for which Paul lays the groundwork and which the Fathers develop, becomes, largely through the influence of Odo Casel,[116] the liturgical theology of the Second Vatican Council.

According to the Fathers of the Council, it is through Baptism that

---

114 Ibid.

115 Bornkamm, TDNT, IV, 826.

116 This is not to deny that Casel's germinal but not infrequently romantic theology of the mystery needs careful refinement. See Charles Davis' and Burkhead Neunheuser's prefaces to the English edition of Casel's The Mystery of Christian Worship. . . .

persons are involved mystically and sacramentally in the mystery of Christ and through the Eucharist that they express their involvement in it.

Thus, by baptism, men are plunged into the paschal mystery of Christ: they die with Him, are buried with Him, and rise with Him. . . . The Church has never failed to come together to celebrate the paschal mystery: reading "in all the scriptures the things referring to himself" (Lk. 24:27), celebrating the Eucharist in which "the victory and triumph of his death are again made present . . ." [117]

. . . .

For it is through the liturgy, especially the divine Eucharistic Sacrifice, that "the work of our redemption is exercised." The liturgy is thus the outstanding means by which the faithful can express in their lives, and manifest to others, the mystery of Christ and the real nature of the true Church.[118]

Moreover, liturgical preaching and participation in the sequence of annual Christian feasts presents the opportunity for engagement in the same mystery.

Its character should be that of a proclamation of God's wonderful works in the history of salvation, that is, the mystery of Christ, which is ever made present and active within us, especially in the celebration of the liturgy.[119]

. . . .

Within the cycle of [the liturgical] year, moreover, [the Church] unfolds the whole mystery of Christ, not only from His incarnation and birth until His ascension, but also as reflected in the day of Pentecost, and the expectation of a blessed, hoped-for-return of the Lord.[120]

Sacramental initiation, liturgical preaching, prayer—all play a part in celebrating the mystery of Christ.

Edward Schillebeeckx explains the theological foundation for the Council's teaching about the liturgy. He describes the sacraments as "ecclesial celebration[s]-in-mystery of the mysteries of Christ's life." [121]

In explaining the "presence of the Mystery of Christ in the sacraments," [122] he insists upon "two aspects of Jesus' redemptive acts: they take place in history, yet they have a perennial character." [123] Since as temporal events they are unrepeatable, the histori-

[117] *DVII*, "Sacrosanctum Concilium," art. 6, p. 140.
[118] *Ibid.*, art. 2, p. 137; cf. "Ad Gentes," art. 16, p. 604.
[119] *Ibid.*, "Sacrosanctum Concilium," art. 35, pp. 149-50.
[120] *Ibid.*, art. 102, p. 168.
[121] Schillebeeckx, *Christ the Sacrament. . .* , 54.
[122] *Ibid.*
[123] *Ibid.*, 55.

cal redemptive acts must have something about them which is perennial. This element lies in their being the personal acts of the eternal
Son of God. Consequently, the acts themselves have an eternally actual
and enduring quality.[124] Ultimately, that quality lies in the fact that
the loving obedience of Jesus for the Father and the pleasure of the
Father in Him which the crucifixion and resurrection express in
historical acts continue in "the mode of glory." [125]

. . . It is precisely [this] eternally actual mystery of worship, Christ himself,
who becomes present to us and is active for our benefit in the sacraments.
This is the authentic and essential factor of the "presence in mystery." [126]

To the degree that participants enter into that mystery of worship
by making their own Christ's loving obedience to the Father, to that
degree is the sacrament full and fruitful for them.[127] That attitude of
the participants is the essence of sacramental prayer and the paradigm
of all Christian prayer.[128]

The meaning of liturgical proclamation of the mystery of Christ;
the meaning of mystical identification with the death and resurrection
of the Lord and incorporation into His Body; the meaning of sacramental participation in the perennial worship of Christ to the Father
through various modes; the meaning of prayer communal and personal: these are but some of the meanings with which the mystery of
Christ as celebration is concerned.

Briefly, then, the mystery of Christ as celebration may be defined as
the *meaning of the Church's participation by the Spirit in the historical and perennial worship of Christ for the Father.*

The Mystery of Christ as Moral Imperative.—In addition to historical,
theological, and liturgical dimensions, the mystery of Christ also has
an ethical dimension. It may be called the meaning of the mystery
of Christ as moral imperative. It concerns the ethical "ought" that
arises from the deed of God in Christ. The moral imperative of the
mystery is also amply expressed in the Scriptures, in the documents
of the Second Vatican Council, and in the work of current theologians.

Biblical justification is summarized by Cullmann's generic statement: "In the Bible, an ethical imperative always follows from an

124 *Ibid.,* 58.
125 *Ibid.*
126 *Ibid.,* 60.
127 *Ibid.,* 133-35.
128 On the relationship between prayer and the mystery of Christ, between
prayer and sacramental attitudes, see Bouyer, *Liturgical Piety,* 229-42.

(or the!) *indicative."* [129] This movement from indicative to imperative is the basis of covenant morality (Ex. 19:3-8; Joshua 24:1-28). It
is central to the Deuteronomic tradition.[130] It is insisted upon by the
prophetic preaching.[131]

Moreover, convenant morality becomes the presupposition of
Christian ethics. In the New Testament, however, the indicative has progressed beyond the Exodus and possession of Canaan
to the death and resurrection of Christ. Mystical death and resurrection in Him become the fact which grounds the "ought" of Christian life (Rom. 6). John puts the principle even more categorically:
"No one who has been begotten by God sins; because God's seed
remains inside him, he cannot sin when he has been begotten by
God" (I Jn. 3:9).

Dead and risen with Christ, reborn with His life, the Christian has
Christ Himself as his principal ethical norm. Especially is Christ's
self-emptying love unto death normative for his followers:

> In your minds you must be
> the same as Christ Jesus:
> His state was divine,
> yet he did not cling
> to his equality with God
> but emptied himself
> to assume the condition of a slave,
> and became as men are;
> and being as all men are,
> he was humbler yet,
> even to accepting death,
> death on a cross (Phil. 2:5-8).[132]

On the voluntary level, the Christian "ought" resides in the com-
pelling fittingness of a love response to a prior divine love.[133] "This
is the love I mean: not our love for God, but God's love for us when

---

[129] Cullmann, *Salvation in History*, 329. The movement from the indicative to
the imperative is not, however, analyzed. See Gustafson, *Christ and the Moral Life*,
260-61.

[130] See Bernhard W. Anderson, *Understanding the Old Testament*, 2nd ed.
(Englewood Cliffs, N.J.: Prentice-Hall, Inc., 1966), pp. 311-325.

[131] See R. E. Clements, *Prophecy and Covenant*, Studies in Biblical Theology
(London: SCM Press Ltd., 1965).

[132] Note that the context is one of urging Christians to fraternal love (Phil. 2:
1-4).

[133] Consequently, not logical reasoning but *sym-pathos* or "connatural" understanding grounds the relationship between the Christian imperative and indicative.
Fundamentally, the same principle is at work in the old covenant ethic. *Hesed*,
"steadfast love," characterizes both divine fidelity and the fitting human response
in the covenant relationship.

he sent his Son to be the sacrifice that takes our sin away" (I Jn. 4:10). "We are to love, then, because he loved us first" (4:19). Consequently love for God and neighbor summarizes and informs the whole Christian ethic (Mk. 12:28-31; Mt. 22:34-40; Lk. 10:25-28; Rom. 13:8-10, I Jn. *passim*). No matter how practical the casuistic codes of the Old Testament [134] nor how parabolic the eschatological demands of Jesus,[135] it is love that makes them imperative for the believer.

The same ethical imperative which appears as an aspect of the mystery of Christ in the Scriptures is expressed in the documents of the Second Vatican Council.

When Christians "help men to attain to salvation by love for God and neighbor. . . . the mystery of Christ begins to shine forth."[136] Besides effecting "a progressive change of outlook [horizon], . . . faith in the mystery of Christ's death and resurrection" brings with it a change in "morals, [which] should manifest itself through its social effects." [137] Moreover, the mystery of Christ gives Christians not only the imperative to transform human culture but also the rationale for their effort:

> Christians, on pilgrimage toward the heavenly city, should seek and savor the things that are above. This duty in no way decreases, but rather increases, the weight of their obligation to work with all men in constructing a more human world. In fact, the mystery of Christian faith furnishes them with excellent incentives and helps toward discharging this duty more energetically and especially toward uncovering the full meaning of this activity, a meaning which gives human culture its eminent place in the integral vocation of man.[138]

These texts display the sensitivity of the Council Fathers to the imperative consonant with the indicative which the mystery of Christ provides.

In current moral theology, Bernard Häring has attempted to recast the tradition of scholastic moral theology on the major premise that "the principle, the norm, the center, and the goal of Christian Moral Theology is Christ." [139] The imitation of Christ, "but not through

---

134 *The Jerome Biblical Commentary*, II, 751.

135 Charles E. Curran, "The Ethical Teaching of Jesus," *Commonweal*, LXXXVII, No. 8 (November, 1967) *(Jesus, Commonweal Papers: 2)* 248-58.

136 *DVII*, "Ad Gentes," art. 12, p. 599.

137 *Ibid.*, art. 13, p. 600.

138 *Ibid.*, "Gaudium et Spes," art. 57, p. 262; cf. art. 38, pp. 235-37.

139 Häring, *The Law of Christ*. . . , I, vii.

mere external copying, even though it be in love and obedience" [140] is for him a fundamental ethical criterion. He shares the Pauline presupposition that for the Christian the ethical imperative lies in "the mystical identification of our whole being in Christ through the sacraments." [141] Consequently, the ethical decisions and acts of the Christian are essentially cultic.[142] In accord with this basic stance, Häring expresses his synthesis of moral theology:

Instead we seek a more comprehensive synthesis in the doctrine of the life in and with Christ, (first volume) in the dialogue of love, with God and with our neighbor (second volume). This dialogue of love with its superabundant endowment and its total commitment continues in the realization of the all-embracing dominion of God's love, a realization of loving dominion in all our spiritual and psychophysical powers and potentialities in all spheres of life (third volume).[143]

Important criticisms can be lodged against Häring's synthesis. For instance, he has forced an earlier division of moral theology arising from a classicist understanding of natural law [144] and conditioned by Canon Law into a Christocentric pattern. The divisions remain largely unchanged, save in sequence, title, and introductions. Needed is a more radical reordering of parts which respects the divine initiative-human response dynamic of Pauline-Johannine ethics, a developmental understanding of natural law,[145] and the primacy of the Sermon on the Mount over the Decalogue. However, the orientation that Häring has given to Roman Catholic Moral Theology by pointing it to the mystery of Christ accords with my interest that the imperative aspect of the mystery be an explicit dimension of the scope of Christian education.

The same interest is cause to welcome James Gustafson's preliminary attempt to focus Protestant ethics upon the centrality of Christ for the moral life.[146] He provides a valuable assessment of the thought

140 *Ibid.*

141 *Ibid.*, I, vii; cf. 51, 94-5; II, xxxv, 126-32.

142 *Ibid.*, II, xxxv, 126-32.

143 *Ibid.*, III, vii.

144 On the classicist understanding of natural law, see Joseph Arntz, "Natural Law and its History," *Concilium*, V, 1 (May, 1965), 23-32.

145 On a developmental understanding of natural law, see Bernard Lonergan, "The Transition from a Classicist World View to Historical Mindedness" in *Law for Liberty: The Role of Law in the Church Today*, ed. James E. Biechler (Baltimore: Helicon Press, 1967), pp. 126-33.

146 Reference here is made especially to his last chapter "Christ and the Moral Life: A Constructive Statement," *Christ and the Moral Life*, 238-71. I expectantly await the "systematic development" promised in a subsequent publication (p. 238, n. 1).

of influential Protestant theologians regarding three ways by which Christ has significance for morality: as the personification of value (chapter II); as the cause and source of man's capacity to be moral (chapters III and IV); and as the exemplar and teacher of ethical norms (chapters V and VI). The tripartite division may be expressed as the significance for ethics of Christ as King, Priest, and Prophet.[147]

In his own statement of "the differences that faith in Jesus Christ *often does make, can make,* and *ought to make* in the moral lives of members of the Christian community" [148] (chapter VII), Gustafson's first section, "Perspective and Posture in the Christian Moral Life," [149] pertains to my meaning of the mystery of Christ as horizon. His other three sections, however, on the attitudes and dispositions evoked and shaped by loyalty to Christ, on the intentions and motives that are consonant with Christian faith, and on the normative force of Christ's example and teachings [150] pertain directly to the mystery of Christ as moral imperative.

I see the shaping of dispositions and the illumination of intentions more dependent upon mystical identification with Christ, after the manner of Bernard Häring, than does Gustafson; but, I agree with Gustafson's explication of Christ as norm: "Thus Christ is the norm for the Christian's theological interpretation of what God wills that life should be among men; Christ is the norm for illumination of what the Christian ought to be and do in his actions; Christ is the central obligatory norm for those who would order their lives in discipleship to him." [151]

Learning the mystery of Christ as moral imperative comprises, then, themes like the basis of covenant morality; apodictic and casuistic law; Christ as the principle, center, and norm of a transposed covenant morality; the parabolic eschatological demands of Jesus' moral teaching; the fruit of Christian ethical experience as it finds articulation in principles and laws and typical cases; and the evolving nature of the human person as a norm for human behavior.

Accordingly, the meaning of the mystery of Christ as moral imperative may be succinctly described as *the demand of a loving response in practical life to God's love in Christ.*

147 *Ibid.,* 5.
148 *Ibid.,* 240.
149 *Ibid.,* 240-48.
150 *Ibid.,* 248-71.
151 *Ibid.,* 265.

FOUR DIMENSIONS OF SCOPE AND THE FOUR CATECHETICAL SIGNS

I have tried to indicate how the mystery of Christ lends itself to four meanings—an historical, a theological, a liturgical, and an ethical meaning—and how these four dimensions are grounded in Scripture's use of the mystery of Christ, echoed in the teaching of the Second Vatican Council, and elaborated upon by contemporary theologians. However, it may be necessary to quiet the suspicion that rather than a fresh ordering of the scope of adult Christian education, these dimensions represent no more than a semantic re-habilitation of the four catechetical signs of Eichstätt.[152] The four signs are expressed in the principle, "Catechesis embraces a fourfold presentation of the faith: through liturgy, Bible, systematic teaching [doctrine] and the testimony of Christian living [witness]." [153] It may be superficially adduced that liturgy equals celebration in my Design, Bible equals event, doctrine equals horizon, and witness equals moral imperative.

The identification of liturgy with celebration and witness with moral imperative can be granted. There are differences, mainly inso-far as celebration and moral imperative are aspects of the one mystery, but the differences are not of crucial significance. The differences between Bible and event, doctrine and horizon, are, however, significant. I think that those differences can meet the objections raised against Bible and doctrine as conceived by Eichstätt. The main objections are that, in a biblical presentation, salvation history becomes a study of past history and that, through systematic presentation, doctrine becomes the study of past formulations of faith.

In my differentiation of scope the Bible is not equivalent to event. The Bible is indeed a past event in that it was produced in the past, and thus belongs to the mystery of Christ as event. However, within its pages there is told the story not only of past events but also of past faith horizons coming to articulation, of past celebration of the mystery of Christ in anticipation and fulfillment, and of past ethical response to the mystery.

[152] The International Study Week on Missionary Catechetics took place at Eichstätt, W. Germany, July 21-28, 1960. Its papers and resolutions are published in Johannes Hofinger (ed.), *Teaching All Nations: A Symposium on Modern Catechetics,* rev. and trans. by Clifford Howell (New York: Herder and Herder, 1961). The four catechetical signs of Eichstätt, which won fairly unanimous agreement among Catholic religious educators after the study week, have fallen largely into disfavor. Their "trivialization" was criticized by Gabriel Moran, *Catechesis of Revelation,* 120-21.

[153] Hofinger (ed.), *Teaching All Nations. . . ,* 398-99.

These meanings, especially as developed in the New Testament, are normative for Christian faith and life now. This fact means that our interpretation of events, formulation of a contemporary faith horizon, liturgical celebration, and moral response must be in positive consistency [154] with those of the New Testament.

Especially in the difference between doctrine and horizon does the accent fall upon present rather than past. As commonly used by Roman Catholics, doctrine refers to inherited formulations of faith sanctioned by a past act of the hierarchical *magisterium*. To learn doctrine is to recover the meanings meant when the formulations were made.

These doctrines are instructive for formulating a contemporary faith horizon. Indeed, if the same question is being raised in the same context with the same data now as before, the answers of the past hold true for the present. But if the question or the context or the data are significantly new, then a new answer is required. The new answer, however, must be in positive consistency with doctrines of the past on related questions. There is an important difference, then, between learning doctrine and learning the mystery of Christ as horizon. The former recovers meanings from the past and asks what meaning they have for the present; the latter begins with the questions of the present and, seeking elucidation from past doctrine, articulates answers out of its present faith perspective. If authenticated by the hierarchical *magisterium,* these answers form part of the normative doctrinal tradition which, passing over into the mystery of Christ as event, can guide the articulation of a future generation's faith horizon.

For these reasons, I find the mystery of Christ as event, as horizon, as celebration, and as moral imperative a more adequate delineation of the scope of Christian education than the four catechetical signs of Eichstätt.[155]

So far I have stressed the distinction between the four meanings of the mystery of Christ. Now it is necessary equally to stress their interdependence. The meanings are distinct but no one meaning nor any combination of three of them exhausts the full meaning of the

---

154 For the meaning of "positive consistency," see *supra,* 94-95.

155 It may be objected that the four catechetical signs make no pretence at being delineations of scope (content). They are put forward as ways of presenting the faith and refer to process (method) rather than scope (content). This is true. However, in their use the four "ways" became four "signs," or four aspects of the "message." See Gabriel Moran, "The Time for a Theology," *The Living Light,* III, No. 2 (Summer, 1966), 18-19. The development seems traceable to a lack of sophistication in curriculum methodology.

mystery. These four meanings—event, horizon, celebration, moral imperative—complement one another.

Not only are the four meanings complementary, they are also interdependent in understanding and appreciating the mystery of Christ. In other words, they are logically interdependent, at least, if logic can be considered to include connaturality.[156] The logical dependency can best be demonstrated by tracing the reciprocity between the various meanings.

The faith perspective which the mystery provides upon oneself and all reality (horizon) rests upon the significance of the deed of God in Christ (event) for oneself and for all reality. Perception of the significance of the deed of God (event) in turn, depends upon an intuition of the implications of that deed for one's self-understanding and one's synthesis of reality (horizon).[157] Moreover, celebration of the mystery depends for its meaningfulness both upon the significance of the event and upon the horizon which faith in the event provides. Correspondingly, celebration of the mystery contributes, by way of "connatural" understanding, a heightened appreciation for the significance of the event and of the horizon which it provides. Furthermore, the perception of the mystery as morally imperative for one's decisions is mystically consonant with sacramental involvement in the event and intellectually consistent with the horizon which faith in the event provides. Reciprocally, ethical response to the mystery heightens an awareness of its historical eventfulness, of the profounder implications of the horizon it provides, and of the rich import of its celebration. Briefly, affirmation of the mystery of Christ as event grounds the horizon from which the Christian views himself and all reality, from which, too, he celebrates his and all creation's relationship to the event, and in keeping with which he ethically contributes to the ongoing history of the event.

The logical interdependence of these four meanings of the mystery of Christ will bear upon solutions to the problems of the selection of scope and the sequence (or lack of it) in which themes of scope are offered. These problems bring us to the last two subordinate questions of scope.

---

[156] *Supra,* 135, n. 133.

[157] The relationship we draw here between event and horizon is similar to that which Lonergan places between "mediating" and "mediated" theology. See "Functional Specialties. . . ," 492-95, and *supra,* 126, n. 86. A difference lies in the fact that L. deals with a doctrinal tradition carried forward mainly by verbal communication. My use of event comprises not only the verbal doctrinal tradition but also deeds, worship, cultural institutions, and any historical form that carries meaning from past to present.

HOW SHALL DIMENSIONS OF SCOPE BE SELECTED
FOR INCLUSION IN A CURRICULUM PLAN?

It is not sufficient to determine the dimensions to which the scope of adult Christian education lends itself. It is also necessary to find a principle that will guide program designers in the choice of those dimensions or themes thereof. Hence the question of selectivity.

The Cooperative/Baptist Design offers the principle that themes will be selected which describe "the intersection of the concerns of the Christian faith with basic persistent life issues." [158]

The Presbyterian Decade Books Design selects all "five abilities" for inclusion in its curriculum plan.[159] The "situational approach" leaves the selection of topics and themes up to participants.

Lansing's selection of courses "is the result of the intersection of student interests (as best that they can be determined), competent personnel availability, and broad diocesan needs." [160]

Baltimore's principle of selectivity is that "dimensions of scope will be determined by understanding the actual life situations of our people and relating the situations to the objective." [161]

All the principles, save that of the Decade Books Design, express, each in its own way, the necessity of scope's being selected in light of the learner's interests and needs. Lansing adds other factors that deserve to be considered—competent resource persons and broad diocesan needs. None of the designs considers another factor—the interdependence of dimensions of scope. Yet if my differentiation of dimensions of scope is acceptable, the interdependence of those dimensions deserves some consideration in selecting scope. In fact, as will be shortly noted, respecting that interdependence figures prominently in solving the problem of sequence. Consequently, I propose the principle of selectivity that *meanings of the mystery of Christ should be selected for inclusion in a curriculum plan according as the interests of learners, competence of resource persons, and broad diocesan or parochial needs permit their interdependence to be observed.*

In a program designed as close to and as much by participants as possible, the felt needs of adults will provide the first and immediate determination of themes and topics of scope. The competence of resource persons and various institutional needs will circumscribe that

[158] *Dissertation,* 171-72.
[159] *Ibid.,* 242-44.
[160] *Ibid.,* 311.
[161] *Ibid.,* 364.

selection somewhat. But if felt needs are to be the principal determinant, then what is to become of sequence and balance in and among curriculum plans? That is the last subordinate question of scope.

IN WHAT SEQUENCE WILL DIMENSIONS OF SCOPE BE OFFERED IN A CURRICULUM PLAN?

The Baptist Design, through its supportive paper, *Learning Tasks in the Curriculum,* offers the principle that sequence might best be provided by matching learning task goals and activities with the modalities of the church's life and work whereby the activities can be most effectively undertaken by the age group to whose dominant learning task they relate.[162] The dominant learning task for adults is "assuming personal and social responsibility in light of the gospel."

Sequence is treated differently in the various Presbyterian designs. The "situational approach," *Trends,* and "The Human Scene" and "Quest" in *Enquiry* leave sequence and continuity of learning for the learner to integrate. The Decade Books also leave sequence up to the learning group but place a value upon the ordered arrangement of related scope. "The Lively Word" in *Enquiry* follows an ordered overview of the Scriptures.[163]

The Lansing principle stipulates that "basically, the learner chooses whatever sequence of learning opportunities he wishes to," but admits "primitive attempts" at sequential courses.[164]

Baltimore asserts that "the attitudinal pace of the learners should determine the sequence (though we haven't always done this), ever aware of the variety of people-paces in the parish and the right balance of guiding and leading for each group toward the Objective." [165]

Each of the designs gives evidence of the difficulty of dealing with sequence. All seem agreed that sequence must strike some balance between the demands of scope and the preference of learners. Each of the principles displays an option for one or the other or a precarious ambivalence between them. Both of the diocesan designs and most of the Presbyterian designs favor the learner's working out his own sequence. In fact, this seems the only option consistent with the curriculum's being planned by learners according to their interests and

---

[162] For an explanation of the principle, see *Dissertation,* 179-80.
[163] *Ibid.,* 267-69.
[164] *Ibid.,* 323-24.
[165] *Ibid.,* 372.

felt needs. Since my proposed Design intends to guide the local planning of curriculum, I adopt the same principle.

However, that adoption does not necessarily preclude scope from exercising an influence upon sequence. Especially if the dimensions of scope are conceived as interdependent, the learning of one may be expected to create an interest in the learning of another. Thus felt needs remain the criterion for selecting dimensions of scope, but with the prospect that needs somewhat satisfied will create different needs that will lead back and forth through all the dimensions of scope at various levels of knowledge, understanding, appreciation, and responsibility.

Consequently, I propose that *the sequence of learning opportunities should be determined by the interests of learners with the expectation that appropriating, however incompletely, one meaning of the mystery of Christ will create interest in appropriating the others at ever deepening levels of knowledge, understanding, appreciation, and responsibility.*

The principle begins with a recognition of the logical interdependence between the dimensions of scope (horizon upon event; celebration upon horizon and event; moral imperative upon celebration, horizon, and event). This order should usually be honored chronologically (event, then horizon, then celebration, then moral imperative). When however, learners reveal a prior interest in, let us say, morality or liturgy, then, these dimensions should be treated out of logical order as the previous principle of selectivity directs. Yet all hope of sequence and balance is not thereby lost.

The principle contends that the logical interdependence of the four meanings of the mystery of Christ is such that one cannot grapple with one aspect of the mystery without raising questions about the other three. For instance, if one's initial interest lies in what a Christian ought to do when faced with injustice (moral imperative), the very effort to answer the question will raise further questions about the origin of the "ought." These questions lead inexorably to the mystery as event, as horizon, and as celebration. If on the other hand, one's initial interest lies in the difference that Christian faith makes for viewing the human situation (horizon), the effort to answer the question leads inevitably to the historical nature of Christianity (event) and paves the way to a consideration of the sacramental and ethical implications of Christian faith (celebration and moral imperative).

The same will be true if one starts with an interest in the historical or liturgical aspects of the mystery (event or celebration). Answering questions regarding them will lead to questions regarding the other aspects of the mystery. The logical interdependence of the meanings of the mystery and the dynamism of human inquiry are such that it could hardly be otherwise. What is especially important is that the resource person perceive the interrelationship between the meanings of the mystery and be sensitive to the questioning process on the part of learners so that he can guide interest from one aspect of the mystery to another.

The principle further contends that the learners' growth can proceed at ever deepening levels of knowledge, understanding, appreciation, and responsibility. These kinds of learning relate respectively to the meanings of the mystery as event, as horizon, as celebration, and as moral imperative. In themselves, however, the kinds of learning pertain to process, not scope, and consequently presume the explanation and justification of principles of process in the next chapter.

SUMMARY AND APPLICATION

This chapter offers a major and four subordinate principles of scope.

The major principle is declarative: the appropriate scope of adult Christian education is the meaning of the Church's experience of the mystery of Christ.

The first subordinate principle is prescriptive: the scope of adult Christian education should be as comprehensive of the meaning of the Church's experience of the mystery of Christ as relevance to adult learners permits.

The second subordinate principle is declarative: distinct dimensions of scope which lend themselves to different kinds of learning are the meaning of the Church's experience of the mystery of Christ as event, as horizon, as celebration, and as moral imperative.

The third subordinate principle is prescriptive: meanings of the mystery of Christ should be selected for inclusion in a curriculum plan according as the interests of learners, competence of resource persons, and broad diocesan or parochial needs permit their interdependence to be observed.

The last subordinate principle is also prescriptive: the sequence of learning opportunities should be determined by the interests of learners with the expectation that appropriating, however incompletely, one meaning of the mystery of Christ will create interest in appropriating the others at ever deepening levels of knowledge, understanding, appreciation, and responsibility.

These principles may not prove acceptable to many planning teams. Planning teams should begin with the questions underlying the principles and come up with answers of their own. My principles can serve as models or examples of the kinds of answers the questions seek.

In framing their principles of scope, teams will find that the major and first and second subordinate principles provide theoretical decisions regarding scope which will stand for quite some time and will be applicable to several practical programs. The last two subordinate principles will practically direct the selection of actual themes and their ordering in various programs.

However, none of the principles of scope is directly applicable to program design save together with the counterpart principles of process. To these principles we now turn.

CHAPTER V

Process—The Learning Dynamics of Adult Christian Education

As scope deals with the "what?" of adult Christian education, process deals with the "how?" The questions to answer are: How does adult Christian learning happen? What kinds of adult Christian learning are to be sought? How is the learner's motivation to be approached in pursuing the kinds of learning desired? What dominant teaching-learning modes give promise of achieving certain kinds of learning.

For scope and process to interrelate properly the answer to the first and major question has to correspond to the major principle of scope. The answers to the second (kinds of learning) and fourth (modes of learning) have to correspond to the second subordinate principle of scope (dimensions of scope).

How Does Adult Christian Learning Happen?

Asked at its most basic level, the question seeks the simplest possible statement of a planning team's learning theory.

The Cooperative/Baptist Design asserts that Christian learning is a complex process involving change under the activating and transforming influence of the Holy Spirit through perception, problem-solving, practice, and identification.[1]

Among the Presbyterian designs, the "situational approach" operates on the principle that adult Christian learning happens through reflection-action. Reflection-action means that "actions in life should provide the stimulus for reflection upon what it means to act that way; and reflection upon the meaning of actions should lead to more responsible ways of acting." [2] The Decade Books and *Enquiry* act on the principle that learning happens through inquiry.

Lansing understands adult Christian learning as "a complex out-

1 *Dissertation,* 155.
2 *Ibid.,* 214. *A New Venture. . . ,* 14.

come, involving many different components" and occuring "in a variety of ways: through the acquiring of information, through the
identifying with another person with a desire to imitate, through
the acquiring of behavioral patterns by practice, through problem
solving, through the change of guiding values by perceiving other
more important values, etc." [3]

Baltimore states that "adult Christian learning takes place when
people are afforded the opportunity to assimilate new knowledge and
experience for which they feel a need and adjust their previous values,
concepts, attitudes and behavior to new syntheses in their daily
lives." [4]

The Cooperative/Baptist and Lansing principles are strikingly similar except that the former explicitly affirms the "activating and transforming influence of the Holy Spirit" which the latter does not.
Baltimore's principle deals mainly with what my methodology understands as kinds of learning and considers under the first subordinate
question. Baltimore's choice of the verbs "assimilate" and "adjust"
pertains more directly to the present question. The Presbyterian
designs, on the other hand, name what my methodology understands to be learning modes or methods and considers under the third
subordinate question.

Even the Cooperative/Baptist and Lansing principles become more
specific regarding kinds of learning and modes of learning than
seem to be required in a general principle indicating the nature of
adult Christian learning. The major principle of process need express
only the intentionality of the learning process and its relation to scope,
leaving to subordinate principles statements regarding the kinds of
learning required by different dimensions of scope and the dominant
learning modes by which those kinds of learning might best be
achieved.

Accordingly, I propose as the major principle of process that *adult
Christian learning happens through interpersonal appropriation by
faith of the meaning of the Church's experience of the mystery of
Christ.* The principle needs ample explanation.

First, a descriptive clarification of the phrase "interpersonal appropriation by faith" is in order. *Appropriation* bespeaks a "making
one's own" the meaning of the mystery of Christ. It may also be
expressed as an affirmation of the meaningfulness of that mystery for
oneself, an internalization of its significance, or a personal integration
of that mystery into one's value system and life orientation.

[3] *Dissertation,* 317.
[4] *Ibid.,* 367.

Further, an appropriation by faith is at issue. More is involved than rational assent. A fiduciary self-commitment to another's veracity and integrity is involved. Accepting another's word, and more profoundly, accepting another's person characterizes appropriation by faith. Consequently, this appropriation is essentially *interpersonal*.

To affirm the mystery of Christ and its meaning for oneself demands witnesses whose integrity of faith and authenticity of life are deeply convincing. The interpersonal aspects of this appropriation also include the supportive climate of encouragement without which a leap of faith is normally impossible. Interpersonal, then, describes the community aspect of Christian learning while appropriation indicates its radically individual aspect. In brief, to designate it as interpersonal appropriation by faith is to say that *adult Christian learning is a profoundly personal process of believing the mystery of Christ to be true and to be truly meaningful for oneself on the word and with the support of fellow believers.*

It is now necessary to move beyond description to explanatory justification. The justification will be modest. Each of the realities—appropriation, faith, interpersonal learning—introduces endless philosophical, theological, and educational positions.[5] All that can be done here is to point ever so sketchily to the cognitional theory which is presuppositional to my meaning of appropriation, the educational implications of my understanding of faith, and the educational foundation of my insistence upon the interpersonal characteristics of Christian learning.

The cognitional theory that grounds and explains my meaning of appropriation is that of Bernard Lonergan. Recently, he has expressed his cognitional theory with utmost brevity:

Our conscious and intentional operations occur on four interlocked levels. There is a level of experiencing, a level of understanding and conception, a level of reflection and judgment, a level of deliberation and decision. We are moved, promoted from one level to the next by questions; from experiencing to understanding by questions for intelligence; from understanding to judging by questions for reflection; from judging to deciding by questions for deliberation. So the many operations are linked together both

[5] For instance, for "appropriation" as it is used in Christian education, see Neely D. McCarter, "The Appropriation of Revelation and Its Implications for Christian Education," an unpublished doctoral dissertation (Yale University, 1961). On faith, see John Henry Newman, *An Essay in Aid of a Grammar of Assent* (Garden City, N.Y.: Doubleday and Co., Inc. 1955) and Juan Alfaro, *Fides, Spes, Caritas: Adnotationes in Tractatum de Virtutibus Theologicis,* (ad usum privatum auditorum), rev. ed. (Rome: Pontificia Universitas Gregoriana, 1964). On interpersonal or synoetic learning, see Phenix, *Realms of Meaning*, 193-211.

on the side of the subject and on the side of the object. On the side of the subject there is the one mind putting the many questions in pursuit of a single goal. On the side of the object there is the gradual cumulation and conjoining of partial elements into a single whole. So insight grasps the intelligibility of what sense perceives. Conception unites what separately sense perceives and intelligence grasps. Judgment pronounces on the truth of the conceiving and on the reality of the conceived. Decision acknowledges the value of actuating potentialities grasped by intelligence and judged to be real. So the transcendental, the intelligible, the true, the real, the good, apply to absolutely every object for the very good reason that they are grounded in the successive stages in our dealing with objects. But they are one in their root as well as in their application. For the intending subject intends, first of all, the good but to achieve it must know the real; to know the real he must know what is true; to know what is true he must grasp what is intelligible; and to grasp what is intelligible he must attend to the data of sense and to the data of consciousness.[6]

Consequently, appropriation (and also learning) is not used here univocally. It applies analogously to learning the meaning of the mystery of Christ on four levels that are dynamically interrelated. It applies to apprehending the data of the mystery of Christ, to understanding its import, to judging its truth and reality, to deciding its validity for oneself.

On each level a person is to some degree learning or appropriating the meaning of the mystery. When he attends to the tradition (event), the doctrines (horizon), the rites (celebration), and the norms (moral imperative) of Christianity, he is involved in Christian learning, but only on a preliminary level. When he sees reasonableness and persuasiveness in the tradition, doctrines, rites, and norms, he has penetrated to a deeper level. When he judges those meanings to be true, he has advanced to a further level. When he decides that those meanings have value for him, embraces them as such, and lives his life accordingly, he has reached the deepest level of Christian learning.[7] Appropriation has come full term.

Appropriation of some sort takes place on all four levels. It happens more properly however on the third (judgment) and fourth (decision) levels.

Moreover, Christian learning is, or at least, tends toward an appropriation *by faith*. As such, it is a unique kind of learning that

6 "Natural Knowledge of God," 63-64. This is a densely compressed statement of L's cognitional theory. For a fuller treatment, see "Cognitional Structure" and *Insight.*

7 Note the similarity between Lonergan's steps in cognitional theory and the "learning tasks" as enunciated in the *CCP*. See *Dissertation*, 154-60.

baffles every effort to explain it adequately.[8] In Catholic Christian tradition it is a graced process, fundamentally reasonable in its movement, but ultimately praeter- or supra-rational in its source, dynamic, object, and firmness of conviction.[9]

Various authors of the New Testament point to the graced aspect of faith descriptively:

At that time Jesus exclaimed, "I bless you, Father Lord of heaven and of earth, for hiding these things from the learned and the clever and revealing them to mere children. Yes, Father, for that is what it pleased you to do. Everything has been entrusted to me by my Father; and no one knows the Son except the Father, just as no one knows the Father except the Son and those to whom the Son chooses to reveal him. (Mt. 11:25-27)

and again:

I still have many things to say to you but they would be too much for you now. But when the Spirit of truth comes he will lead you to the complete truth . . . (Jn. 16:12-13) [10]

and again:

Because it is by grace that you have been saved, through faith; not by anything of your own, but by a gift from God . . . (Eph. 2:8)

The Scriptural witness is echoed by Protestant Christian educators. Wyckoff expresses a veritable consensus:

There is no Christian education if it is not conducted "in the Spirit." . . . The Spirit is the initiator, director, sustainer, and corrector of education that is Christian, for God is the teacher, and the human teacher properly knows and assumes his role only as an aide.[11]

It is precisely the special character of Christian learning as a learning in and by faith that persuades Boelke of the inadequacy of every current major learning theory to explain the dynamics of Christian learning.[12] It is also the demands of faith, that encourage him to outline his own learning theory of "creation-engagement."

8 See Alfaro, *Fides.* . . , 359-72.

9 Council of Trent, *DS,* 1525, 1526, and 1553; First Vatican Council, *DS,* 3010, 3035. More fully, Newman, . . . *Grammar of Assent,* 318-79, and Alfaro, *Fides.* . . , 212-358.

10 For other Joannine texts where the specialness of faith-learning is described, see *Dissertation,* 500, n. 2. For a procession of Scriptural witness, see Alfaro, *Fides.* . . , 215-19.

11 "Instruction, the Person and the Group," 12. See *Dissertation,* 160.

12 Boelke, *Theories of Learning.* . . , 146.

" 'Creation' is intended to communicate the divine participation while 'engagement' symbolizes the active thrust of the whole person in learning." [13] More succinctly, *"The concerns of Christian nurture are learned as God creates new selves through the engagement of persons with their field of relationships."* [14]

Boelke's further elaboration of creation-engagement,[15] so far as I can see, provides descriptive rather than analytic justification. It translates the Scriptural data into the language of current learning theory. It does not analyze the theological ingredients of the divine initiative (creation) as they relate to the cognitional and psychological dynamics of the learning process (engagement). I shall not attempt to undertake that task here.[16] Boelke's outline of a theory is valuable insofar as it expresses in educational terms the inability of general learning theory adequately to explain Christian learning, the dependency of Christian learning upon divine grace, and yet the fully human process which the act of Christian learning remains.

The *interpersonal* aspects of Christian learning also deserve some preliminary explanation, at least in terms of their educational foundation. That foundation would seem to be what learning theorists refer to as learning by identification. Identification means "the appropriation into the self of the characteristics of an admired group or person." [17] Wyckoff illustrates how heavily the learning of Christian values, attitudes, and appreciations depends upon identification.[18] By having "interpersonal" modify "appropriation by faith," I wish to go further and assert that learning by identification colors and influences the entire process of Christian learning. In short, there is never an arrival at Christian assent which does not rely to some degree upon the integrity and authenticity of other believers [19] not to speak of their encouragement and support.[20]

---

[13] *Ibid.*, 186.

[14] *Ibid.*, 188.

[15] *Ibid.*, 188-201.

[16] Alfaro, *Fides.* . . , 234-80, 322-33, supplies useful data on the influence of grace upon the psychological dynamism of faith. I await, however, Bernard Lonergan's further analysis of belief. See Tracy, *The Achievement.* . . , 175-82. Of special moment is L.'s insistence that the final product of the faith process is "not judgment (as immanently generated assertion of truth) but assent (as reasonable act of believing)." *Ibid.*, 180.

[17] So Wyckoff, *Theory and Design.* . . , 103, quoting the *Dictionary of Education.*

[18] *Ibid.*, 104-05.

[19] Following Lonergan's analysis that belief does not rely upon evidence which exhausts the subject's questions upon the matter under consideration but upon the evidence of another's integrity. See *supra*, n. 16.

[20] Their encouragement and support, would, according to my categories, pertain to context rather than to process.

The dynamics of learning by identification are very much a *terra incognita*. It has close affinity to that realm of meaning for which Phenix coins the name 'synnoetics.' "Briefly this term refers to meanings in which a person has direct insight into other beings (or oneself) as concrete wholes existing in relation." [21] Confessing the novelty of the enterprise and the absence of a specialized discipline,[22] Phenix surveys the foundations for synnoetics in the reflections of Martin Buber, the data of depth psychology, and the preoccupations of existentialist philosophy.[23]

One result of Phenix' investigation is to place in bold relief an aspect of the interpersonality of Christian learning not yet touched upon. Noting that synnoetics involves a concrete engagement of subject to subject rather than the detachment which is a condition of "objective" knowledge,[24] one is struck by the clarity this lends to that learning which faith most mysteriously is, namely, the direct learning of God through Christ. So far, we have spoken only of the interpersonal aspects of Christian learning insofar as it depends upon the integrity and support of other believers. We must reckon as well with that other interpersonal aspect insofar as it engages the learner in an intersubjective identification with God through Christ.[25] This union which faith creates is the very meaning of the Christian tradition *credimus Deum* as well as *in Deum* and *Deo*.[26]

Such, in brief, is my explanation for the major principle of process that *adult Christian learning happens through interpersonal appropriation by faith of the meaning of the Church's experience of the mystery of Christ*. "Interpersonal appropriation by faith" denotes the process at its most theoretical level; "the meaning of the Church's experience of the mystery of Christ"—scope at its most theoretical level—is precisely that which is appropriated. Hence the theoretical interrelationship of scope and process.

---

21 Phenix, *Realms of Meaning*, 193.

22 *Ibid.*, 187-90.

23 *Ibid.*, 197-211.

24 *Ibid.*, 193-94.

25 I Jn. 1:3 expresses concisely both the vertical and horizontal dimensions of this synnoetic learning of God through one's fellow believers: "What we have seen and heard we are telling you so that you too may be in union with us, as we are in union with the Father and with his Son Jesus Christ."

26 *Credimus in Deum* expresses a fiduciary adherence to the person of God; *credimus Deo* expresses an assent to God because of His truthfulness; and *credimus Deum* expresses the unitive presence to God which faith inaugurates. See Alfaro, *Fides. . .* , 94-98, 185-97. For a treatment of the interpersonal aspects of faith-learning not unlike that presented here, see Van Caster, *The Structure of Catechetics*, 111-23.

WHAT KINDS OF ADULT CHRISTIAN LEARNING
ARE TO BE SOUGHT?

The answer to this question looks to the second subordinate principle of scope (dimensions of scope).

The Cooperative/Baptist Design seeks altered concepts, skills, attitudes, and appreciations.[27]

Of the Presbyterian designs, that of *Trends* seeks awareness and those of Decade Books and *Enquiry* seek understanding.[28]

Lansing specifies its kinds of desired learning as information, formation, initiation, and transformation. The last is equivalent to its objective of adult Christian education.[29]

Baltimore states, in addition to the kinds of learning already named in its general principle of process, that "adult Christian learning should include personal and inter-personal (i.e., cognitive, affective, and experiential) forms of learning." [30]

Each design's way of expressing kinds of learning is different. In my methodology, Lansing's identification of kinds of learning pertains more to modes of learning than kinds. The Cooperative/Baptist, Presbyterian, and Baltimore principles all name kinds of learning but express them so differently as to evidence the variety of ways by which kinds of learning can be conceived. Moreover, none of the designs expressly relates kinds of learning to dimensions of scope. I should like to suggest a principle which attempts to relate them.

It is that *adult Christian learning should seek historical knowledge of the mystery of Christ as event, cognitive understanding of the mystery of Christ as horizon, appreciation for the mystery of Christ as celebration, and responsibility to the mystery of Christ as moral imperative.*

Before moving to an explanatory justification of the principle, it is well to point out that, in accord with the major principle of process, each of these is conceived as an interpersonal kind of learning by faith at some level of appropriation. Moreover, just as the meanings of the mystery of Christ are interdependent, so too these kinds of learning complement one another. Here the effort is to identify "more or less" which kinds of learning most correspond to the specified meanings.

[27] *Dissertation*, 156.
[28] *Ibid.*, 237-38, 245-46, and 254-55.
[29] *Ibid.*, 318.
[30] *Ibid.*, 368.

Historical Knowledge of the Mystery of Christ as Event.—The meaning of the mystery of Christ as event has been described above as *the eventful tradition of human acts initiated by God, integrated by the death and resurrection of Christ, contributed to by all those who are moved by the Spirit of Christ, and purposed by God for a consummation that will be man's as well as His.*

I consider historical knowledge as the kind of learning that best corresponds to this meaning. Knowledge here means to indicate a kind of learning which has reached the level of judgment rather than remaining on the level of experience or understanding.[31] Moreover, it is knowledge which for the most part has not passed over into decision. True, the knowledge of which we speak here is faith-knowledge and consequently partakes of value judgment and choice.[32] It may be called more properly, then, assent or affirmation. However, this assent or affirmation is precisely of the truth value in contrast to the goodness value of the tradition. Consequently, knowledge of the event characterizes the level of appropriation more accurately than any other level.

Moreover, knowledge of the eventful tradition is in the order of historical knowledge. Various theories of history cannot, of course, be entered into here. I favor the view which considers history an interpretative art rather than a science. To call the knowledge historical, then, is to point out that what is knowingly affirmed by the believer is both the facticity of the eventful tradition and the interpretation of that facticity as salvific.[33] For all its limitations and conflicting usages, historical, in the sense of factual and interpretative of fact, seems best to describe the kind of knowing by which the mystery of Christ as event is appropriated by faith.

Cognitive Understanding of the Mystery of Christ as Horizon.—I have presented as a working definition of the mystery of Christ as horizon that it constitutes *a call to analyze the basic perspective by which one perceives oneself and the whole of created and historical reality as changed by the deed of God in Christ, to articulate that analysis, and to relate those articulations to one another in a coherent synthesis.* Cognitive understanding seems to be the kind of learning that corresponds to this undertaking. Understanding belongs to the second level of appropriation. It is the product of insight. It is the "bright

---

[31] Lonergan in Crowe (ed.), *Collection.* . . , 222-24.
[32] Tracy, *The Achievement.* . . , 180.
[33] This seems the special concern of both Cullmann and Barr which we have employed above at length. See *supra,* 121-23.

idea" or constellation of "bright ideas" that have yet to be verified.[34]

When one does theology, some few insights will reach the virtually unconditioned stage where, given adequate evidence, they will be judged true, real, objective. But such will not usually be the case. As one tries to work out and systematize his faith-horizon, he will have to make do with provisional, tentative formulations. Indeed, insofar as "not new answers but new questions" are central to horizon-analysis, the case can hardly be otherwise.

Cognitive understanding is specified in contrast to affective "understanding." The use of cognitive wishes expressly to caution against the naive expectation that feeling, imagination, and intuition will best serve to learn the mystery of Christ as horizon. These qualities of the human spirit are important in adult Christian education and in the whole of life. But given their head, they engender highly romantic but equally unverifiable theological insights in the name of horizon expansion.[35] The systematic, critical, and methodical exigencies [36] that both prompt horizon analysis and promise its best development clearly demand an intellectual and not a primarily emotional exercise.

In short, to learn the mystery of Christ as horizon is to undertake the classical task of theology—*fides quaerens intellectum.*

Appreciation for the Mystery of Christ as Celebration.—The mystery of Christ as celebration has been described above as *the meaning of the Church's participation by the Spirit in the historical and perennial worship of Christ for the Father.* The kind of learning for which celebration calls is more than an historical knowledge of rites and their development and more than cognitive understanding of the theological principles of worship. Rather, celebration calls for value learning. It calls for affective, emotional appropriation. To excite the desire for worship, to invite to meaningful participation, to inspire the heart as well as the head is the kind of learning that celebration demands.

Appreciation as value learning lies beyond experiencing, understanding, and judging. It approaches the level of decision. It relies upon freedom and choice. It enters the level of love. Too little is known about the structure of value judgment.[37] Notwithstanding,

[34] Lonergan in Crowe (ed.), *Collection.* . . , 222-24. See Tracy, *The Achievement.* . . , 105-13.

[35] See Tracy, *The Achievement.* . . , 4.

[36] *Ibid.,* 224-31.

[37] The analysis of value and value judgment is one of Bernard Lonergan's present preoccupations. See *ibid.,* 229, n. 30.

appropriating the mystery of Christ as celebration seems to belong on the level of value learning. Appreciation, then, seems best able to describe the kind of learning that the mystery of Christ as celebration seeks.

Responsibility to the Mystery of Christ as Moral Imperative.—The meaning of the mystery of Christ as moral imperative has been described above as *the demand of a loving and free response in practical life to God's love in Christ.* Already the description suggests the kind of learning appropriate to the meaning of the mystery as moral imperative—responsibility.

Responsibility lies on the deliberative level of appropriation. Freedom and love are here engaged most fully. Value is even more seriously at issue than with respect to the appreciation of the mystery as celebration. For upon the level of responsibility to the mystery as moral imperative, values are believed and clung to, not just on the level of value judgments or liturgical expression, but on the level of practical decisions frequently at the cost of pain, persecution, and sometimes death. Lonergan well describes the movement beyond judgment to decision, beyond fact to value, beyond affirmation to responsibility:

Though being and the good are coextensive, the subject moves to a further dimension of consciousness as his concern shifts from knowing being to realizing the good. Now there emerge freedom and responsibility, encounter and trust, communication and belief, choice and promise and fidelity. On this level subjects both constitute themselves and make their world. On this level men are responsible, individually, for the lives they lead and, collectively, for the world in which they lead them.[38]

With responsibility to the mystery as moral imperative, interpersonal appropriation by faith of the meaning of the Church's experience of the mystery of Christ comes full circle. Only to the degree that responsibility develops do historical knowledge of the mystery as event, cognitive understanding of the mystery as horizon, and appreciation for the mystery as celebration make their proper contribution to the growth of an informed, thinking, praying, ethical Christian. Continuous growth in these four kinds of learning at ever deeper levels of knowledge, understanding, appreciation, and responsibility specify the ongoing, interpersonal appropriation of the meaning of the Church's experience of the mystery of Christ which characterizes the adult Christian as a lifelong learner.

[38] Crowe (ed.), *Collection.* . . , 237.

It is not enough to specify these kinds of learning and the various dimensions of scope to which each relates. It is also necessary to tackle the problem of motivating persons toward these kinds of learning.

How Is the Learner's Motivation to Be Approached in Pursuing the Kinds of Learning Desired?

The Cooperative/Baptist Design presumes that motivation will be forthcoming from the learner because themes of scope are drawn from persistent life issues.[39]

Among the Presbyterian designs, the "situational approach" leaves motivation to learners who will on principle only study what they wish. Motivation will be elicited by *Trends,* Decade Books, and *Enquiry* by the perennial or current relevance of the topics of scope they treat.[40]

Lansing's statements regarding motivation are reducible to the principle that felt needs of the learner supply the motivation to which curriculum planning must respond.[41]

Baltimore states: "To motivate the learner we should honestly listen to the learner's attitudes, values, concepts and behavior; and develop motivation out of this base, as well as generate an atmosphere that is friendly, personal, and communal, so as to give every possible support and reassurance." [42]

The designs which encourage planning close to the learner, namely the Presbyterian "situational approach," Lansing, and Baltimore all allow for intrinsic motivation on the part of the learner by insisting that existential needs of the learner should determine the selection of dimensions of scope. Even designs which guide planning somewhat removed from the learner—the Cooperative/Baptist, Decade Books, and *Enquiry*—hope to meet felt needs by their selection of themes which correspond to persistent life issues, to current concerns, or to perennial interests of the Christian.

Following the lead of those designs which encourage planning close to the learner but conscious also of broader kinds of learning for which learners might not initially feel a need, I propose the principle that *in order to capitalize upon the intrinsic motivation of adult learners, kinds of learning should be selected which correspond to the felt needs*

39 *Dissertation,* 144-45.
40 *Ibid.,* 265-66.
41 *Ibid.,* 319.
42 *Ibid.,* 368.

of learners in the hope that, once achieved, the need may be experienced for other kinds of learning to which other meanings of the mystery of Christ lend themselves.

This principle, like the fourth subordinate principle of scope (sequence of learnings), relies upon the interdependence of the meanings of the mystery of Christ for its cogency.

There is, however, a more profound problem that lurks beneath the principle itself. What if adults feel no need for any Christian learning? The principle presumes that adult Christians feel some need for it. Suppose they do not—and the evidence is that most do not. Then what intrinsic motivation does adult Christian education have to capitalize upon?

It seems that most adults have to be stimulated to a conscious desire for Christian learning. Many must be helped to raise the distinctively religious questions. To a great extent, the religious upheaval of the present stimulates persons to ask religious questions. But more encouragement of the questioning process seems necessary especially for Catholic Christians who have been discouraged in the past from asking real questions of their faith.

The only practical process I know of to stimulate adults to raise the religious questions and to seek solutions to them in the scope of Christian education is GIFT—Growth in Faith Together. It begins with a survey of religious beliefs and concerns calculated to have adults examine their personal beliefs. The process then provides for those who have filled out the survey to gather in reflection groups where once a week for five weeks they sharpen their questions of faith and open themselves to liturgical and educational responses to these questions.[43] It seems that some process such as GIFT is necessary for this principle of motivation to be operative. There remains the question of learning modes.

What Dominant Teaching Modes Give Promise of Achieving Certain Kinds of Learning?

The Cooperative/Baptist Design responds with the principle that learning modes are reducible to one or other or a dynamic combination of the learning tasks:

Listening with growing alertness to the gospel and responding in faith and love

43 See my article "GIFT—an Adult Program That Works."

Exploring the whole field of relationships in light of the gospel

Discovering meaning and value in the field of relationships in the light of the gospel

Appropriating personally the meaning and value discovered in the field of relationships in light of the gospel

Assuming personal and social responsibility in light of the gospel [44]

The Presbyterian designs do not specify learning modes other than the generic reflection-action which supplies their major principle of process.[45]

Answering a question which sought methods and not modes, Lansing replies that:

> Different programs use a variety of different teaching-learning methods: formal classes use lectures, questions, discussions, audio-visual materials, text and resource books, visiting lecturers, projects, etc. Workshops utilize all of the above methods, plus small group discussions and the general initiative and transformative effects of a community experience. Home discussion programs rely heavily on small group dynamics.[46]

Answering the same question, Baltimore responds with the principle that "the dynamics used to achieve learning should be any meaningful form of cognitive, affective and experiential learning that will stimulate and encourage the learner." [47]

The operative principles of the Presbyterian designs and the Lansing statement are too limited to practical teaching-learning methods to offer a principle which responds to the question. Baltimore states the more general type of principle which the question seeks, but its "any meaningful form" is too broad to give positive guidance to the selection of methods. It begs the question rather than answers it.

The Cooperative/Baptist principle is suitably general yet sufficiently positive to act as a criterion for the selection of practical methods. Especially as developed in *Learning Tasks in the Curriculum*, the three basic modes—exploration, discovery, and appropriation—are guides to practical methods.[48] The Cooperative/Baptist principle also has the advantage of relating the learning modes directly to the Design's general principle of scope. The principle of learning

---

44 *Dissertation*, 156-59.
45 *Ibid.*, 214-15.
46 *Ibid.*, 319.
47 *Ibid.*, 369.
48 *Ibid.*, 157-58.

tasks is apparently meant to apply equally and indiscrimately to each of the Cooperative areas of scope.[49] Against the Cooperative Design's analysis of scope, this seems a legitimate application of the principle. Against my analysis of scope, however, the application of the principle would not be legitimate. The Cooperative Design understands areas of scope to be "distinct perspectives upon the whole scope." I understand dimensions of scope to be aspects of scope which lend themselves to distinct kinds of learning each with its distinctive mode of learning. Acceptable, then, as the Cooperative/Baptist principle of learning tasks is to the Design's own analysis of scope, it is not applicable to my analysis of scope and of the scope-process relationship.

Instead, I suggest as a principle regarding learning modes that *historical knowledge of the mystery of Christ as event gives promise of being learned especially through the teaching-learning mode of disclosure; cognitive understanding of the mystery of Christ as horizon through inquiry; appreciation for the mystery of Christ as celebration through initiation; and responsibility to the mystery of Christ as moral imperative through problem-solving.* Each learning mode deserves explanation and application to various teaching-learning dynamics.

Before proceeding to each mode singly, however, it must be pointed out that just as the kinds of learning and the dimensions of scope to which they relate are interdependent so too are the modes of learning. Accordingly, the word "especially" has been added to the principle. Its addition indicates that only the *dominant* mode which relates to each kind of learning is sought.

Disclosure: A Way of Gaining Historical Knowledge of the Mystery as Event.—Applied to learning the mystery of Christ as event, historical knowledge wishes to indicate assent to the fact and salvific interpretation of the fact mediated by Christian tradition. The principal means by which such knowledge is learned and taught can be described as disclosure. By disclosure is meant the unfolding of the eventful tradition in such a way as to invite another to affirm for himself the truthfulness of the tradition and its salvific importance. Disclosure, then, happens between one who knows more and one who knows less of the tradition. Disclosure means to be, however, invitatory not impositional. Disclosure wishes to create the favorable climate wherein one can freely chose to affirm the Christian fact and its salvific significance.

[49] This same statement applies indirectly to the Baptist three "annual perspectives" which restructure *CCP* areas of scope. See *ibid.*, 142-43.

By disclosure a teacher carried out the transmissive task of Christian education.[50] Disclosure was the mode employed by apostolic heralds of the *kerygma* [51] and favored by catechetical leaders until quite recently.[52] I contend that disclosure retains its importance among other equally important modes which are necessary for learning the other meanings of the mystery of Christ.

Disclosure as a learning mode pervades the teaching-learning dynamics that are usually considered informational or didactic. Listening to lectures, participating in seminars led by a resource person, viewing informational (not primarily attitude-forming) films, reading exegetical and historical books are all learning methods which employ disclosure. The mode and its derivative methods have a special place in learning the meaning of the mystery of Christ as event.

Inquiry: A Way of Gaining Cognitive Understanding of the Mystery as Horizon.—Understanding bespeaks the tentative, probing search to articulate one's faith horizon. Cognitive describes the process as distinctively intellectual. Questions are the invariable entrance to cognitive understanding, just as meaningful questions are the boundaries of one's present horizon.[53] Accordingly, "the raising and answering of questions" [54] —inquiry—is the mode of learning which gives promise of gaining cognitive understanding of the mystery of Christ as horizon.

Inquiry, then looks to such methods as group discussion, debate, and panel presentations, where questions can be frequently raised or

50 See Wyckoff, *The Task. . .* , 34-36 and *supra*, 38-39.

51 See Domenico Grasso, "The Core of Missionary Preaching" in Hofinger (ed.), *Teaching All Nations*, 39-58.

52 Usually under the name of "proclamation" or "catechesis." See Johannes Hofinger, *The Art of Teaching Christian Doctrine: The Good News and Its Proclamation*, rev. ed. (Notre Dame, Ind.: University of Notre Dame Press, 1962); Josef A. Jungmann, *Handing on the Faith: A Manual of Catechetics*, trans. and rev. by A. N. Fuerst (New York: Herder and Herder, 1962), esp. pp. 387-405; and Alfred McBride, *Catechetics: A Theology of Proclamation* (Milwaukee, Wis.: The Bruce Publishing Company, 1966). A counter move set in with Alfonso M. Nebreda's *Kerygma in Crisis* (Chicago: Loyola University Press, 1965) and Moran's *Theology of Revelation* and *Catechesis of Revelation*. At present the emphasis upon "experience-oriented" curriculum and "discovery" learning leaves little room for disclosure of an inherited fact and its accumulative interpretation.

53 See Tracy, "Horizon Analysis. . . ," 169, "As a first approximation, therefore, horizon may be called the limit or boundary between my docta and docta ignorantia. As a second approximation, it is to be noted that what lies beyond my horizon consists not principally of answers but rather of *questions* that are meaningless and insignificant to me." Also, *Idem, The Achievement. . .* , 10.

54 *Idem, The Achievement. . .* , 9.

where the presentation of positions and counter-positions can stimulate questions in the minds of participants. Contrariwise, didactic lectures on horizon-analysis contribute little to the analysis of one's own horizon, save perhaps by planting the initial question which prompts one to learn what horizon-analysis means.[55] Dynamics, then, which excite questions in the learner, especially questions which lead to a theoretical, critical, and methodical understanding of oneself as believer and of the relationship of all reality to God are the methods which give most promise of understanding the mystery of Christ as horizon.

Initiation: A Way of Gaining Appreciation for the Mystery of Christ as Celebration.—Appreciation consists in value judgment. To set so much a value upon worship that one wishes enthusiastically and joyfully to celebrate God's deed in Christ demands a special way of learning. It must be a way by which one not so much *learns about* as *learns* worship. Such a way would seem to be initiation.

Initiation is selected for its obviously liturgical connotations. The sacraments of initiation—Baptism, Confirmation, Eucharist—immediately come to mind. However, the mode implies a more profoundly personal involvement which lies at the heart of worship. Marcel Van Caster describes it well.

Catechesis has the task of *initiation* into the mystery of God, who gives himself to us in a Word which is at once actual and efficient. It is an initiation that is an invitation to share actively in the activities of Jesus Christ in his Church, especially that of knowing the Father.[56]

For Van Caster, then, initiation is an invitation to encounter God through Christ.[57] If sacramental initiation fails to engender that encounter, it remains an educational technique whereby rites are learned about, but worship is not learned.

The dynamics which initiation suggests are those of meaningful participation in sacramental and para-liturgical worship. Perhaps, this is but another way of saying that to learn to pray, one must pray; to learn to worship, one must worship; to learn to celebrate, one must celebrate. Only by favorable introduction to these experiences and sensitive reflection upon the experiences is it likely that

[55] I speak from my own experience in hearing David Tracy's lecture on "Horizon Analysis and Eschatology," understanding little, and learning much from the eventual publication of the piece and discursive conversation with the author.

[56] *The Structure of Catechetics*, 14.

[57] *Ibid.*, 114.

one will come to appreciate the meaning of the mystery of Christ as celebration.

Problem-solving: A Way of Approaching Responsibility to the Mystery as Moral Imperative.—Responsibility lies on the level of decision. It can only be learned by exercise. Consequently, the most suitable context for learning responsibility to the mystery as moral imperative is in the crucible of practical challenge and under the demand for decisive action. However, this test can be educationally prepared for. I suggest that educational preparation for ethical responsibility lies especially in the learning mode of problem-solving.

Problem-solving is here meant in the sense described by Campbell Wyckoff:

Learning through problem-solving assumes that the person will learn when he is presented with a situation that is somewhat baffling and has to find his way through it. In the process it is thought that he learns to think and that he "learns" the resources that he has to use to solve the problems. The procedure is, as a rule, to define, analyze, suggest possible answers, select the most promising ones, gather the facts, choose the best answer, test it in action, and evaluate it.[58]

So described, problem-solving with respect to ethical situations corresponds well to the themes currently stressed in moral theology. Not so much moral principles as practical contexts are emphasized at present. More correctly, moral principles only as they bear upon the practical context with its unique circumstances and demands are stressed.[59] Accordingly, the contextual learning of moral values through an enlightened casuistry [60] seems called for. Problem-solving is the basic mode of learning involved in such a process.

In practice, a resource person or discussion leader would present cases, situations, or contexts, whether real or contrived, so that learners might wrestle with the complexity of ethical decision in

---

58 *Theory and Design. . . ,* 103.

59 John C. Bennett *et al., Storm over Ethics* (Philadelphia: The United Church Press, 1967). Paul L. Lehmann, *Ethics in a Christian Context* (New York: Harper and Row, 1963).

60 Casuistry is not used here in the pejorative sense of presenting cases in order to show a principle's application as used, for instance, by Edwin F. Healy in *Medical Ethics* (Chicago: Loyola University Press, 1956), but in the complimentary sense of presenting situations and contexts through which the complexity of ethical decision and the interplay of circumstances and normative values can be seen.

weighing the unique demands of a given situation against the more or less constant values that moral principles attempt to affirm. Problem-solving of this kind offers some hope of learning responsibility to the mystery of Christ as moral imperative.

THE INTERRELATIONSHIP OF THE PRINCIPLES OF SCOPE AND PROCESS

Scope has been distinguished from process and dimensions of scope from kinds of learning. Moreover, the modes of learning by which these kinds of learning might be learned have been specified. The distinguishing and specification may have appeared labored and excessive. But as Lonergan well observes "the alternative to distinguishing is confusion." [61] Distinction is necessary to make sound curriculum decisions regarding what to learn and how to learn it. However, it is equally necessary to realize how closely interrelated the principles of scope and process are.

First, the major principles of process and scope are directly related to one another. It is precisely the meaning of the Church's experience of the mystery of Christ (scope) that the learners appropriate interpersonally by faith (process).

Moreover, the second subordinate principle of scope is directly related to the first subordinate principle of process. The learner seeks historical knowledge (process) of the mystery as event (scope); cognitive understanding (process) of the mystery as horizon (scope); appreciation (process) for the mystery as celebration (scope); and responsibility (process) to the mystery as moral imperative (scope).

Furthermore, the modes of learning (third subordinate principle of process) are immediately determined by the kinds of learning specified. Disclosure gives promise of engendering historical knowledge of the mystery as event. Inquiry gives promise of stimulating cognitive understanding of the mystery as horizon. Initiation gives promise of creating appreciation for the mystery as celebration. Problem-solving gives promise of inviting responsibility to the mystery as moral imperative.

This interrelationship of the principles of scope and process at various levels of specification is reinforced by the interdependence that obtains among the four dimensions of scope and among the four kinds of learning. It is only by keeping the interrelationship of the

[61] Crowe (ed.), *Collection. . .* , 231.

principles and the interdependence of the dimensions of scope and kinds of learning firmly in mind that this solution of the scope-process nexus is viable in the fluid situation of curriculum planning close to and as much by the adult learner as possible.

SUMMARY AND APPLICATION

I have suggested a major and three subordinate principles of process.

The major principle is declarative: adult Christian learning happens through interpersonal appropriation by faith of the meaning of the Church's experience of the mystery of Christ.

The first subordinate principle is prescriptive: adult Christian learning should seek historical knowledge of the mystery of Christ as event, cognitive understanding of the mystery of Christ as horizon, appreciation for the mystery of Christ as celebration, and responsibility to the mystery of Christ as moral imperative.

The second subordinate principle is also prescriptive: in order to capitalize upon the intrinsic motivation of adult learners, kinds of learning should be selected which correspond to the felt needs of learners in the hope that, once achieved, the need may be experienced for other kinds of learning to which other meanings of the mystery of Christ lend themselves.

The last subordinate principle is prescriptive, too: historical knowledge of the mystery of Christ as event gives promise of being learned especially through the teaching-learning mode of disclosure; cognitive understanding of the mystery of Christ as horizon through inquiry; appreciation for the mystery of Christ as celebration through initiation; and responsibility to the mystery of Christ as moral imperative through problem-solving.

As the principles of scope, so these principles of process serve as examples to planning teams how they might answer the questions of process. If these principles are acceptable, then the problem of their joint application along with principles of scope remains. It is the task of the organizing principle to guide this application to actual program design. But since the organizing principle hangs so heavily upon the solution to the scope-process nexus, it is not out of place to begin that application here.

The principles of scope and process will be more applicable if translated into scope-process goals. These goals act as a specification of the overall objective of adult Christian education and as practical criteria for program planning:

Mature persons are invited to learn:

historical knowledge of the Christ event through disclosure;
cognitive understanding of Christian faith through inquiry;
appreciation for Christian worship through initiation;
and responsibility to the mind of Christ through problem-solving.

Perhaps the following diagram can illustrate how the principles of scope and process specify the objective and follow upon the major principle of personnel.

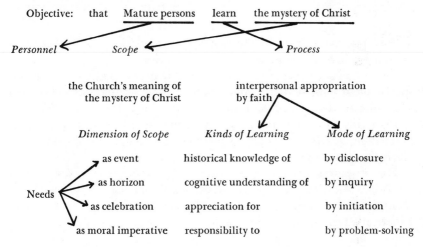

CHAPTER VI

Context—
The Social and Spatial Environment
of Adult Christian Education

FROM THE INTRICACIES of the scope-process relationship we move to the more practical factors of context and timing.

It will be recalled that context was defined above as the social and spatial environment of learning. Moreover, a setting was defined as a specifically structured and situated group for learning. The purpose of this chapter is to work out principles which can guide program designers in creating and selecting favorable settings for adult Christian education.

The questions this chapter deals with are: Where does adult Christian learning take place? How shall persons be grouped for adult Christian learning? How should the group be structured? and Where shall the group meet?

WHERE DOES ADULT CHRISTIAN LEARNING TAKE PLACE?

This major question of context seeks a theoretical answer that will have practical consequences for the selection of actual settings. Let us first consider the principles which two Protestant and two Catholic designs offer.

The Cooperative/Baptist principle is that the context of curriculum is the worshiping, witnessing, nurturing fellowship of persons who owe allegiance to Jesus Christ, that is, the church, especially as realized in the local congregation and in the Christian home.[1]

The Presbyterian designs do not express a general principle of context explicitly but imply that the church membership especially as gathered in a local church is the context for adult Christian learn-

1 *Dissertation*, 147-50.

ing. The "situational approach," however, acknowledges that Christian learning takes place in a variety of secular settings, too.[2]

Lansing enunciates the principle that "adult Christian learning generally and ideally takes place within the context of some kind of Christian community."

Lansing's justification for the principle is very instructive:

From the pedagogical point of view, that aspect of education which may be sociologically labeled "socialization" occurs mainly by the process of imitation within a social environment. From the practical point of view, efficiency dictates that people be educated by groups instead of individually.

From the empirical point of view, the most striking successes in adult Christian education have been found to occur where a living Christian community has been built up.[3]

Baltimore maintains that "adult Christian learning takes place wherever the Christian person and community can consciously mature." The principle does not intend to beg the question but to say, in effect, that the Christian person and community can consciously mature anywhere.[4]

The Protestant designs consider the church as gathered in a local congregation to be the context for adult Christian learning. Lansing agrees substantially but does not specify the local parish as the learning environment *par excellence*. A community of Christians, whether stably organized as a parish or temporarily gathered, is the kind of environment Lansing considers favorable and conducive to Christian learning. Though subtle, the difference seems to indicate variant popular ecclesiologies at work. Lansing's principle seems to rest on the presumption that Catholics, in general, identify primarily with the Church universal and secondarily with the local parish. The Cooperative/Baptist and Presbyterian principles seem to presume that Protestants, in general, identify primarily with the local congregation and secondarily with a national or supranational denomination.[5] If this is true, then a statement of the major principle of context for a Catholic design need not specify the local parish as the especially favorable environment for adult Christian learning.

Baltimore's principle differs in direction from the other three

2 *Ibid.*, 224 and 229-30.
3 *Ibid.*, 312-13.
4 *Ibid.*, 364.
5 This reason was suggested by Richard Gladden, speaking especially for the free church tradition of American Baptists. Interview, January 23, 1969.

principles. The other three wish positively to indicate where adult Christian education "generally and ideally" takes place. Baltimore wishes to state negatively that no environment should be considered alien to the possible maturation of "the Christian person and community." Parenthetically, Baltimore does not say to what degree the maturation of the Christian person is dependent upon Christian community. The principle coincides with that of the Presbyterian "situational approach."

Consequently, the principles of Lansing and Baltimore are divergent but not mutually exclusive. Insofar, however, as Lansing's principle indicates positively the environment where adult Christian learning "generally and ideally takes place," it is more directive as a guide to planning programs than the negative Baltimore principle. Therefore, I subscribe to the Lansing principle nuancing it in the light of my overall objective. Accordingly, I propose the principle that *the usual and most favorable context for adult Christian learning is a community of persons who try to believe and live, however, imperfectly, the mystery of Christ.*

The principle indicates only "the usual and most favorable context" of adult Christian education. It does not imply that this is the only context. Adult Christian learning can go on anywhere. Perhaps one of its most fruitful settings is the corner of one's room where one can curl up with a good book. Quiet, reflective reading remains one of the most effective means of Christian learning. Even in this instance, however, a community of persons is involved: the author and the reader. The author provides the best crystalization of his thought and feeling. The reader enters into dialogue with him: probing, searching, testing, appropriating.

The matter of "the usual and most favorable context" raises again the distinction between "live curriculum" and curriculum which is the result of intentional and explicit planning.[6] Christian learning, as most learning, takes place everywhere. It takes place at bridge clubs, at cocktail parties, at work, at worship, at play, before the television set, at the theater, in the neighborhood, and at meetings of all kinds. Only a small fraction of learning happens as a result of explicit and intentional planning. Yet it is that small fraction for which we design programs and for which a community of persons who try to believe and live the mystery of Christ form the most suitable context.

6 *Supra,* 6.

HOW SHALL PERSONS BE GROUPED FOR
ADULT CHRISTIAN LEARNING?

This question begins to get down to the practicalities of the setting. It asks for a principle that will guide the creation or selection of various kinds of grouping.

The Cooperative Design does not articulate a principle of grouping but implies that the past experience of the local church or denomination will determine grouping.[7]

The reason is that the Cooperative Curriculum Project considers settings part of the operational stage of program design which denominations and local congregations should manage directly.

The Baptist Design gets more practical. It does so especially when enlarging upon the term "setting" in its glossary:

SETTING—a particular structure planned and organized to provide teaching-learning opportunities within the total educational ministry. It is a construct, the form of which is determined by such factors as:

function (the purpose and distinctive contribution of the setting to the total educational ministry)

relationship of the setting to other defined settings

duration (the span of time between the beginning of the first and the conclusion of the last of the activities assumed in the plan for the setting)

frequency (the number and schedule of meetings or engagements in the plan for the setting)

time-span of a gathering (the length of time for each meeting assumed, or provided for, in the plan for the setting)

location (the assumed situation or locality for each meeting in the setting)

constituency (the persons assumed to compose the population for which the setting is planned)

grouping (the mode of assembling or delimiting the gathering of persons in the population for which the setting is planned)

resources (physical objects, the printed and projected materials, skilled, knowledgeable persons, community institutions and forms which help to give direction to the educational engagement in the setting)

administrative connection (the manner in which the persons, the programs, and the resources for the setting are related to a coordinating/governing body in the church polity)

leadership (the persons assumed either to be indigenous to the constituency, or to be specifically designated to assist constituents in initiating and carrying out the educational engagements planned for in the setting)

[7] *Dissertation,* 149-54.

A particular setting derives its form from the interplay among the various factors.

A setting serves as a vehicle for bringing into coordinated relationship the components of the curriculum design. Hence the setting is [a] manifestation of the organizing principle in operation. The teaching-learning experiences planned for a setting are derived from the components of the design and selected in the light of the form of the particular setting.[8]

The principle which emerges from the foregoing is that adult learnings will be tailored to the settings available and not settings to the learning desired. The reason is that American Baptists inherit a tradition of adult Christian education from the Uniform Lessons concept and hope to divert that tradition and its traditional church settings to more creative uses.

Among the Presbyterian designs the Decade Books suggest an explicit principle of grouping. It is that persons should be grouped according to their interest in topics or their involvement in a common task in the church.[9] For instance, persons interested in the same book would gather to study it together or persons desirous of becoming leaders or teachers in the church school would all study the Foundations of Christian Faith and Action, the eight books which form the nucleus of the Decade Books.

Guided Group Study offers further direction for grouping:

The optimum size for a class dealing with printed content with an inquiry and discussion method is fifteen to twenty people. It is preferable for such groups to meet in a face-to-face arrangement around a large table.[10]

The "situational approach" also offers principles with respect to grouping.

FLEXIBLE GROUPINGS 8. The laity require flexible groupings according to their diverse interests, competence, commitment, and constantly changing situations.

Temporary groups for a short-term exploration should be offered, based on interest rather than on age or sex.[11]

Trends and *Enquiry* look to private study or to groupings based on interest in their topics.

[8] *Foundations for Curriculum,* 48; cf. *CCP,* 807-09.
[9] *Dissertation,* 244-45.
[10] P. 10.
[11] Kempes, *Lay Education. . . ,* 50, 77-80.

Lansing first insists that grouping should arise "from the actions of the participants rather than from the action of any administrator" and then offers a variety of principles that might govern grouping in various programs. In some, persons group themselves according to interest in scope; in others, by reason of a shared apostolate or responsibility. In still others, learners are grouped by leaders (by way of exception to the basic principle) according to the contribution they can make to one another's learning. Although it operates as a determinant for grouping in one of Lansing's most promising programs, interest primarily in process is not explicitly stated in the principle of grouping. It seems it should be.[12]

Baltimore's principle is that the "grouping of adults for learning will be accomplished by learner-interest." It is not specified whether interest in scope and/or process is meant.[13]

In the designs which have specific principles, interest in scope figures most prominently in the determination of grouping. In two designs, a common ministry in the church determines grouping. Interest in process is an operative determinant in one design and possibly in another. In no design are age, sex, occupation, or competence stated as determinants of grouping. Yet it is not unlikely that certain topics of scope or kinds of process would require a certain age, sex, occupation, or competence. Except for the case which Lansing cites, grouping in all the designs is presumed to arise from the initiative of learners. That presumption were better expressed in the principle.

Combining these mutually complementary aspects of the various principles and the other considerations that have been raised, I propose as a principle of grouping that *persons should group themselves for adult Christian learning according to their interest in scope and/or process or by reason of their desire to receive preparation for a common Christian service save when the characteristics of scope and/or process require learners of a certain age, sex, occupation, or competence.*

Most often persons will choose to join a group because they are interested in the topic that the group is going to pursue: racial justice, formation of conscience, what it means to be a Catholic today, etc. On other occasions persons will choose to become involved in a desirable process: seminar, encounter group, prayer group, etc. Sometimes it is a combination of both which will attract adults.

At other times, persons will be grouped because they are to receive

12 *Dissertation*, 314-16. The program which attracts adults largely because of its process is the two day workshop especially for CCD teachers. *Ibid.*, 286-90.
13 *Ibid.*, 365.

preparation for a common task. This principle is at work when adults gather for a catechist training course, or when parents participate in a learning program to fit them to introduce their children to the sacraments of Baptism, Eucharist, Penance, and Confirmation. The same principle operates when young persons gather for pre-Cana courses, married persons for Cana experiences, and widows and widowers for post-Cana.

An obvious example of scope and/or process determining the grouping rather than the group choosing scope/process itself is a golden age program offered expressly for senior citizens. Other examples are medical ethics courses offered for physicians, business ethics for businessmen, or legal ethics for lawyers.

How Should the Group Be Structured?

It is one thing to gather a group. It is another to determine how the interrelationships between participants will operate. A lecture depends upon one structure of relationships, a buzz group upon a different structure of relationships, and so forth. The present question seeks a principle for structuring groups.

The Cooperative/Baptist Design does not address the question directly but implies that the past experience of the local church or the denominational board of Christian Education will determine the structuring of the group.[14]

Of the Presbyterian designs only that of the Decade Books has an explicit principle of structuring. It is that the size of the group and its structure should be determined by the process elected.[15]

Lansing's principle is that "the groupings of people which occur within the various kinds of adult education should be structured, as much as the various types of programs allow, to make the formation of Christian community as easy as possible."

Dr. Martin's justification and application of the principle are especially illuminating:

   a. Why are they structured this way?
      The general principle articulated above (Section C, major question 1) states that adult Christian education ideally occurs within the context of some kind of Christian community. Adult Christian education is more than just the experience of being in a community, however. It

---

14 *Dissertation*, 149-54 and 172-73.
15 *Ibid.*, 263-64 and 244.

also involves the acquisition of knowledge, the evolution of one's personal values and goals, and the acquiring or abandoning of some behavioral patterns. Not all means to attain the latter objectives are equally conducive to the building of a Christian community. A lecture type course, for example, will rarely engender the same intimacy among participants that a small discussion group will. But lectures are much more effective at conveying information that a discussion group generally is.

The principle stated in the answer above (to question 3) therefore directs that each different type of program be made as conducive to Christian community as its inherent characteristics allow. Examples of this are given immediately below.

b. Describe some concrete settings which demonstrate the application of this principle.

Coffee breaks are the rule between two lectures which make up an evening adult education formal course program.

Name tags are commonly used in almost every different type of program. Large workshop groups are subdivided into small discussion groups of 6 to 8 people.

Initial sessions of small discussion groups, whether in homes or within the context of a workshop, are taken up with each person introducing himself, telling something about himself and why he enrolled in the program.

All these, as well as other means, have proven to be effective in helping to build some kind of community among the participants in the various programs.[16]

In light of the justification and application of the principle, it might be more accurately stated: Of the structures suited to the kind of learning desired those should be selected which best facilitate the formation of Christian community.[17]

Baltimore states that "the principle for group structuring is found in structuring so that it will include dialogue and stimulate growth for adults." [18]

All the explicit principles agree that the structuring of the group should derive from or contribute to process. For the Decade Books Design, process should determine structure. For Lansing and Balti-

[16] These are good examples of how structures which do not significantly engender an experience of community can be supplemented to do so. *Dissertation*, 315-16.

[17] *Ibid.*, 314-16, esp. 315, n. 1.

[18] *Ibid.*, 366.

more, structure should facilitate a process of communal dialogue and growth. Lansing alone raises the problem of the interrelationship between process as determinant and process as goal.

The distinction is important. By process as determinant is meant that the process selected determines the kind of learning that is possible. For instance an informal buzz session without well informed resource persons present is not likely to achieve a sophisticated understanding of transubstantiation, transignification, and transfinalization even if the topic is the Eucharist. Or as Dr. Martin points out, a lecture process is suitable for informational learning but ill-suited to attitudinal or behavioral learning. Process becomes a goal when to experience a certain process, such as free and open sharing with other persons, is the very learning desired. In this sense, process as goal facilitates a sense of community. Some processes as determinants facilitate a sense of community; others do not.

Sometimes a kind of learning is desirable (*e.g.,* information) whose process of communication is not as conducive to communal dialogue and growth as others. The second and more accurate statement of Lansing's principle maintains the tension between process as determinant and process as goal but insists that the former cede to the latter as much as possible. Even when a structure is employed which is not conducive to communal dialogue and growth, Lansing stresses that supplementary methods should be used to facilitate them.

Because of its ability to guide the selection of structure when process as determinant and process as goal are in conflict, I agree with the Lansing principle. Rephrased, it can be put: *Of the structures suited to the kind of learning desired those should be selected which best facilitate communal dialogue and growth and those structures which of themselves do not foster them should be supplemented by other methods which do.* Dr. Martin has already provided a number of examples of the application of this principle in the passages quoted above.

WHERE SHALL THE GROUP MEET?

Once the principle upon which grouping will be based is established and its structure decided upon, then the practical question of place comes up.

The Cooperative/Baptist Design does not take up the question directly but implies that the past experience of the local church should determine where groups should meet.[19]

19 *Ibid.,* 149-54 and 172-73.

The Decade Books Design which considers only groups of less than twenty in a discussion structure suggests that the location should be determined by accessibility and comfort.[20]

Lansing's principle is that "within the limits of possibility, facilities used for programs of adult education should be conducive to the type of learning desired." [21]

Baltimore states that "places are selected so that they should readily provide a physical atmosphere where the Christian person and the community can consciously mature." [22]

The Decade Books principle names some practical considerations which must condition any principle of place. In fact, in their statements of justification or application, both Lansing and Baltimore qualify their principles in terms of availability and accessibility.[23] Upon inspection, Lansing's and Baltimore's principles complement one another after the manner of process as determinant and process as goal. For Lansing, the kind of learning desired should determine the place. For Baltimore, suitability for communal dialogue and growth should determine the place. The choice of place, then, is parallel to the choice of structure. In fact, it seems apparent that once the choice is made regarding structure, the choice regarding place directly follows. There is no need, then, for the principle of place to reassert the tension between process as determinant and process as goal which is already expressed in the principle of structure. It is only necessary for the principle of place to assert that the place must be as consistent with the characteristics of structure as possible and practicable.

Consequently, this Design proposes as a principle of place that *of the places which are available and accessible, those should be selected which best accommodate the characteristics of the structure of the learning group.*

The principle is simple and obvious. But it is frequently neglected in practice. Too often administrators assign learning centers first: classrooms, lecture halls, libraries, lounges without regard to the learning group or its structure. The anticipated size of the group seems the only influencing factor. It is just as practical and far sounder educationally to receive a description of the learning group and its structure before assigning locations. Thus the incongruity may be avoided of small group discussions meeting in large auditoriums while lectures are offered in lounges.

[20] *Ibid.*, 244.
[21] *Ibid.*, 316.
[22] *Ibid.*, 366.
[23] *Ibid.*, 316-17 and 366-67.

SUMMARY AND APPLICATION

I have proposed a major and three subordinate principles of context.

The major principle is declarative: the usual and most favorable context for adult Christian learning is a community of persons who try to believe and live, however imperfectly, the mystery of Christ.

The first subordinate principle is prescriptive: persons should group themselves for adult Christian learning according to their interest in scope and/or process or by reason of their desire to receive preparation for a common Christian service save when the characteristics of scope and/or process require learners of a certain age, sex, occupation, or competence.

The second subordinate principle is also prescriptive: Of the structures suited to the kind of learning desired those should be selected which best facilitate communal dialogue and growth and those structures which of themselves do not foster them should be supplemented by other methods which do.

So too is the third subordinate principle prescriptive: of the places which are available and accessible, those should be selected which best accommodate the characteristics of the structure of the learning group.

When each of the principles was set forth in the body of this chapter, the practical application of each was indicated. Here it is appropriate to reinforce the importance of moving from a principle of grouping to a principle of structure to a principle of placement. The opposite movement is the more usual but less inventive. It is usual to treat context and settings as a purely practical matter. "What locations are available?" "Let's assign a group to each." It is educationally more fruitful to determine first what kind of group is being formed, then what kind of structure is to be employed, and finally to assign the group to the best available place. Even when one follows this movement, he finds that the available places are not suitable to the kind of group and its structure. At least, the leader of the group will know what limitations he labors under and can compensate for some ingeniously while he empathetically apologizes to participants for the other limitations that are unavoidable.

Timing—The Succession of Events and Experiences During Which Adult Christian Learning Occurs

Ask ten persons to design a program and nine will come up with a schedule. Scheduling is the last, not the first ingredient of program design. Yet, it is only when dates and hours and minutes are alloted for learning experiences that the design becomes practical and realistic. Moreover, it is usually under the hammer of deadlines that design proceeds from the luxury of considering possibilities to the discipline of making choices.

Even within the category of timing itself, however, scheduling is the last not the first element to be considered.

The questions with which timing deals are the following: The major question is: When does adult Christian learning occur? Subordinate questions are: What principle governs the responsiveness of a curriculum plan to God's present activity? What principle governs the responsiveness of a curriculum plan to current events in the Church and in the world? How shall the readiness which is conditioned by age, experience, and responsibility influence a curriculum plan? and What determines the frequency and duration with which related adult learning opportunities will be offered?

WHEN DOES ADULT CHRISTIAN LEARNING OCCUR?

While admitting that much if not most Christian learning occurs in unplanned ways and at unscheduled times, the Cooperative/Baptist Design, in accord with its principle of learning tasks, sees adult Christian learning occurring when the learner undertakes the learning tasks and sees them through to the assumption of personal and social responsibility in the light of the gospel.[1]

1 *Dissertation,* 176.

The Presbyterian designs operate on the general principle that adult Christian learning occurs when learners choose to pursue it.[2]

Lansing states that "adult Christian learning . . . is an ongoing, almost evolutionary process, admitting of no terminal cutoff date, and of vaguely defined beginning point." [3]

Baltimore's principle is that "adult Christian learning takes place when people consciously respond to the opportunity expressed in the dynamics of process." [4]

The principles seem to complement one another. The learning in unplanned ways and at unscheduled times by which the Cooperative/ Baptist Design qualifies its principle of timing is given primary and exclusive emphasis in the Lansing principle. The Cooperative/Baptist, Presbyterian, and Baltimore principles accentuate the promise which the learner's free and conscious involvement in the learning process holds for the occurrence of adult Christian learning.

Utilizing the insights expressed in the various principles and adapting them to my own principles of scope and process, I propose as the major principle of timing that *although adult Christian learning is an ongoing process which happens in unplanned ways at unscheduled times, it gives special promise of occurring when adult learners freely and consciously choose to appropriate personally the meaning of the Church's experience of the mystery of Christ.*

The principle is based upon the distinction between "live curriculum" and planned curriculum.[5] Dr. Martin enlarges upon the difference:

To paraphrase the words of one secular adult educator, "Adult Education (in its broadest sense) goes on 18 hours a day in the life of a person." [If the Freudian principle is correct that much experience is appropriated and worked through in dream life, that period could fairly be extended to 24 hours a day.] Adult education more narrowly conceived is a continual necessity in the rapidly changing world. Adult Christian education, in the context of a changing Church in a changing world is also continually necessary, even precinding from the fact that the Christian life is meant to be one of growth, of continual transformation into the likeness of Christ.[6]

The designer of adult programs who feels that to educate adults he has to deal with the whole continual stream of experience in which

2 *Ibid.*, 267-69.
3 *Ibid.*, 320.
4 *Ibid.*, 370.
5 *Supra*, 6.
6 *Dissertation*, 320-21.

and through which the adult learns [7] is likely to doom his efforts to frustration. He proliferates himself too broadly. It is more realistic to appreciate that the vast majority of learning goes on through experiences outside the influence of the professional educator and plan in the light of that fact for the relatively limited learning that occurs through intentionally and explicitly planned learning opportunities.

WHAT PRINCIPLE GOVERNS THE RESPONSIVENESS OF A CURRICULUM PLAN TO GOD'S PRESENT ACTIVITY?

The Cooperative/Baptist Design acknowledges the necessity of weighing "what God is doing in the world" but offers no principle which may guide curriculum planning in reckoning with His activity.[8]

Implicit in the Designs of *Trends* and of "The Human Scene" in *Enquiry* is the principle that in being responsive to current events, a curriculum plan is being responsive to God's present activity.[9]

Lansing states that the first subordinate question should be combined with the second but, in doing so, gives evidence of an implicit principle that in responding to current events in the Church and in the world, curriculum planning responds as much as can be expected to God's present activity in history.[10]

Baltimore states that "awareness of God's presence is found in the realization that man should be concerned to discover the presence of God in life's situation." [11]

Baltimore's statement, though true, is a general directive to all who would wish to develop a basic Christian perspective on life but hardly serves as a principle for curriculum planning. It is much like the acknowledgement of the Cooperative/Baptist Design. The implicit principles of the Presbyterian designs and Lansing, which substantially agree with one another, seem to offer the beginnings of an explicit principle. They give, however, the impression that current events in Church and world may simply be equated with God's present activity. Current events may be as much the result of man's evil as of God's will. Only the most naive theology of secularity would

[7] This seems the view of Fr. Kevin Coughlin. See *The National Catholic Reporter*, November 12, 1971, p. 15.

[8] *Dissertation*, 176-77.

[9] *Ibid.*, 267-69.

[10] *Ibid.*, 321.

[11] *Ibid.*, 370.

equate them.[12] What seems needed, then, is a tempering of the equation between current events and God's activity with a criterion that might sift the two. The only criterion that seems available is God's past activity and promise of future activity to which Judaeo-Christian tradition imperfectly gives witness.[13] In the light of God's past and promised activity, curriculum planners, who do not for the most part enjoy the special inspiration of Israel's prophets,[14] can hazard but tentative judgments about God's present activity.[15]

Joining this last consideration to the implicit principles of "Christian Faith and Action" and Lansing, I propose the principle that by

---

[12] It is not possible to rehearse here all the issues of the "secular city debate." By a naive theology of secularity, I mean a complete identification of the New Testament figure of the Kingdom of God with the secularization process. Thomas J. J. Altizer, *The Gospel of Christian Atheism* (Philadelphia: The Westminster Press, 1966), pp. 105-07, propounded this identification after Harvey Cox, *The Secular City*, 110-13, first, but less categorically, suggested it. Moreover, I do not consider conscious refusal to engage in the evolutionary process as the cardinal sin (see Heimo Dolch, "Sin in an Evolutive World," *Concilium*, VI, No. 3 [June, 1967], 36-40) nor the discipline to build the secular city as the primary repentance demanded by the in-breaking of God's Kingdom. Rather, I understand the imminence of the Kingdom's establishment as both relativizing and criticizing the building of the secular city after the manner of Johannes Baptist Metz' "The Church's Social Function in the Light of 'Political Theology,'" *Concilium*, VI, No. 4 (June, 1968), 3-11. Further I consider the in-breaking of the Kingdom to comprise a healing as well as an eschatological dynamic—a healing at their source of the seven deadly sins which the medievals sagely categorized (of which sloth—refusal to engage in the evolutionary process—is but one) and which Archbishop Helder Câmara has recently redrawn for the contemporary world (see "Response to Crisis," *Herder Correspondence*, VI, No. 6 [June, 1969], 175-77). It is especially the failure to recognize man's manifold selfishness and the consequent necessity for the healing dynamic of God's Kingdom which renders an otherwise exciting theology of secularity naive.

[13] This statement wishes to be mindful of the strictures that, on the one hand, "whoever tries to save God from involvement in present history usually ends by idolizing elements of past human history" and, on the other, "there must be on our part a readiness *always* to look for God in historical happenings but never to equate our human judgment of the event with the divine will" (Gabriel Moran, "The God of Revelation," *Commonweal*, LXXXV, No. 18 [February 10, 1967] [*God: Commonweal Papers: 1*], 502-03). It seeks to express a criterion that will be dependable for curriculum planning without pretending to be privy to the divine purpose. The criterion rests upon an expectation that God will not be altogether inconsistent with his past activity and not untrue to his promises (against Altizer, *The Gospel. . .*, 27-28).

[14] Accepting the position of Bruce Vawter ("Introduction to Prophetic Literature" in *The Jerome Biblical Commentary*, I, 224) that "by prophecy we understand . . . the mediation and interpretation of the divine mind and will." Carl Pfeiffer would seem to place this burden upon religious educators. See "The Role of the Catechist in Religious Education," for distribution in the Know Your Faith Series, N. C. News Service, Washington, D.C. [1969].

[15] On the intricacies of judging the theological meaning of but one aspect of current religious experience, the "underground church," see David Tracy, "Holy Spirit as Philosophical Problem," *Commonweal*, LXXXIX, No. 6 (November 8, 1968) (*Holy Spirit: Commonweal Papers: 3*), 205-13.

attempting to interpret current events in the Church and in the world against the record of God's past and promised deeds, curriculum planning responds as best it can to God's present activity in history.

The meaning of the principle should be clear from the argumentation that precedes it. It will become clearer in answering the next subordinate question which is complementary to the present one.

What Principle Governs the Responsiveness of a Curriculum Plan to Current Events in the Church and in the World?

The Cooperative/Baptist Design, especially through its supportive paper, *Learning Tasks in the Curriculum,* raises the question but does not express a principle that can guide a centrally planned curriculum in responding to current events.[16]

The Presbyterian "situational approach," especially as supported by *Trends,* operates on the principle that current events in the world will largely determine the scope of curriculum.[17]

Lansing states that "an adult Christian education curriculum should be attentive to and responsive to the 'signs of the times.' "[18]

Baltimore appeals to its principles of scope to meet the present question. If the comprehensiveness of scope is limited to the felt needs of learners and dimensions of scope are selected according to the life situations of learners, Baltimore argues that a curriculum plan will be as responsive to current events as it realistically can be.[19]

The Cooperative/Baptist Design demonstrates a serious liability of the centrally planned, life-long curriculum plan. It cannot respond flexibly to current events. It must rely almost exclusively on perennial Christian concerns as these meet persistent life issues. Locally planned curriculums can respond more directly to current events. For locally planned curriculums Lansing expresses a general directive which is true as far as it goes but which gives less pointed guidance to curriculum planning than the principles of the "situational approach" and Baltimore. Both of the latter identify scope as the curriculum component which should be especially responsive to current events. In *Trends,* the scope is determined by an editorial board's

16 *Dissertation,* 177.
17 *Ibid.,* 267-69.
18 *Ibid.,* 321.
19 *Ibid.,* 371.

judgment as to which current events provide opportunities for adult Christian learning. For the "situational approach" itself, however, and for Baltimore, the scope is determined by the felt needs of learners.

Baltimore's principle seems especially helpful in assessing how current events affect curriculum planning. They do so only to the extent that current events create in learners felt needs for dimensions of scope. This principle narrows down the potential learning opportunities that current events provide to those which learners themselves find relevant. The approach, however, is only valid for curriculums planned by learners or very close to learners. National boards and diocesan offices can only guess or sample opinions as to what felt needs current events create.

Both the "situational approach" and Baltimore principles limit the influence of current events to decisions regarding scope. It seems legitimate to ask why they might not be as influential in determining process. Current experiences, it may be argued, like psychedelic celebrations and sensitivity sessions, can create felt needs for certain modes of process in adult Christian education.[20]

The popularity of Lansing's workshops seems attributable to a desire for a personal sharing process conditioned by current trends in interpersonal experience.[21] Felt needs, then, for certain learning dynamics also seem worthy of mention in a principle guiding the responsiveness of a curriculum plan to current events.

Thus, developing Baltimore's principle with respect to process as well as scope, I propose that *curriculum planning should respond to current events in the Church and in the world insofar as those events create in learners an interest in appropriating certain meanings of the mystery of Christ or participating in certain modes of process.* Because scope and process are interrelated, interest in the one can provide entrance to the other.

HOW SHALL THE READINESS WHICH IS CONDITIONED BY
AGE, EXPERIENCE, AND RESPONSIBILITY
INFLUENCE A CURRICULUM PLAN?

With a centrally planned, lifelong curriculum in mind, the Cooperative/Baptist Design offers the principle that only the readiness

20 Witness the current popularity of religious "happenings" such as those created by Miss Corita Kent. See Celia Hubbard, "Corita—Myth or Maid," *The Living Light*, V, No. 4 (Winter, 1968-69), 101-09. (For a correction, see *ibid.*, VI, No. 1 [Spring, 1969], 154.)

21 *Dissertation*, 286-90.

which derives from a generic consideration of age levels and broadly shared experiences can influence denominational planning of curriculum; individual readiness must be judged and capitalized upon by the teacher in the concrete situation of live curriculum.[22]

The Presbyterian designs do not consider readiness conditioned by age or experience. Their resources are directed to learners of sixteen years through old age indiscriminately.[23]

Lansing states the principle: "Each program within the curriculum should be designed to match up with the abilities and background of the potential learners that it attracts, or is meant to attract." Dr. Martin offers useful justification:

This principle may be interpreted in two ways. On the one hand, it states that, given a particular type of program, a particular kind of learner is likely to be attracted—and hence, the program should be aimed at this general type of learner. On the other hand, it states that, given a certain kind of learner as a target group, programs should be designed to attract him and match up with his abilities and background. Research has been done in this area. (*Cf.* for example, Matilda Rees and William Paisley, "Social and Psychological Predictors of Adult Information Seeking and Media Use" *Adult Education*, Vol. XIX, No. 1 [Fall, 1968], pp. 11-29.) A certain type of program will generally attract a certain type of person: "When classroom and lecture hall activities are combined across all subjects of study, formal education (= number of years previously spent in classrooms) joins with age (e.g. youth) to predict the behavior (multiple correlation = .47)." (*art. cit.*, p. 39). In other words, formal evening courses can be expected to attract young to middle aged people, generally with some college or college graduates—and the subject matter and level of difficulty of the courses should be fixed accordingly.

On the other hand, "If one has a target audience but no commitment to a medium or institution, then predictor profiles can be studied to discover the seeking/use behaviors on which the target audience 'peaks'." (*art. cit.*, pp. 26-27)

In summary: learner's age and experience influence his participation in programs in generally determinable ways, and program content should be gauged accordingly.[24]

Baltimore considers the question invalid.

Baltimore's reason for considering the question invalid is instructive. Basing the selection of dimensions of scope on felt needs includes

22 *Ibid.*, 178.
23 *Ibid.*, 267-69.
24 *Ibid.*, 322-23.

weighing the readiness which age and experience condition. The approach seems legitimate for programs planned by or as close to the learner as possible. The Cooperative/Baptist and Lansing Designs consider curriculum planning somewhat removed from the learner. Each Design's principles fundamentally agree that age and experience influence participation in generally determinable ways and scope and process should be gauged accordingly. Sophisticated statistical studies render readiness "generally determinable." The addition of the Baptist principle regarding individual readiness seems incontrovertible in light of the uniqueness of each person.

Combining the Cooperative/Baptist and Lansing principles and qualifying them with Baltimore's reasons for considering the question invalid, I propose that *when learners do not have a direct role in curriculum planning, their readiness, as best it can be determined from a statistical consideration of age and background, should influence decisions regarding scope and process, with the realization that individual readiness can only be appraised and used to the advantage of the learner by the leader or fellow learners in the actual learning situation.*

WHAT DETERMINES THE FREQUENCY AND DURATION WITH WHICH RELATED ADULT LEARNING OPPORTUNITIES WILL BE OFFERED?

The Cooperative/Baptist Design considers frequency and duration administrative matters.

Among the Presbyterian designs, the Decade Books Series suggests that "the number of sessions . . . arise out of the nature of the subject as reflected by the author's approach to it." *Enquiry* also operates on the principle that duration and frequency of related learnings depend upon the scope to be mastered.

Lansing states that "frequency and duration of related learning opportunities are decided on the basis of availability of teachers and of learners."

Baltimore's principle is that "the frequency and duration of learning opportunities are determined by the attention span, life cycles, resources, and organizational competence of the people involved."

Lansing fundamentally agrees with the Cooperative/Baptist Design that administrative practicality determines frequency and duration. Baltimore agrees in large part but adds explicitly that the interest and capacity of learners must also be weighed. The Presbyterian designs raise another consideration that may be overlooked because of its very obviousness, that is, that the scope to be learned is the principal criterion which should determine frequency and duration of learning opportunities. Putting the emphases together it seems reasonable that scope determines what frequency and duration should obtain and practicality determines what can obtain. Administrative practicality, then, limits the frequency and duration which the desired scope (and consequently, process) of a learning opportunity would find ideal.

Expressing these considerations in a principle, I propose that *the frequency and duration of related learning opportunities should be determined by the time needed by the learner to appropriate the intended scope insofar as practical limitations of personnel and space permit.*

SUMMARY AND APPLICATION

The major principle of timing is declarative: Although adult Christian learning is an ongoing process which happens in unplanned ways at unscheduled times, it gives special promise of occurring when adult learners freely and consciously choose to appropriate personally the meaning of the Church's experience of the mystery of Christ.

The first subordinate principle is also declarative: By attempting to interpret current events in the Church and in the world against the record of God's past and promised deeds, curriculum planning responds as best it can to God's present activity in history.

The second subordinate principle is prescriptive: Curriculum planning should respond to current events in the Church and in the world insofar as those events create in learners an interest in appropriating certain meanings of the mystery of Christ or participating in certain modes of process.

The third subordinate principle is also prescriptive: When learners do not have a direct role in curriculum planning, their readiness, as best it can be determined from a statistical consideration of age and background, should influence decisions regarding scope and process, with the realization that individual readiness can only be appraised and used to the advantage of the learner by the leader or fellow learners in the actual learning situation.

The fourth subordinate principle is prescriptive too: The frequency and duration of related learning opportunities should be determined by the time needed by the learner to appropriate the intended scope insofar as practical limitations of personnel and space permit.

With respect to application, there are two kinds of principles here.

The major and first three subordinate principles guide decisions that need to be taken near the beginning of the planning process. The fourth subordinate principle guides decisions that should be taken only at the end of the planning process.

The first three subordinate principles may appear too complex to follow in practice. Their complexity derives from the delicacy of decisions with respect to timing. However, they are relatively simple in application to actual program design when one considers that all three principles revolve around the priority of meeting felt needs in adult education. Only those current events deserve to be dealt with in which learners demonstrate an interest. Only that readiness needs to be considered which learners actually evidence. This simplicity of application pertains only to programs designed as close to and as much by learners as possible. A centrally designed curriculum faces a much more complex problem in dealing with current events and readiness levels. It is with these national and diocesan planning teams in mind that the principles are as intricately nuanced as they are.

The fourth subordinate principle finally gets down to the practicalities of scheduling. The principle is obvious in theory but often difficult to apply in practice.

Frequently it is not how long the learning experience should take but how much time participants can afford that determines scheduling. The availability of resource persons and facilities is also a major determinant with respect to scheduling. But it is important that the planning team first work out an "ideal" schedule where the time is allotted according to the experience planned and then make only the most necessary concessions to practical necessities.

CHAPTER VIII

General Curriculum Concerns— The Organizing Principle, Evaluation, Administration

THIS CHAPTER ACTS first as a summary and secondly as an application of the curriculum design for adult Christian education which has been developed through the preceding seven chapters. A summary occupies the opening section. Application is treated under different aspects when explaining the organizing principle and when addressing the problem of administration. Evaluation is reserved for the end because it looks to the future improvement both of this curriculum design and its underlying methodology.

SUMMARY

A summary of the methodology upon which this curriculum design is based ends Chapter I.[1] It would help to read that summary again before proceeding. It identifies six factors of program design and three general concerns that affect all the factors. It raises irreducible and unavoidable questions with respect to each factor and concern. It suggests the data sources from which principles which answer the questions may be framed.

At the end of each succeeding chapter (II-VII) can be found summaries of principles regarding the factors of program design with which the chapters respectively deal. However, it may prove convenient to marshal all the principles together here with a capsule justification for each. This summary may be especially helpful as a prelude to treating the organizing principle which by its very nature is meant to be a statement embodying the evaluative judgment which relates the principles of objective, personnel, scope, process, context,

[1] *Supra,* 64-69.

and timing one to another in such a way that each exercises its proper guidance upon curriculum planning.

Principles Regarding Objective

The *major principle* is that the objective of adult Christian education is that mature persons learn the mystery of Christ.

"Mature persons" summarizes the learners and resource persons who engage in adult Christian education. "The mystery of Christ" summarizes the scope of adult Christian education and "learn" its process.

The *first subordinate* principle is that the objective should provide the direction for all the educational experiences in a program; act as a criterion for planning and negotiating with participants short-term goals, learning activities, and resources; and serve as a means of evaluating a program.

The principle is proposed both because it crystallizes the long experience of Protestant Christian educators in developing systematic curriculum plans and because of its obvious logic.

The *second subordinate* principle is that the objective of adult Christian education agrees with the purpose of the Church materially but differs from it formally insofar as the objective of the former is that [mature] persons learn the mystery of Christ whereas the purpose of the latter is that persons live the mystery of Christ.

The principle is proposed because it locates the identity between the objective of Christian education and the mission of the Church in the mystery of Christ but differentiates the formalities of learning and living by which one may be involved in the mystery.

Principles Regarding Personnel

The *major principle* of personnel is that those persons interrelate in teaching and learning adult Christian education who, through various roles, intend to assist one another in learning the mystery of Christ and whose needs, interests, capacities, and competencies largely determine the scope and process of a particular curriculum plan.

The principle owes its justification to Baltimore's insights that willingness to achieve the objective characterizes real participants in adult Christian education and that the needs and competencies of learners and resource persons should largely determine the scope and process of a program.

The *first subordinate* principle is that God's role in adult Christian education is to be the center of its scope, the enabling power of its process, the creator of its context, and the provider of its timing.

This principle incorporates the various affirmations of the designs analyzed and draws upon principles of scope and timing articulated and justified later in this proposed Design.

The *second subordinate* principle is that being the persons upon whom the visible context of adult Christian education depends, the role of the College of Bishops is to pass final human judgment on the consistency of formulations of scope with the meaning of the Church's experience of the mystery of Christ and the fittingness of methods to convey that meaning.

Justification relies upon the historical position of bishops in Catholic tradition as touchstones of unity and final human judges of orthodoxy and orthopraxis.

The *third subordinate* principle is that the learner's role should vary according to the characteristics of the teaching-learning mode(s) and the structure(s) of the setting in a curriculum plan.

The *fourth subordinate* principle is that the teacher's role should vary according to the characteristics of the teaching-learning mode(s) and the structure(s) of the setting in a curriculum plan.

Both principles rely upon the obvious logic followed in all four designs that choices as to process determine the roles of learners and resource persons. This Design proposes that it is more precisely the learning mode which determines the structure of the setting and correspondingly the roles of learners and resource persons.

The *fifth subordinate* principle is that the persons closest to the learning situation—learners, leaders, planners, administrators—should plan curriculum as much as possible for themselves guided by theologically and educationally sound principles and stimulated by broad possibilities as to scope, process, context, and timing which a central coordinating staff can make available.

The principle incorporates the general conclusions derived from studying all four designs. It reiterates the cardinal principle of the Presbyterian "situational approach" but insists further upon commonly thought through principles.

The *sixth subordinate* principle is that the proper task of administration is to implement a curriculum plan.

The principle adopts the reasoning of the two Protestant designs and Lansing that the task of curriculum planning differs from the task of administration as policy differs from practice.

Principles Regarding Scope

The *major principle* is that the appropriate scope of adult Christian education is the meaning of the Church's experience of the mystery of Christ.

This principle relies upon the anthropological presupposition that man is an incarnate subject who discovers, creates, and expresses meaning and upon the theological presuppositions that the deed of God in Christ is the integrative event of history and that the Church is the extension of the Christ event.

The *first subordinate* principle is that the scope of adult Christian education should be as comprehensive of the meaning of the Church's experience of the mystery of Christ as relevance to adult learners permits.

The principle acknowledges the experience of the Presbyterian, Baltimore, and Lansing designs that demonstrated need and interest on the part of learners limit the "broadest potential scope" of adult Christian education.

The *second subordinate* principle is that the distinct dimensions of scope which lend themselves to different kinds of learning are the meaning of the Church's experience of the mystery of Christ as event, as horizon, as celebration, and as moral imperative.

Justification for this principle lies in the fourfold aspects of the mystery of Christ intimated in Scripture, expressed in the Second Vatican Council documents, and elaborated by contemporary theologians.

The *third subordinate* principle is that meanings of the mystery of Christ should be selected for inclusion in a curriculum plan according as the interests of learners, competence of resource persons, and broad diocesan or parochial needs permit their interdependence to be observed.

The principle acknowledges the practical experience of the four designs that needs and competencies determine what dimensions of scope can be treated but it goes on to stress that the reciprocity between various meanings of the mystery of Christ should also be respected.

The *fourth subordinate* principle is that the sequence of learning opportunities should be determined by the interests of learners with the expectation that appropriating, however incompletely, one meaning of the mystery of Christ will create interest in appropriating the others at ever deepening levels of knowledge, understanding, appreciation, and responsibility.

This principle like the third subordinate principle of scope and the second subordinate principle of process attempts to resolve the problem of following the preference of learners while respecting the demands of scope. It relies upon the experience of "situational approaches" in giving priority to learners' immediate interests but it also alerts resource persons in the actual learning situation to guide felt needs into needs for other meanings of the mystery of Christ.

Principles Regarding Process

The *major principle* is that adult Christian learning happens through interpersonal appropriation by faith of the meaning of the Church's experience of the mystery of Christ.

The principle rests upon the epistemological presupposition that appropriation consists in experience, insight, judgment, and decision and the anthropological-theological presuppositions that Christian learning is a graced process created by a mutual sharing of faith and terminating in the persons of God.

The *first subordinate* principle is that adult Christian learning should seek historical knowledge of the mystery of Christ as event, cognitive understanding of the mystery of Christ as horizon, appreciation for the mystery of Christ as celebration, and responsibility to the mystery of Christ as moral imperative.

Justification lies in locating the cognitional and decisional operations to which each dimension of meaning of the mystery of Christ most relates.

The *second subordinate* principle is that in order to capitalize upon the intrinsic motivation of adult learners, kinds of learning should be selected which correspond to the felt needs of learners in the hope that, once achieved, the need may be experienced for other kinds of learning to which other meanings of the mystery of Christ lend themselves.

The principle relies upon the experience of those designs (Presbyterian "situational approach," Lansing, Baltimore) which construct curriculum close to the learner. That experience is that if curriculum grows out of felt needs, adequate motivation is already present. The principle incorporates, however, the further potential for learning which other meanings of the mystery have and for which learners may not yet feel needs.

The *third subordinate* principle is that historical knowledge of the mystery of Christ as event gives promise of being learned especially through the teaching-learning mode of disclosure; cognitive understanding of the mystery of Christ as horizon through inquiry; appreciation for the mystery of Christ as celebration through initiation; and responsibility to the mystery of Christ as moral imperative through problem-solving.

The justification rests upon an identification of modes of learning which give more promise than others of achieving given kinds of learning.

Principles Regarding Context

The *major principle* of context is that the usual and most favorable context for adult Christian learning is a community of persons who try to believe and live, however imperfectly, the mystery of Christ.

The principle relies upon Lansing's reasoning, supported, though out of a different ecclesiology, by the Cooperative/Baptist and Presbyterian designs. The reasoning is that a supportive climate of Christian believers gives more promise than other environments of the occurrence of Christian learning.

The *first subordinate* principle is that persons should group themselves for adult Christian learning according to their interest in scope and/or process or by reason of their desire to receive preparation for a common Christian service save when the characteristics of scope and/or process require learners of a certain age, sex, occupation, or competence.

Justification reflects the combined experience of the four designs under study and adds mention of special instances where the demands of scope and process rather than the interests of learners would determine grouping.

The *second subordinate* principle is that, of the structures suited to the kind of learning desired, those should be selected which best facilitate communal dialogue and growth and those structures which of themselves do not foster them should be supplemented by other methods which do.

The principle relies upon Lansing's solution to the dilemma of process as determinant and process as goal. It places priority upon process as goal, that is, a process of mutual sharing which creates community.

The *third subordinate* principle is that, of the places which are available and accessible, those should be selected which best accommodate the characteristics of the structure of the learning group.

The principle recognizes that the tension between process as determinant and process as goal should have been resolved in the decision as to the structure of the group and that consequently the place should accord with the structure chosen. The principle combines the insights of Lansing and Baltimore regarding setting.

Principles Regarding Timing

The *major principle* of timing is that although adult Christian learning is an ongoing process which happens in unplanned ways at unscheduled times, it gives special promise of occurring when adult learners freely and consciously choose to appropriate personally the meaning of the Church's experience of the mystery of Christ.

Justification draws upon a combination of insights stated in the major principles of timing in the four designs under investigation.

The *first subordinate* principle is that by attempting to interpret current events in the Church and in the world against the record of God's past and promised deeds, curriculum planning responds as best it can to God's present activity in history.

Justification relies upon the consistency which may fairly be expected to characterize God's dealings with man and his history.

The *second subordinate* principle is that curriculum planning should respond to current events in the Church and in the world insofar as those events create in learners an interest in appropriating certain meanings of the mystery of Christ or participating in certain modes of process.

The justification draws upon Baltimore's insight that if curriculum is responsive to the felt needs of learners, it will automatically respond to the current events that shape those felt needs.

The *third subordinate* principle is that when learners do not have a direct role in curriculum planning, their readiness, as best it can be determined from a statistical consideration of age and background, should influence decisions regarding scope and process, with the realization that individual readiness can only be appraised and used to the advantage of the learner by the leader or fellow learners in the actual learning situation.

The principle relies upon Lansing's use of statistical data in planning programs and the obvious logic of the Cooperative/Baptist Design's insistence that only in the actual learning situation can the teachable moment be recognized and acted upon.

The *fourth subordinate* principle is that the frequency and duration of related learning opportunities should be determined by the time needed by the learner to appropriate the intended scope insofar as practical limitations of personnel and space permit.

Justification follows the obvious logic of the Presbyterian principle that scope and process should determine the frequency and duration of learning periods. The principle also respects the practical issues raised by the other designs.

THE ORGANIZING PRINCIPLE

No less than six major principles and twenty-two subordinate principles have been proposed. Are they consistent? Do they hang together? Can they be realistically applied?

It is the task of an organizing principle to demonstrate their consistency and to provide a key to application. The question which asks for the organizing principle can be put in two ways. If scope is seen as the key to curriculum organization, the question may be put: What dimensions of *scope* shall *persons* master through a *process timed* and *situated* so as to achieve the *objective?* If process is seen as the key, the question can be put: How shall the *process* be *timed* and *situated* so as to involve the *persons* in mastering the *scope* in order to fulfill the *objective?* [2] I prefer to consider scope the key to curriculum organization and consequently choose the first formulation of the question.

By way of answer, I propose this as the organizing principle of the twenty-eight principles: *in order to learn the mystery of Christ (objective), adults should choose according to their needs and competencies (personnel) what dimensions of the meaning of the Church's experience of that mystery (scope) they wish to appropriate through the learning modes (process) in the settings (context) and at the times (timing), which give most promise of learning those dimensions.*

The principle begins with learners' needs and resource persons' competencies. This is not to deny that learners have competencies and resource persons needs. However, the former are usually described in terms of needs and the latter in terms of competencies.

These needs, according to the psychological, cognitional, and epistemological presuppositions already explained, are fulfilled by meanings. When the meanings desired pertain to the Church's experience of the mystery of Christ, then distinctively Christian education can take place. These Christian meanings may be variously historical, theological, liturgical, ethical, or a combination of some or all of them. When the meanings are identified which respond to expressed

2 *Supra,* 54.

needs, then the kinds of learning needed either singly or in combination are also apparent. These kinds of learning, in turn, suggest the modes of learning required—disclosure, inquiry, initiation, or problem-solving either singly or in combination as the dimensions of meaning and kinds of learning are single or combined.

Interest in the meanings will also determine which learners learn together (grouping). The corresponding kinds of learning and learning modes will suggest the structure of the learning group—lecture, panel, discussion, debate, seminar, etc. The grouping and structure together will determine the place. The kinds and modes of learning, in turn, determine the time it will take to learn the desired meanings.

Let me try to describe the process more practically and simply. First the planning team should agree upon the overarching purpose of adult Christian education—either the one proposed here or another one.

Then the team should research the learning needs of the adults it hopes to serve as well as the competencies of the available resource persons to respond to those needs. The research, however, must be done in such a way that the prospective participants involve themselves in the research process so as to become more conscious of their learning needs and feel a sense of responsibility in satisfying them. It does little good for the planning team to know these needs if prospective participants are not conscious of them too. Otherwise motivation to participate is nil. Clues to these needs may be found in current events in the Church and in society-at-large or in the generic readiness levels of adults but until evidence exists that these are the strongly felt needs of these particular adults, they remain in the realm of possible and not practical "take-hold" points for learning.

Once both the planning team and participants have determined the learning needs they are in a position together to choose the themes and topics which respond to those needs. Here the cooperation of planning team and participants becomes intricate and acute. Most participants will not have a detailed understanding of the various meanings of Christianity that can provide a satisfactory resolution of their needs and still less an idea of the processes by which these meanings can be best appropriated. The planning team must work out in advance possible constellations of themes and processes to present to participants by way of options. The principles of scope and process elaborated in this Design provide guides to working out those options. Once participants have chosen the themes, then planners can work on the actual program offerings.

It is the planners' task rather than the participants to devise the best processes which fit with the themes, to provide for the kinds of groups and places which best fit with each process and to determine the frequency and duration of the sessions. The actual time at which the sessions can be held will have to be worked out with participants. Only the amount of time the process will take is the responsibility of planners to decide.

I have already alluded to GIFT [3] as a process of doing adult Christian education which utilizes this organizing principle. It may help to elaborate here.

GIFT begins with an overarching purpose for which its name is an acrostic: Growth In Faith Together. The promotional material expands upon its meaning of faith: "Faith is what GIFT is all about: faith in the Father through the Son in the Spirit; faith in one another; faith in the leaders of the Church during this time of change." Participants work toward the purpose through a three step process: research, reflection, and response.

First, prospective participants are invited to search their own hearts and minds as to where they presently stand with respect to personal belief and ethical convictions. The practical tool for accomplishing this self-research is a "Survey of Religious Beliefs and Concerns" mailed to the home. The survey presents sixty statements arranged in four categories: beliefs; prayer; church life; and morality. Some are simple statements of traditional beliefs; others are provocative statements of counter-belief. Some are clear statements; others are purposely ambiguous. Participants are asked to mark their agreement or disagreement with the statements. They are also encouraged to discuss the statements with the whole family. Thus the survey acts as a stimulant to self examination and as an inducement to discuss serious questions of faith with others. When filling out the survey, participants are invited to join reflection groups to discuss these concerns with small groups of other adults.

The surveys are turned in to the planning team and analyzed by computer so that it can be known how the young, middle-aged, and elderly compare on various statements; how men and women compare; what difference educational backgrounds and frequency of Mass attendance makes in the responses. Consequently, in addition to acting as a tool for self-research, the survey results provide a means for the planning team to find out "where people are" in varying degrees of belief. The results are then publicized so that all can learn where they stand in relation to one another.

3 *Supra,* 104 and 159.

After research, reflection begins. The purpose of this phase is to gather participants in groups of ten or twelve so they can reflect upon their faith together. They meet once a week for five weeks at a time convenient to the group. For the first two weeks they try to get as many concerns of faith—either those suggested by the survey or others—out on the table. During the third week they synthesize these concerns and send them in to the planning team for placement on a ballot. During the fourth week they set a priority among the concerns—"first we are interested in formation of conscience; second we are interested in the divinity of Christ; third we are interested in what our children are being taught in religion, etc." At the end of the fourth week, all the groups come together, report on the priorities of each, and then vote on their priority concerns as a total community. During the fifth week the groups meet separately to negotiate their individual priorities with the whole community's priorities and to motivate themselves to participate in the response phase.

Once the priority concerns of the whole community have been voted upon, the planning team begins to design the educational and liturgical programs which will occupy the response phase of the process. They can use the principles of scope and process explained in this book as a short cut to that design. The participants have identified themes and topics of scope by voting upon their faith and morality concerns. The planning team then notes whether the themes relate more or less to the historical, theological, liturgical, or ethical dimensions of faith. Depending upon which they relate to, educational and worship experiences using disclosure, inquiry, initiation, or problem-solving are used. Usually six sessions are offered during the two weeks of immediate response and an undetermined number during the months and years of continuing response.

The process takes thirteen weeks to complete: a week to fill in the survey; three weeks to prepare for reflection groups; five weeks of reflection; two weeks to prepare response; and two weeks of immediate response followed by as lengthy a period of continuing response as is deemed necessary.

With respect to the organizing principle stated above, "Growth in Faith Together" expresses the overall objective. The research and reflection phases are an extended effort for participants and planners to determine needs together and to choose the dimensions of Christian faith and life that will satisfy those needs. During response these needs are met by using processes, settings, and times which are required to satisfy those growth and learning needs.

GIFT is but one application of this organizing principle. I use it only as a concrete illustration of how the Master Design presented in this book can be practically applied. Once, however, the methodology that underlies this Design and its principles are grasped, an infinite variety of programs can be designed from it.

Administration

Applying the Master Design to practical application raises the general concern of administration. Here I speak, not so much of the role of administration as described above under Personnel,[4] but of the administrative practicality of the Master Design itself or of any particular designs based upon it.

The concern for administrative practicality can be expressed in the question: How administratively practical are the principles enunciated in answer to each question in objective, personnel, scope, process, context, and timing as organized by the organizing principle?[5] This is a constantly recurring preoccupation that must influence the framing of every principle of the Master Design and every application of the principles to the decisions that make up a particular program. The effort has been made to make each principle practical in the foregoing Design. I have found them practical in experience when designing particular programs.

I am quite aware, however, that the fruit of analytic planning can become frightfully unstuck in practice. Planned learning is only infrequently the learning which happens. However, more frequently, the unexpected learning which happens would not have occurred had not other learnings, perhaps unfulfilled, been planned.

Evaluation

Evaluation can be made either of the results of a program or of the very process by which a program is planned. The results of a program in terms of learning outcomes, satisfied and unsatisfied expectations of participants, and future directions for learning should always be a part of adult programs. It will be most valuable to planners and participants to the degree that participants themselves evaluate their own growth. This kind of evaluation is most important for future programs.

4 *Supra*, 102-03.
5 *Supra*, 57-58.

However, the kind of evaluation that concerns us most here is ongoing evaluation of the planning process itself. It is crystalized by three constantly recurring questions as planning goes on: Are these categories of curriculum inquiry necessary and sufficient to raise all the significant curricular questions? Are the questions within each category necessary and sufficient to deal with the distinct problem that the category faces? and Are the answers to the questions in each category adequately reflective of the most reliable data sources? [6] I can only answer that, with respect to the Design explained in this book, the categories, questions, and principles are as adequate as I can arrive at for the present. How they will stand the test of time I do not know.

The principles themselves which make up this Master Design will probably last but briefly. Data from the increasing experience of adult educators and from the foundational disciplines will call for their constant revision.

The methodology, however, which is used to arrive at the principles may endure longer. It is developed out of the sound educational tradition which sired the Cooperative Curriculum Project. However, because of the very principle of self-criticism which is built into the methodology, it is destined to be transcended by more pointed curricular questions and more adequately delineated categories of inquiry.

What may endure longest is the process which this study has followed and the example it has given. The study has been an exercise in arriving at curriculum principles. First, it demands an open disclosure of one's methodology. Second, it asks an analysis of the experience of adult Christian education. Third, it requires a searching review of the foundational disciplines for guidance in framing these principles. I have found this exercise of great benefit in sorting out the factors that interrelate in program design and in making decisions about them. I invite others to pursue the same exercise of systematic and analytic planning for adult Christian education for the benefit of all of us who labor in the profession but especially of all adults who deserve the opportunity to grow to full maturity in Christ.

6 *Supra*, 55-57.

Appendix A

Table of Contents of

A PROPOSED CURRICULUM DESIGN FOR ADULT CHRISTIAN EDUCATION FOR USE IN CATHOLIC DIOCESES

A DISSERTATION

By

JAMES R. SCHAEFER

The Catholic University of America
Washington, D.C.
1971

Table of Contents

PART III. ANALYSES OF CATHOLIC DIOCESAN
PLANNING AND COORDINATION OF ADULT
CHRISTIAN EDUCATION PROGRAMS

PART IV. DEVELOPMENT OF A CURRICULUM
DESIGN FOR ADULT CHRISTIAN EDUCATION
FOR USE IN CATHOLIC DIOCESES

Appendix B

QUESTIONS TO ASK IN PLANNING A PROGRAM

This is a slightly revised version of my article incorrectly titled "Questions to Ask before Planning a Program" which first appeared in *PACE—Professional Approaches for Christian Educators,* ed. by Sheila Moriarty (Winona, Minn.: St. Mary's College Press, [n.d.]), Planning-Tactics-A-pp. 1-12.

Questions to Ask in Planning a Program

You are going to plan a program of religious education. It is for adults. Good. You won't have to tailor it to a scholastic schedule and an academic setting. You can start fresh. You have few models to imitate. The pain as well as the promise of creativity is yours.

Immediately questions begin. Shall we have a six week course? Shall we use the Dutch Catechism as a discussion guide? Who will teach? Who is likely to come? How much should we charge for books? Are we going to have books? Is the hall free Wednesday nights? Maybe we can have a home discussion program. What about a race relations workshop? What speakers can really draw people? What is the best time to hold classes? Why do we want a program? Who is responsible for registering people? Should we write to Gabriel Moran and ask him what to do? Should we have refreshments before or after? Why not use the Christian Experience Series? Who should be involved in this planning anyway? Wait a minute. Questions are tumbling out all over the place. We'll stumble over ourselves in answering them. Likely as not the answers will contradict one another.

What is needed is to reduce the questions to an unavoidable minimum and then ask them in an efficient sequence. Here I presume that those doing the asking are a group somewhat representative of the persons for whom the program is being planned. Hopefully, at a later stage, the prospective participants will share in the planning process.

In looking for irreducible questions, it is difficult to improve upon the basic "who? what? where? why? when? how?" Asking the questions in an efficient sequence, that is, in a sequence which attends to first things first and avoids the necessity of skipping to later questions for answers to former ones, is a more delicate matter. I have a sequence to suggest. But it depends upon a more thorough development of the questions. Accordingly, let me develop the questions first, and then indicate why the sequence in which I ask them makes sense.

The first question for the planning team to ask is "why?" It seeks the overall purpose of the program. Perhaps the question can be put more explicitly, "What is the purpose of the program we are designing?" In answering the question, all kinds of goals and sub-goals will spill out—goals as to the persons the program hopes to attract, goals as to its content and methods, goals as to target dates, etc. All these, however, will receive their proper attention in answers to later questions. Here is desired a succinct statement of overall purpose for the program—the general direction it will take, the final objective it hopes to achieve. To avoid getting into goals and sub-goals, it is important to express the objective in as few words as possible—five or ten at most. The statement will be frustratingly general and vague. An overall orientation cannot be otherwise. Also, it cannot be but tentative and provisional at the outset. Every decision taken at later stages of questioning will hone the objective more sharply. But, however provisional, the initial statement of purpose gets the planning process rolling in a definite direction.

Once sharpened through the rest of the planning process, the statement of objective functions significantly through the execution of the program. It becomes a rule of thumb by which all themes, topics, learning dynamics are considered appropriate or inappropriate, germane or extraneous. Moreover, the overall purpose provides the criterion of evaluation for the program's success or failure. If the participants achieve the objective, the program is successful for the purpose for which it was designed. If not, it has failed. Such statements of objective might be: "that persons become aware of God's continuing revelation" or "that they become more fully human" or "that they learn more fully the mystery of Christ." Each of those statements reveals how different theological and educational presuppositions determine a program's purpose. Part of the reason for stating an initial objective is to get those presuppositions out in the open.

The next question for the planning team to address is "who?" It has to be asked in several ways. "Who will be the 'learners' in this program?" As much as possible they must be known in terms of their individual needs. Questionnaires, exploratory discussions, sample surveys, all may be helpful in finding out who the participants are in terms of their interests and concerns. Also, the question must be asked "Who are the resource persons who can best respond to the participants' needs?" The resource persons may be the learners themselves, but more often than not a learner is considered in terms of needs and a resource person in terms of competency to meet those needs. Hopefully, the resource person welcomes the resources of learners and admits needs himself which can be met even in the learning situation where he fills the role of resource person.

The roles of learners and resource persons in the program also pertain to the question "who?" Shall the resource person be a seminar director and the learner a questioner? Shall the resource person be a facilitator and the learner a discoverer? Perhaps the question can be generically phrased: "What will be the roles of learners and resource persons in the program?" Obviously, the answer must await answers to the "what?" and the "how?" of the program.

The next question, then, is "what?" The question seeks what some may call the content or subject matter of the program. I prefer to call it scope and to define scope as the meanings which the program hopes to explore or communicate. To conceive of scope in terms of meanings rather than content or subject matter seems more promising in avoiding the impression of learning just facts, or information, or a set of "right beliefs." This conception of scope is based upon the independent efforts of Philip Phenix [1] and Bernard Lonergan [2] to redefine the classic "man is a rational animal" into "man is an incarnate subject who discovers, creates and expresses meaning(s)." To recover old meanings, to discover new ones, to share meanings provide the "what?" of a religious education program. Moreover, it provides the "what?" in such a way as to open and not constrict the way to the "how?" of recovering, discovering, and sharing meaning. Consequently the interrelationship of scope and process (content and method) becomes a practical possibility.

These presuppositions stated, it becomes possible to ask questions regarding the "what?" of the program. It is too limiting to ask immediately "What shall we teach or what shall we learn in this program?" The theoretical question should first be addressed "What is appropriate scope for adult religious education?" In reply, the planning team must come clean with its judgment, explicit or implied, as to what is germane to religious education. I have found the following delineation of scope useful: the scope of Christian education is the meaning of the Church's experience of the mystery of Christ; more broadly, the scope of religious education is the meaning of mankind's experience of the mystery of God; and still more broadly, the scope of human education is the meaning of mankind's experience of the mystery of man. You may not agree with the distinctions but at least they illustrate the kind of latent judgment the question wishes to unearth.

1 *Realms of Meaning*, 21.
2 "Theology in Its New Context" in Shook (ed.), *Theology of Renewal*, I, 39-40.

So broad theoretical answers as these are still quite removed from the practical task of selecting meanings for the program to explore and communicate. Additional questions are necessary. One is "What dimensions of meaning or themes or topics does your broad description of scope (content) lend itself to?" For instance, the field of theology is frequently divided into dogma, moral, liturgy, scripture, catechetics, etc. Almost an infinite number of themes and topics belong to each division. You may wish to treat one or several of these.

Any convenient division which you find in the scope of religious education is a step but only a step in deciding what meanings to aim for in the program. An additional question must be asked: "How are these dimensions, themes, or topics to be selected for inclusion in the program?" If you have done your homework on the needs of participants and competence of available resource persons, negotiation between the two will determine what you finally select from the whole range of possible meanings. It is important, however, to have considered the whole range before limiting your selection to the possible and practical.

Another important question regarding scope is "How shall the continuity of learning be provided for chronologically?" More often than not, educational planners dismiss the question. They feel that learners will build their own sequence and interrelationships of meanings. Perhaps that is the only realistic stance to take in adult education but the manner in which learnings may be built one upon another deserves some attention all the same.

It is not sufficient, of course, to ask what meanings shall be explored and communicated. It must also be asked "how?" Recovering the meaning of Paul in the Epistle to the Romans might be achieved through informative exegetical lectures or seminars. Discovering the meaning of love may not be found except through interpersonal sharing in a supportive group process. Learning dynamics differ greatly according to the kinds of meanings that are to be explored and communicated.

Just as the "what?" questions begin on the theoretical level and work to the practical, so should the "how?" questions. The first is "How do we expect learning to happen in this program?" What one expects, of course, may be quite different from what happens; but, it is important from the outset for the planning team to get hidden learning theories out in the open. Latent rules of thumb that never get aired have a way of prejudicing whatever processes are planned or attempted. Persons who think most learning happens through listening plan lectures; those who think it happens through seeing plan films; those who think it happens through inquiry plan buzz sessions; those who think it happens through unstructured interchange (if there is such a thing) don't plan anything beyond inviting persons to get together. There are uses to all these dynamics. It depends what kinds of learning are desired.

Consequently the next question in moving the "how?" of the program from theory to practice is "What kinds of learning will this program seek?" If informational learning is sought, lectures will do. If in-depth cognitive learning is desired, group inquiry will be better. If affective learning is hoped for, sensitivity techniques may be required. If attitudinal learning is to be achieved, warmth and trust must condition the process. If value learning is the goal, the integrity and authenticity of the resource person are all important. Notice that the kinds of learning desired must exactly correlate to the kinds of meaning selected for scope if there is to be effective interrelationship between the scope (content) and process (methods) of the program.

If the meanings to be explored and consequently the kinds of learning desired have arisen from the felt needs of learners, motivation to achieve those learnings should be high. However, frequently there are meanings and corresponding kinds of learnings for which persons feel no need and yet for which they have a need. This is the often made distinction between felt and real needs. When such is the case the further question arises "What motivation will be conducive to these kinds of learning?" It is far easier to ask the question than to answer it. But the question must be asked whenever there is a gap between the felt needs of learners and the meanings which planners think important to communicate.

The remaining question under "how?" brings theory finally to the level of practice: "What learning dynamics give promise of achieving the kinds of learning desired?" As the examples in the last paragraph indicate, the learning dynamics or techniques—the practical "how?" or methods—are determined by the kinds of learning desired which are in turn determined by the kinds of meaning to be explored or communicated. That, at least, is the usual flow in program design. However, sometimes a certain process, especially a group dynamic, is the very learning that is desired. When that is so, then the meaning to be explored or communicated must be the kind that accords with that process. For instance, if the decision is first taken that the dynamic will be one of facilitating the affective feelings of group members one for another, the meaning to be communicated could hardly be that of transignification as compared to transubstantiation in the Eucharist.

The questions of "what?" and "how?" are the thorniest to resolve in planning a program. Yet, even if answered most ingeniously, their effect can largely be negated by failing to give adequate consideration to questions regarding "where?" and "when?"

"Where?" has to do with the context and environment for learning. Like questions of "what?" and "how?" the questions can begin on a theoretical level, especially if the planning teams wish to appreciate the larger context of life within which planned learning takes place. However, it usually suffices to ask three practical questions regarding grouping, structure, and place. "How shall the learners group themselves or be grouped in the program?" Interest in a topic, common age group, common sex, common profession—all provide different principles of grouping. "How shall the group be structured?" A seminar provides one structure, a small discussion another, the usual classroom situation another. Paul Bergevin, Dwight Morris, and Robert Smith [3] describe an endless variety of such structures. "Where will the learning sessions take place?" completes the practical questions of context. A living room, a theater, a lecture hall, a slum might be chosen.

Usually decisions as to grouping, structure, and place should follow upon decisions regarding scope ("what?") and process ("how?"). Contrariwise, the unavailability of space not infrequently limits possibilities as to scope and process. The advantage of planning for adult religious education programs is that questions of context can be decided after questions of scope and process. In the academic setting, the environment, usually a school, is inherited and the scope and process must be tailored accordingly.

Questions of "when?" deserve consideration last despite the fact that scheduling is frequently the first thing done in planning a program. As with questions of "where?" the advantage of planning adult programs is that one does not have to fit learnings into a predetermined academic calendar. One is free to work out scheduling in accord with the time it will take to achieve the learnings decided upon. However, it is usually the practicalities of time—how much learners and resource persons can afford, when the facilities are available—that restrict a program to manageable limits. Likewise, it is usually only under the gun of target dates that the planning team abandons the luxury of speculation for the discipline of practical planning.

A theoretical question of timing, "When does learning occur?" can help the planning team realize that learning is an ongoing occurrence

[3] *Adult Education Procedures.*

of which planned learning is but a small part. Another serious question of timing which also comes before the mechanics of scheduling is "How can this program respond to current events in the Church and in society at large?" Conflict situations and crises frequently provide special "learnable moments" in the lives of adults. To seize upon them is the mark of alert program planners. Seven thousand adults in the diocese of Lansing responded to an invitation to study the Kerner Report in group sessions two weeks after the assassination of Dr. Martin Luther King, Jr. in 1968.

These are some of the questions regarding timing before the practical question of scheduling is met: "What will be the frequency and duration of learning sessions in the program?"

These are the questions I consider irreducible and unavoidable regarding the factors of objective (why?), personnel (who?), scope (what?), process (how?), context (where?), and timing (when?) in planning educational programs. There are two additional concerns to keep in mind as the planning team goes about answering them. The first is that the answers must be consistent with one another. In curriculum theory, this is referred to as the concern for an organizing principle. The second is that the answers must be administratively practical. Otherwise the program will present an edifying design doomed to failure.

It remains to indicate why I suggest this and not another sequence of questions. It is important, of course, that all the questions be understood and considered before answering any of them. The reason is that decisions taken with respect to one question affect decisions that can be taken in response to others. For example, timing ought to be the last question answered but the anticipation of answering it severely limits choices that can be made with reference to scope and process.

The sequence which I propose depends upon these considerations. First, it is not possible to begin planning without at least a hunch as to the end in view (objective). Secondly, persons such as adults who are not forced to go to school by law, usually learn what they feel a need to learn. Accordingly, personnel, especially the person of the learner, deserves attention after the objective. Thirdly, needs find their solution in the discovery, recovery, or creation of meaning. Therefore, scope belongs next. Fourthly, meanings are discovered, recovered, and created by processes, by learning dynamics. Consequently, process should receive attention next. Both the meanings decided upon and the processes by which they are learned determine the social and spatial environment (context) in which they can be learned and how long (timing) it will take to learn them. To repeat, it is necessary to run back and forth through the questions because answers to some influence answers to others. For instance the needs of learners and competencies of resource persons should be sought prior to making decisions about scope and process. Yet decisions as to scope and process determine the roles of learners and resource persons in the program. So also, the availability of time and facilities largely limit options as to scope and process. Every step of the planning process refines or even corrects the original objective. However, the flow of planning runs predominantly from initiating purpose, to needs, to meanings, to learning dynamics, to learning environment, to scheduling. For that reason I suggest a sequence of questions which runs why? who? what? how? where? when?

Perhaps the following schematic outline of planning factors and questions within each factor will clarify the sequence of steps in planning a religious education program:

Objective (why)? —The purpose which the program hopes to help the learner achieve.
What is the purpose of this program?

Personnel (who?)—The persons who learn from and teach one another through the program.
Who are the learners and teachers?
What are their needs and competencies?
How shall they interrelate in the program (what will be the roles of the learners and teachers)?

Scope (what?)   —The meanings which the program hopes to explore and communicate.
What is appropriate scope for religious education?
What dimensions, themes, or topics does this scope lend itself to?
How are these dimensions, themes, or topics to be selected for inclusion in the program?
In what sequence can they be most fruitfully offered?

Process (how?)   —The dynamics by which learning is expected to happen in the program.
How is learning expected to happen in the program?
What kinds of learning will this program seek?
What motivation will be conducive to these kinds of learning?
What learning dynamics give promise of achieving the kinds of learning desired?

Context (where?)—The social and spatial environment of learning.

Where does learning take place?

How shall the participants be grouped or group themselves?

How shall the learning session be structured?

Where shall the learning session take place?

Timing (when?) —The succession of events and experiences by which learning is expected to occur in the program.

When does learning occur?

How does the program respond to current events in the church and in society at large?

What shall be the frequency and duration of learning sessions in the program?

Appendix C

A REVISED QUESTIONNAIRE TO EXPLORE CURRICULUM PRINCIPLES WHICH GUIDE AN ADULT CHRISTIAN EDUCATION PROGRAM

This instrument can be used by a planning team to uncover its latent theory of adult Christian education and to frame the principles which will guide the team in designing programs. The questionnaire is adapted from the one used in the Dissertation (pp. 578-85) in light of a refined methodology.

Questionnaire to Explore Curriculum Principles Which Guide an Adult Christian Education Program

Please do not answer any questions until you thoroughly understand the following methodology and concepts upon which they are based.

PRELIMINARY CONCEPTS

Adult A person of the age of twenty-five years or more having commensurate maturity.

Christian education The ways and means by which, in accord with the character of Christianity and the process of education, persons freely participate in teaching and learning the Christian faith and life.

Curriculum The sum of all learning experiences provided for in the curriculum plan.

Curriculum plan An intentional and explicit provision of learning opportunities.

Other necessary concepts will be defined in outlining the following methodology.

METHODOLOGY

This questionnaire rests upon the conviction that the task of planning curriculum is that of reducing curricular questions to an unavoidable minimum and answering these questions with principles capable of guiding concrete curriculum decisions.

It understands those questions to be ultimately reducible to six: why; who; what; how; where; and when. To each of these questions corresponds a *category of curriculum inquiry:* objective; personnel;

scope; process; context; and timing. Within each category a *major question circumscribes the general but distinct problem with which the category deals.* Several *subordinate questions contribute to or draw out the implications of the major question.*

The *objective* is *the purpose which the curriculum plan seeks to help the learner achieve.* The category of objective comprises the irreducible and unavoidable questions which seek that purpose. It wishes to know the "why" of curriculum.

Personnel are *the persons who learn from and teach one another in the educational process.* The category of personnel comprises the irreducible and unavoidable questions needed to discover the persons who learn from and teach one another in the educational process and the roles according to which they interrelate. It asks the "who" of curriculum.

The *scope* is *the meanings (subject matter, content) which the curriculum plan intends to explore and communicate.* The category of scope includes the irreducible and unavoidable questions which seek those meanings and their communicability. It asks the "what" of curriculum.

Process is *the dynamics by which the teaching-learning experience happens.* The category of process consists of the irreducible and unavoidable questions needed to arrive at the methods that will best ensure the desired teaching-learning experience. It seeks the "how" of curriculum.

The *context* is *the social and spatial environment of learning.* A *setting* within the context is *a specifically structured and situated grouping for learning.* The category of context embraces the irreducible and unavoidable questions needed to arrive at the overall and particular social and spatial environment for learning. It searches the "where" of curriculum.

Timing is *the succession of events and experiences during which learning occurs.* The category of timing considers the irreducible and unavoidable questions needed to discover the succession of events and experiences that will best promise the occurrence of learning. It explores the "when" of curriculum.

The questions in each category seek by way of answers curriculum principles. By a *curriculum principle* is meant *a judgment expressing the dependable relationship between two or more educational variables which guides curriculum planning and practice.* Principles are major or subordinate depending on whether they answer major or subordinate questions. A principle is *declarative if it states a relationship of fact based upon a theological and/or philosophical interpretation of the variables and their interrelation.* It can usually be expressed by the present tense of the copulative verb. A principle is *prescriptive if it relies upon an analysis of the functions of the educational variables between which it expresses the dependable relationship.* It can usually be expressed by "should" or "must." A principle is *selective if it chooses among the many relationships that may obtain between variables one that will govern a particular curriculum plan.* It can usually be expressed by the future tense. The cast of a curricular question usually indicates whether a declarative, prescriptive, or selective principle is appropriate. The foregoing are stated principles. Also to be considered are operative principles. An *operative* principle is *one which, whether stated or implied, actually and effectively guides concrete* curriculum decisions. Not all stated principles are operative in actual curriculum planning and not all principles actually operative in curriculum planning are stated.

Curriculum principles deserve justification. They receive it from the experience of curriculum planners including learners insofar as they participate in the planning process. This experience, however, should be broadened, informed, criticized, and corrected by those systematically organized bodies of experience which form the foundational disciplines of Christian education. These include, at least, theology, philosophy, education, history, sociology, psychology, and communications. *Justification of curriculum principles are here referred to as foundational presuppositions.*

The curricular problems which the categories of inquiry address are distinct but not independent. So, too, the curriculum principles which answer them are interdependent. Thus arises the *general concern of organizing the curriculum.* This concern wishes to know how the answer given to each major and subordinate question will exercise its proper influence in planning the entire curriculum. The concern of organizing the curriculum seeks, then, an *organizing principle, that is, a statement embodying the evaluative judgment which relates the principles of objective, personnel, scope, process, context, and timing one to another in such a way that each exercises its proper guidance upon curriculum planning.*

There are two other general curriculum concerns that cut across the categories of inquiry. One is evaluating the very process of planning the curriculum; the other is the concern for administering the curriculum plan. Although these concerns can be put in the form of curricular questions, they are more properly continual preoccupations for the validity and administrative practicality of both the questions and the answers in the six categories and in the concern of organizing the curriculum.

Curriculum decisions, curriculum principles, and foundational presuppositions have been differentiated. They depend on one another. The reasons for curriculum decisions are found in curriculum principles; the reasons for curriculum principles in foundational presuppositions. *Considered another way, principles mediate presuppositions from the foundational disciplines to curriculum practice.* Decisions, principles, and presuppositions are not easy to differentiate in the actual planning of curriculum. This questionnaire asks you to try to identify them.

In the questionnaire, numbered questions (1, 2, 3, etc.) seek major or subordinate curriculum principles. Questions lettered small case "a" seek foundational presuppositions. Questions lettered small case "b" seek curriculum decisions.

When the operative principles which guide curriculum practice are identified and justified then the *curriculum design* upon which a program is based is revealed. Once revealed it can be critically improved. A *curriculum design is the systematic articulation, justification, and explanation of the principles which effectively guide a particular curriculum plan and their correlation by an organizing principle.* To arrive at the curriculum design of your adult Christian education programs is the purpose of this questionnaire.

DIRECTIONS

Since this questionnaire explores the curriculum principles which guide your practical planning, it is important that all the persons who make significant planning decisions collaborate in answering the questions.

However, it is suggested that each person first answer the questionnaire independently and then that the leader of the planning team try to collate the answers. Then the team members should come together to examine individual responses and the collated reply and to negotiate differences until a commonly agreed upon curriculum design is reached.

In answering the questionnaire, team members are asked first to read all the questions several times to gain an understanding both of the distinct thrust of each major and subordinate question and of the interrelation of the questions one to another. It is especially necessary to have a grasp of all the questions within a given category before answering a single question in that category.

It will help if answers are typewritten and if, following the sequence in which the questions occur, they are lettered and numbered accordingly.

QUESTIONS IN SIX CATEGORIES

A. *Objective*

1. *Major question:* Why (what is the purpose of) adult Christian education?
   a. What is your justification for this statement?
2. Subordinate question: What is (are) the function(s) of this objective?
   a. Give evidence of the objective's influencing actual curriculum planning and practice.
3. Subordinate question: What is the relationship between the objective and the purpose of the Church?
   a. Why do you conceive this relationship as you do?
   b. How has this conviction practically influenced your cooperation with other church agencies and ministries?

B. *Personnel*

1. *Major Question:* Who are the learners and teachers in adult Christian education?
   a. What is the justification for this statement?
2. Subordinate question: What do you consider God's role in adult Christian education?
   a. What is your justification for this statement?
   b. What evidence is there of its practical influence upon your program planning?
3. Subordinate question: What do you consider the role of the College of Bishops to be in adult Christian education?
   a. What is your justification for this statement?
   b. How does it influence practical curriculum decisions?
4. Subordinate question: What principle governs the learner's role in your programs?
   a. Why this principle?
   b. What practical consequences does this principle have upon the learner's engagement in your programs?
5. Subordinate question: What principle governs the teacher's role in your programs?

a. Why this principle?

b. What evidence is there that teachers actually operate according to this principle in your programs?

6. Subordinate question: What are the roles of participants in building your programs?

a. How do you justify this principle?

b. How is it evidenced in your process of curriculum decision-making?

7. Subordinate question: What determines the roles of administrative personnel with respect to your programs?

a. How is this principle justified?

b. How is it seen at work in practice?

C. *Scope*

1. *Major Question:* What is appropriate scope for adult Christian education?

a. What is your justification for this statement?

2. Subordinate question: How comprehensive should the scope of an adult Christian education program be?

a. What is your reason for this statement?

b. What concrete curriculum decisions evidence the influence of this statement upon them?

3. Subordinate question: What dimensions of scope lend themselves to different kinds of adult Christian learning?

a. What is your justification for this statement?

4. Subordinate question: How do you select dimensions of scope for inclusion in programs?

a. What is your justification for this criterion?

b. What concrete learning opportunities do you provide which give evidence of this criterion at work?

5. Subordinate question: What principle governs the sequence of learnings in your programs?

a. What is the justification for this principle?

b. How does it influence the sequence with which learning opportunities are actually offered in your programs?

D. *Process*

1. *Major Question:* How does adult Christian learning happen?

a. What is your justification for this statement?

2. Subordinate question: What kinds of adult Christian learnings do you seek through your programs?

a. Why these kinds?

3. Subordinate question: How do you elicit the learner's motivation in pursuing these kinds of learning?

    a. Why this way?

    b. What evidence have you that motivation is actually elicited?

4. Subordinate question: What teaching-learning modes do you use to help the learner achieve these kinds of learning?

    a. Why these modes?

    b. Give examples of concrete educational methods which incorporate these modes.

E.   Context

1. *Major Question:* Where does adult Christian learning take place?

    a. What is your reason for this statement?

2. Subordinate question: What principle do you follow in grouping persons for adult learnings?

    a. What is your reason for this statement?

    b. Give examples of this principle at work in actual settings.

3. Subordinate question: What principle do you follow in structuring adult learning groups (lecture, class, seminar, group discussion, etc.)?

    a. Why are they structured this way?

    b. Describe some concrete settings which demonstrate the application of this principle.

4. Subordinate question: What principle do you follow in selecting places where the learning group meets?

    a. What is your justification for this principle?

    b. How is it followed in practice?

F.   Timing

1. *Major Question:* When does adult Christian learning occur?

    a. What is the justification of this statement?

2. Subordinate question: What principle governs the responsiveness of your programs to God's present activity in history?

    a. What is the justification of this principle?

    b. What is the evidence that this principle influences programs in practice?

3. Subordinate question: What principle governs the responsiveness of your programs to current events in the Church and in the world?

    a. What is the justification of this principle?

b. What is the evidence that this principle influences programs in practice?

4. Subordinate question: What principle governs the responsiveness of your programs to the readiness conditioned by the learner's age and experience?
   a. What is the reason for this principle?
   b. What is the evidence that it influences programs in practice?

5. Subordinate question: What determines the frequency and duration with which you offer learning sessions?
   a. What is your justification for this principle?
   b. How has it influenced practical decisions as to the frequency and duration of actual program offerings?

QUESTIONS REGARDING THREE GENERAL CONCERNS

AA. *Organization*

Please answer one of the following questions:
If you consider scope the key to organizing curriculum:
What dimensions of *scope* shall *persons* master through a *process timed* and *situated* so as to achieve the *objective?*
If you consider process the key to organizing curriculum:
How shall the *process* be *timed* and *situated* to enable *persons* to master the *scope* in order to achieve the *objective?*
The answer to either of these questions should express in a single sentence the interrelationship of the principles you framed in each category.

BB. *Evaluation*

What evidence is there that your process of planning curriculum is under continuous reevaluation?

CC. *Administration*

What evidence is there that your asking and answering of curricular questions continually respects administrative practicality?

Appendix D

AN ACTUAL PROGRAM DESIGN BASED UPON THE
MASTER DESIGN PROPOSED IN THIS BOOK

PRACTICUM IN PLANNING ADULT CHRISTIAN EDUCATION

Objective: to introduce adult religious educators to a methodology of designing programs of adult Christian education, to explore the theological and educational principles upon which that design is based, and to provide a supervised experience of planning such programs.

For whom: leaders and members of teams who plan adult Christian education programs. (limit 30)

| | | FIRST DAY |
| | | Context and |
Scope	Process	Timing
Get acquainted; review of participants' expectations; negotiation between expectations and pre-arranged practicum design.	—Round table discussion	classroom 9-11 AM
An exercise in random identification of curriculum questions by participants.	—Brainstorming—three recorders at blackboard	
A methodology of arranging curriculum questions.	—Explanation illustrated by overhead transparencies	
Clarification	—Discussion	
An exercise in random identification of personal, audio-visual, and printed resources for adult Christian education.	—Brainstorming—three recorders with newsprint and magic markers	classroom 2:30-4:30 PM
The need for criteria of selection.	—Explanation illustrated by overhead transparencies	
Determining the felt needs of participants.	" "	
Determining the dimensions of scope (content) of adult Christian education.	—Explanation illustrated by overhead transparencies	
Selecting the appropriate process.	" "	
The scope-process interrelationship.	" "	
Clarification	—Discussion	

Scope	Process	SECOND DAY Context and Timing
An experience of learning historical knowledge of the Christ event through disclosure.	—Filmstrip on salvation history	theater 9-11 AM
Reflection upon the experience and its learning value.	—Discussion	
Interrelationship between eventful dimension of Christianity, historical knowledge, and disclosure.	—Explanation illustrated bv overhead transparencies	
Learning dynamics which use the mode of disclosure.	" "	
Clarification	—Discussion	
An experience of learning cognitive understanding of Christian faith through inquiry.	—Fishbowl discussion, eight in center circle discussing, rest in outer circle observing; question "Does the war in Vietnam have anything to do with the death and resurrection of Jesus?"	lounge 2:30-4:30 PM
Reflection upon the experience and its learning value.	—Discussion by all	
Interrelationship between Christianity as a faith-horizon, cognitive understanding, and inquiry.	—Explanation illustrated by overhead transparencies	
Learning dynamics which use the mode of inquiry.	" "	
Clarification	—Discussion	

		THIRD DAY
		Context and
Scope	*Process*	*Timing*
An experience of learning appreciation for liturgical celebration through initiation.	—Shared prayer before the exposed Eucharist	chapel 9-11 AM
Reflecting upon the experience and its learning value.	—Discussion	
Interrelationship between celebrating the mystery of Christ, appreciation, and initiation.	—Explanation illustrated by overhead transparencies	
Learning dynamics which use the mode of initiation.	″ ″	
Clarification	—Discussion	
An experience of learning responsibility to Christian moral imperative through problem-solving.	—Buzz groups to solve ethical "case"	lounge 2:30-4:30 PM
Reflection upon the experience and its learning value.	—Discussion	
Interrelationship between moral imperative, responsibility, and problem-solving.	—Explanation illustrated by overhead transparencies	
Learning dynamics which use the mode of problem-solving.	″ ″	
Clarification	—Discussion	

		FOURTH DAY
		Context and
Scope	*Process*	*Timing*
Interrelationship of objective, personnel, scope, process, context, timing.	—Explanation illustrated by overhead transparencies	classroom 9-11 AM
Organizing principle of a design.	" "	
The key: The scope-process interrelationship.	" "	
Assignment of tasks: teams of six persons each to plan five different original designs for adult Christian education.	—Explanation and negotiation	
Designing adult Christian education programs.	—Participants work in groups of six to plan one design in each group	Participants' rooms or any other convenient place; afternoon and evening, if needed

		FIFTH DAY
		Context and
Scope	*Process*	*Timing*
Review of first three designs.	—Each team presents its own design; other participants critically assess	classroom 9-11 AM (40 minutes each design)
Review of second three designs.	" "	classroom 2:30-4:30 PM (40 minutes each design)
Evaluation of Practicum.	—Written and oral by participants	

Bibliography

This is not a full bibliography on curriculum design for adult Christian education. Rather, it only contains the complete works, articles, curriculum resources, and unpublished works consulted in writing the Dissertation. Sources quoted in this book and in the Dissertation are marked by asterisks (*) and sources quoted in this book but not found in the bibliography of the Dissertation are marked by plus signs (+).

COMPLETE WORKS

* *The Age Group Objectives of Christian Education.* Prepared in connection with the Long-Range Program of Lutheran Boards of Parish Education. [Philadelphia:] The Boards of Parish Education of The American Evangelical Lutheran Church, The Augustana Lutheran Church, The Suomi Synod, The United Lutheran Church in America, 1958. Pp. 97.

* Alfaro, Juan. *Fides, Spes, Caritas: Adnotationes in Tractatum de Virtutibus Theologicis.* (Ad usum privatum auditorum.) Revised edition. Rome: Pontificia Universitas Gregoriana, 1964. Pp. 650.

* Altizer, Thomas J. J. *The Gospel of Christian Atheism.* Philadelphia: The Westminster Press, 1966. Pp. 157.

* Anderson, Bernhard W. (ed.) *The Old Testament and Christian Faith.* New York: Harper & Row Publishers, 1963. Pp. xiv+271.

* ———. *Understanding the Old Testament.* Second edition. Englewood Cliffs, N.J.: Prentice-Hall, Inc., 1966. Pp. xxi+586.

* Anderson, Vernon E. *Principles and Procedures of Curriculum Improvement.* Second edition. New York: The Ronald Press Company, 1965. Pp. xii+498.

Ban, Joseph D. *Education for Change.* Valley Forge, Pa.: The Judson Press, 1968. Pp. 126.

* Barr, James. *Old and New in Interpretation: A Study of the Two Testaments.* London: SCM Press Ltd., 1966. Pp. 215.

Batchelder, Richard L. and Hardy, James M. *Using Sensitivity Training and the Laboratory Method: An Organizational Case Study in the*

Development of Human Resources. New York: Association Press, 1968. Pp. 128.

Benne, Kenneth D. and Muntyan, Bozidar (edd.). *Human Relations in Curriculum Change.* New York: The Dryden Press, 1951. Pp. xx+363.

* Bennett, John C. *et al. Storm over Ethics.* Philadelphia: The United Press, 1967. Pp. vii+183.

Benson, Clarence H. *A Popular History of Christian Education.* Chicago: Moody Press, 1943. Pp. 355.

Bergevin, Paul. *A Philosophy for Adult Education.* New York: The Seabury Press, 1967. Pp. xi+176.

* ———; Morris, Dwight; and Smith, Robert M. *Adult Education Procedures: A Handbook of Tested Patterns for Effective Participation.* Greenwich, Conn.: The Seabury Press, 1963. Pp. viii+245.

* ——— and McKinley, John. *Design for Adult Education in the Church.* Greenwich, Conn.: The Seabury Press, 1958. Pp. xxviii+320.

* Betts, George H. *The Curriculum of Religious Education.* New York: The Abingdon Press, 1924. Pp. 535.

Bischof, Ledford J. *Adult Psychology.* New York: Harper and Row, Publishers, 1969. Pp. x+310.

* Black, Matthew and Rowley, H. H. (edd.). *Peake's Commentary on the Bible.* London: Thomas Nelson and Sons Ltd., 1962. Pp. xvi+1126+ 4+16 maps.

* Boelke, Robert R. *Theories of Learning in Christian Education.* Philadelphia: The Westminster Press, 1962. Pp. 221.

* Bouyer, Louis. *Liturgical Piety.* Liturgical Studies. Notre Dame, Indiana: University of Notre Dame Press, 1955. Pp. xii+284.

Bovard, William Sherman. *Adults in the Sunday School: A Field and a Force.* New York: The Abingdon Press, 1917. Pp. 196.

* Bower, William C. *The Curriculum of Religious Education.* New York: Charles Scribner's Sons, 1928. Pp. xii+283.

——— and Hayward, Percy Roy. *Protestanism Faces Its Educational Task Together.* Appleton, Wisconsin: C. C. Nelson Publishing Company, 1949. Pp. xi+292.

* Brien, André. *La cheminement de la foi.* Paris: Éditions du Seuil, 1964. Pp. 240.

Brown, Arlo Ayres. *A History of Religious Education in Recent Times.* New York: The Abingdon Press, 1923. Pp. 282.

* Brown, Raymond E., Fitzmyer, Joseph A., and Murphy, Roland E. (edd.) *The Jerome Biblical Commentary,* Vol. I: *The Old Testament* and Vol. II: *The New Testament and Topical Articles.* Englewood Cliffs, New Jersey: Prentice-Hall, Inc., 1968. Pp. xxxvi+637+889.

* Bruner, Jerome S. *The Process of Education.* Cambridge, Mass.: Harvard University Press, 1963. Pp. xvii+97.

———. *Toward a Theory of Instruction.* Cambridge, Mass.: The Belknap Press of Harvard University Press, 1966. Pp. xi+176.

Brunner, Edmond deS. *et al. An Overview of Adult Education Research.*

234   PROGRAM PLANNING FOR ADULT CHRISTIAN EDUCATION

Chicago: Adult Education Association of the U.S.A., 1959. Pp. viii+279.
* Bultmann, Rudolph. *et al. Kerygma and Myth.* Ed. by H. W. Bartsch,
rev. ed. and trans. by R. H. Fuller. New York: Harper and Row,
Publishers, 1961. Pp. xiv+228.
Bushnell, Horace. *Christian Nurture.* New Haven: Yale University, 1888.
Pp. xl+351.
Cantor, Nathaniel. *Dynamics of Learning.* Third Edition. Buffalo, N.Y.:
Henry Stewart, Inc. Publishers, 1956. Pp. xx+296.
* Cartwright, Dorwin and Zander, Alvin (edd.). *Group Dynamics: Research
and Theory.* Second edition. New York: Harper & Row, Publishers,
1960. Pp. xii+826.
Case, Adelaide Teague. *Liberal Christianity and Religious Education: A
Study of Objectives in Religious Education.* New York: The Mac-
Millan Company, 1924. Pp. x+194.
* Casel, Odo. *The Mystery of Christian Worship and Other Writings.* Ed.
by Burkhard Neunheuser. Westminster, Md.: The Newman Press,
1962. Pp. xx+212.
* Casteel, John L. (ed.) *Spiritual Renewal through Personal Groups.* New
York: Association Press, 1957. Pp. 220.
Chamberlin, J. Gordon. *Freedom and Faith: New Approaches to Christian
Education.* Philadelphia: The Westminster Press, 1965. Pp .156.
————. *Parents and Religion: A Preface to Christian Education.* Phila-
delphia: The Westminster Press, 1961. Pp. 111.
* *The Church in Our Day.* A statement of the National Conference of
Catholic Bishops. Distributed by the United States Catholic Conference,
1312 Massachusetts Ave., Washington, D.C., 1968. Pp. 79.
* *The Church's Educational Ministry: A Curriculum Plan.* The Work of the
Cooperative Curriculum Project. St. Louis: The Bethany Press, 1965.
Pp. xxxii+848.
* Clements R. E. *Prophecy and Covenant.* Studies in Biblical Theology.
London: SCM Press Ltd., 1965. Pp. 135.
Clemmons, Robert F. *Dynamics of Christian Adult Education.* New York:
Abingdon Press, 1958. Pp. 143.
Coe, George Albert. *A Social Theory of Religious Education.* New York:
Charles Scribner's Sons, 1928. Pp. xiii+361.
* ————. *What is Christian Education?* New York: Charles Scribner's Sons,
1929. Pp. xii+300.
*The Constitution of the United Presbyterian Church in the United States
of America,* Part I: *Book of Confessions.* Published by the Office of the
General Assembly, Witherspoon Building, Philadelphia, 1967. Pp.
x+1.1-3-99.18.
* Cox. Harvey. *The Secular City: Secularization and Urbanization in Theo-
logical Perspective.* New York: The Macmillan Company, 1965. Pp.
276.
* Crowe, F. E. (ed.) *Collection: Papers by Bernard Lonergan S. J.* New
York: Herder and Herder, 1967. Pp. xxxviii+280.

* Cullmann, Oscar. *Salvation in History.* Trans. by Sidney G. Sowers. New York: Harper & Row, Publishers, 1967. Pp. 352.
* *The Design for the Curriculum of Education in the Ministry of Christian Churches (Disciples of Christ).* [St. Louis:] Christian Board of Publication, 1966. Pp. 48.
* *Design for Methodist Curriculum: A Statement of the Curriculum Committee, General Board of Education, The Methodist Church.* Nashville: Editorial Division, General Board of Education, 1965. Pp. 30.
* Dewey, John. *Democracy and Education: An Introduction to the Philosophy of Education.* New York: The Macmillan Company, 1916. Pp. xiv+434.
* DeWolf, L. Harold. *Teaching Our Faith in God.* Nashville: Abingdon Press, 1963. Pp. 188.
* *The Documents of Vatican II.* Ed. by Walter M. Abbott with an introduction by Lawrence Cardinal Shehan. Trans. ed. Joseph Gallagher. New York: Herder and Herder, 1966. Pp. xxii+793.
Doll, Ronald C. *Curriculum Improvement: Decision-Making and Process.* Boston: Allyn and Bacon, Inc., 1964. Pp. xiv+337.
Doniger, Simon. (ed.) *Becoming the Complete Adult.* New York: Association Press, 1962. Pp. 222.
Douglass, Paul F. *The Group Workshop Way in the Church.* New York: Association Press, 1956. Pp. xvi+174.
Douty, Mary Alice. *How to Work With Church Groups.* New York: The Abingdon Press, 1957. Pp. 170.
* *Educational Guide.* Prepared for the Educational Plan of the Church of the Brethren. [Elgin, Ill.: Christian Education Commission of the General Brotherhood Board, 1968]. Pp. 131.
* *Enchiridion Symbolorum: Definitionum et Declarationum de Rebus Fidei et Morum.* Ed. by Adolphus Schönmetzer, (originally ed. by Henricus Denziger). Thirty-second Edition. Freiburg im Breisgau: Herder, 1963. Pp. xxxi+907.
* Erikson, Erik H. *Childhood and Society.* Second edition revised and enlarged. New York: W. W. Norton & Company, Inc., 1963. Pp. 445.
* ———. *Identity: Youth and Crisis.* New York: W. W. Norton & Company, 1968. Pp. 336.
Ernsberger, David J. *A Philosophy of Adult Christian Education.* Philadelphia: The Westminster Press, 1959. Pp. 172.
Essert, Paul L. *Creative Leadership of Adult Education.* New York: Prentiss-Hall, Inc., 1951. Pp. xii+333.
* Ferré, Nels F. S. *A Theology for Christian Education.* Philadelphia: The Westminster Press, 1967. Pp. 224.
* Flavell, John H. *The Developmental Psychology of Jean Piaget.* With a foreword by Jean Piaget. The University Series in Psychology. Ed. by David C. McClelland. Princeton, N.J.: D. Van Nostrand Company, Inc., 1963. Pp. xvi+472.
* *Foundations for Curriculum.* American Baptist Approved Documents for

Curriculum Building. Valley Forge, Pa.: American Baptist Board of Education and Publication, 1966. Pp. 51+chart.

Fry, John R. *A Hard Look at Adult Christian Education.* Philadelphia, 1961. Pp. 150.

* Fuller, Reginald H. *The Foundations of New Testament Christology.* New York: Charles Scribner's Sons, 1965. Pp. 268.

The Functional Objectives for Christian Education. Vol. I. Prepared by the Joint Staff for a Long-Range Program of Parish Education. [Philadelphia: The Luthern Church in America], 1959. Pp. 437.

* Funk, Robert. *Language, Hermeneutic, and Word of God: The Problem of Language in the New Testament and Contemporary Theology.* New York: Harper & Row, Publishers, 1966. Pp. xviii+317.

* Goldbrunner, Josef. *Realization: Anthropology of Pastoral Care.* Liturgical Studies, No. 10. Trans. by Paul C. Bailey and Elisabeth Reinecke. Notre Dame, Ind.: University of Notre Dame Press, 1966. Pp. ix+221.

* Goodlad, John I. *School, Curriculum, and the Individual.* Waltham, Mass.: Blaisdell Publishing Company, 1966. Pp. viii+259.

Gorham, Donald R. *Understanding Adults.* Philadelphia: Judson Press, 1948. Pp. viii+141.

* Gustafson, James. *Christ and the Moral Life.* New York: Harper & Row, Publishers, 1968. Pp. xii+275.

* Häring, Bernard. *The Law of Christ: Moral Theology for Priests and Laity,* Vol. I: *General Moral Theology,* Vol. II: *Special Moral Theology: Life in Fellowship with God and Fellow Man.* Vol. III: *Special Moral Theology: Man's Assent to the All-embracing Majesty of God's Love.* Trans. by Edwin G. Kaiser. Cork: The Mercier Press, 1963-67. I, pp. xxxii+615. II, pp. xiv+573. III, pp. xxvi+735.

Hare, A. Paul; Borgatta, Edgar F.; Bales, Robert F. (edd.) *Small Groups: Studies in Social Interaction.* New York: Alfred A. Knopf, 1955. Pp. xv+666.

Havighurst, Robert J. *The Educational Mission of the Church.* Philadelphia: The Westminster Press, 1965. Pp. 159.

* ———. *Human Development and Education.* New York: David McKay Company, Inc., 1953. Pp. ix+338.

* Healy, Edwin F. *Medical Ethics.* Chicago: Loyola University Press, 1956. Pp. xxii+440.

* Hilgard, Ernest R. *Theories of Learning.* Second Edition. The Century Psychology Series. Ed. by Richard M. Elliott and Kenneth MacCorquodale. New York: Appleton, Century, Crofts, Inc., 1956. Pp. ix+563.

* ———. (ed.) *Theories of Learning and Instruction: The Sixty-Third Yearbook of the National Society for the Study of Education, Part I.* Chicago: The University of Chicago Press, 1964. Pp. xi+430+vi.

* Hofinger, Johannes. *The Art of Teaching Christian Doctrine: The Good News and Its Proclamation.* Revised edition. Notre Dame, Ind: University of Notre Dame Press, 1962. Pp. 290.

* ———. (ed.) *Teaching All Nations: A Symposium on Modern Catechetics.* Rev. and trans. by Clifford Howell. New York: Herder and Herder, 1961. Pp. xvi+421.

Howe, Reuel L. *The Creative Years.* New York: The Seabury Press, 1959. Pp. ix+239.

* *Human Life in Our Day.* A Statement of the National Conference of Catholic Bishops. Distributed by the United States Catholic Conference, 1312 Massachusetts Ave., Washington, D. C., 1968. Pp. 47.

Inlow, Gail M. *The Emergent in Curriculum.* New York: John Wiley and Sons, Inc., 1966. Pp. 353.

* *The Jerusalem Bible.* Ed. by Alexander Jones. Garden City: New York: Doubleday & Company, Inc., 1966. Pp. xvi+1548+498+8 maps.

* Jungmann, Josef A. *The Good News Yesterday and Today.* Trans. and ed. by William A. Huesman. New York: W. H. Sadlier, Inc., 1962. Pp. xii+228.

* ———. *Handing on the Faith: A Manual of Catechetics.* Trans. and rev. by A. N. Fuerst. New York: Herder and Herder, 1962, Pp. xiv+445.

Kant, Immanuel. *Critique of Pure Reason.* Trans. by F. Max Müller. Garden City, N.Y.: Doubleday & Company, Inc., 1966. Pp. xlvi+543.

Khoobyar, Helen. *Facing Adult Problems in Christian Education.* Philadelphia: The Westminster Press, 1963, Pp. 140.

* Kidd, J. Roby. *How Adults Learn.* New York: Association Press, 1959. Pp. 324.

Knowles, Malcolm S. *Informal Adult Education: A Guide for Administrators, Leaders, and Teachers.* New York: Association Press, 1950. Pp. xvi+272.

+ ———. *The Modern Practice of Adult Education.* New York: The Association Press, 1970. Pp. 384.

+ Küng, Hans. *Infallible? An Inquiry.* Tr. by Edward Quinn. Garden City, N.Y.: Doubleday and Company, Inc., 1971. Pp. 262.

LeFevre, Perry. *Understanding of Man.* Philadelphia: The Westminster Press, 1966. Pp. 187.

* Lehmann, Paul L. *Ethics in a Christian Context.* New York: Harper and Row, 1963. Pp. 384.

Lentz, Richard E. *Making the Adult Class Vital.* St. Louis: The Bethany Press, 1954. Pp. 112.

* Liégé, Pierre-André. *Adultes dan le Christ.* Brussels: La Pensée Catholique, 1958. Pp. 88.

Liston, Walter M. *Working with Groups: Group Process and Individual Growth.* New York: John Wiley and Sons, Inc., 1961. Pp. ix+238.

* Little, Lawrence C. (ed.) *The Future Course of Christian Adult Education.* Selected Addresses and Papers Presented in a Workshop on the Christian Education of Adults, Pittsburgh, Pennsylvania, June 15-17, 1958. Pittsburgh: University of Pittsburgh Press, 1959. Pp. xii+322.

* ——— (ed.). *Wider Horizons in Christian Adult Education.* Selected Addresses and Papers Presented in a Workshop on the Curriculum of

Christian Education for Adults, Pittsburgh, Pennsylvania, June 19-30, 1961. Pittsburgh: University of Pittsburgh Press, 1962. Pp. x+338.

* Lonergan, Bernard J. F. *Insight: A Study of Human Understanding.* London: Longmans, Green and Co., 1957. Pp. xxx+785.

* Lundström, Gösta. *The Kingdom of God in the Teaching of Jesus.* Trans. by Joan Bulman. Richmond, Va.: John Knox Press, 1963. Pp. xiv+300.

* McBride, Alfred. *Catechetics: A Theology of Proclamation.* Milwaukee, Wis.: The Bruce Publishing Company, 1966. Pp. xii+154.

* McKenzie, John L. *Dictionary of the Bible.* Milwaukee: The Bruce Publishing Company, 1965. Pp. xx+954.

McKinley, John. *Creative Methods for Adult Classes.* St. Louis: The Bethany Press, 1960. Pp. 96.

Macquarrie, John. *Principles of Christian Theology.* New York: Charles Scribner's Sons, 1966. Pp. xiv+477.

Manual for the Parish Confraternity of Christian Doctrine. Tenth ed. rev. Paterson, New Jersey: Confraternity Publications, 1961. Pp. vi+187.

Maves, Paul B. *Understanding Ourselves as Adults.* New York: The Abingdon Press, 1959. Pp. 217.

+ McKinley, John and Smith, Robert M. *Guide to Program Planning.* New York: The Seabury Press, 1965. Pp. 30.

* Mersch, Emile. *The Theology of the Mystical Body.* Trans. by Cyril Vollert. St. Louis: B. Herder Book Co., 1951. Pp. xviii+663.

* ————. *The Whole Christ: The Historical Development of the Doctrine of the Mystical Body in Scripture and Tradition.* Trans. by John R. Kelly. London: Dennis Dobson Ltd., 1938. Pp. xvi+623.

Minutes of the General Assembly of The United Presbyterian Church in the United States of America, Part III: *The Statistical Tables and Presbytery Rolls, January 1-December 31, 1967.* Published by the Office of the General Assembly, Witherspoon Building, Philadelphia, 1968. Pp. 898.

* Moran, Gabriel. *Catechesis of Revelation.* New York: Herder and Herder, 1966. Pp. 174.

* ————. *Theology of Revelation.* New York: Herder and Herder, 1966. Pp. 223.

National CCD Survey: January-April, 1968. Submitted by the Research Committee of the National Council of Diocesan Directors, Confraternity of Christian Doctrine and the CCD National Center. Prepared by Census Management, Inc., Washington, D.C., n.d. [1968]. Pp. 30.

* Nebreda, Alfonso M. *Kerygma in Crisis.* Chicago: Loyola University Press, 1965. Pp. xiv+140.

* *A New Catechism: Catholic Faith for Adults.* Trans. by Kevin Smyth from *De Nieuwe Katechismus* produced by the Higher Catechetical Institute at Nijmegen. New York: Herder and Herder, 1967. Pp. xviii+510.

* Newman, John Henry. *An Essay in Aid of a Grammar of Assent.* Garden City, N.Y.: Doubleday and Co., Inc., 1955. Pp. 396.

* ————. *An Essay on the Development of Christian Doctrine.* London: Longmans, Green, and Co., 1894. Pp. xvi+445.

* *The Objective of Christian Education for Senior High Young People.* Published for the Division of Christian Education National Council of the Churches of Christ in the U.S.A. by the Office of Publication and Distribution, 120 East 23rd Street, New York 10, New York, 1958. Pp. 44.

The Objectives of Christian Education. Distributed by the Lutheran Church of America, Board of Parish Education, Philadelphia, Pa., 1957. Pp. 13+chart.

* *The Objectives of Christian Education: A Study Document.* Published for the Commission on General Christian Education National Council of the Churches of Christ in the U.S.A. by the Office of Publication and Distribution, 120 East 23rd Street, New York 10, New York, n.d. [1958]. Pp. 22.

* Ochoa, Xaverius (ed.). *Index Verborum cum Documentis Concilii Vaticani Secundi.* Rome: Commentarium pro Religiosis, 1967. Pp. 847.

Official 1969 Directory for the Archdiocese of Baltimore. Published by The Catholic Review, 320 Cathedral St., Baltimore, Md., 1969. Pp. 228.

Outlines of Curriculum. A Supplement to the Report of the Curriculum Committee of the General Board of Education, the Methodist Church, 1965-66. Published by the Editorial Division of the General Board of Education of the Methodist Church [Nashville, Tenn.], 1964. Pp. 431.

* Pannenberg, Wolfhart (ed.) *Revelation as History.* Trans. by D. Granskow. New York: The Macmillan Company, 1968. Pp. x+181.

* ———. *Theology and the Kingdom of God.* Philadelphia: The Westminster Press, 1969, Pp. 143.

Parsch, Pius. *Learning to Read the Bible.* Trans. by H. E. Winstone. A reprint from *The Bible Today.* Collegeville, Minnesota: The Liturgical Press, 1963. Pp. 19.

* Phenix, Philip H. *Realms of Meaning: A Philosophy of the Curriculum for General Education.* New York: McGraw-Hill Book Company, 1964. Pp. xiv+391.

* Pope Pius XII. "Mystici Corporis," *Acta Apostolicae Sedis,* XXXV (1943), 193-248.

The Proposed Book of Confessions of The United Presbyterian Church in the United States of America. Published by the Office of the General Assembly, Witherspoon Building, Philadelphia, 1966. Pp. 186.

* Rahner, Karl. *Theological Investigations.* Vol. I: *God, Christ, Mary and Grace* and Vol. V: *Later Writings.* Trans. with an introduction by Cornelius Ernst. New edition with indexes. London: Darton, Longman, & Todd, 1961, 1966. I, pp. xxii+394. V, pp. x+525.

Reinhart, Bruce. *The Institutional Nature of Adult Christian Education.* Philadelphia: The Westminster Press, 1962, Pp. 242.

+ Rhodes, Eloise Roth. *Planning in the Local Setting.* Distributed by Central Distribution Service, Box 7286, St. Louis, Missouri, 63177, 1970. Pp. 104.

* Robinson, James M. and Cobb, John B., Jr. (edd.) *New Frontiers in*

Theology: Discussions among Continental and American Theologians.
Vol. II: *The New Hermeneutic.* New York: Harper & Row, Publishers,
1964. Pp. xii+243.

Rosalia, Sister M. [Walsh]. *Teaching Religion the Adaptive Way: Post
Vatican Edition.* Saint Paul, Minnesota: Catechetical Guild Educational Society, 1966. Pp. 416.

* Saylor, J. Galen, and Alexander, William M. *Curriculum Planning for
Better Teaching and Learning.* New York: Rinehart & Company, Inc.,
1954. Pp. xiv+624.

* Scheeben, Matthias J. *The Mysteries of Christianity.* Trans. by Cyril
Vollert. St. Louis: B. Herder Book Co., 1947. Pp. ix+834.

* Schillebeeckx, Edward. *Christ the Sacrament of the Encounter with God.*
Trans. by Paul Barrett *et al.* New York: Sheed and Ward, 1963. Pp.
xviii+222.

* Schnackenburg, Rudolph. *God's Rule and Kingdom.* Second enlarged edition. Trans. by John Murray. New York: Herder and Herder, 1968.
Pp. 400.

* Scott, Vaile J. *Catholic Adult Education,* NCEA Papers, No. 4. Ed. by
Russell Shaw. Dayton, O.: Geo. A. Pflaum, Publisher, Inc., 1968. Pp.
48.

Sherrill, Lewis J. *The Gift of Power.* New York: The Macmillan Co., 1955.
Pp. xiv+203.

Shinn, Roger, L. *The Educational Ministry of Our Church.* Boston: United
Church Press, 1962. Pp. 176.

* Smith, B. Othanel; Stanley, William O.; Shores, J. Harlan. *Fundamentals
of Curriculum Development.* Revised edition. Yonkers-on-Hudson,
N.Y.: World Book Company, 1957. Pp. xviii+685.

* *Specialized Resources for National Curriculum Developers in the Educational Ministry.* The Work of Cooperative Curriculum Development.
New York: Division of Christian Education, National Council of the
Churches of Christ in the United States of America, 1967. (Multilithed.) Pp. xx+4+L160+R205+S223+V134+C193+101.

* Stone, L. Joseph and Church, Joseph. *Childhood and Adolescence: A Psychology of the Growing Person.* Second edition. New York: Random
House, 1968. Pp. xvi+616.

* Stratemeyer, Florence B.; Forkner, Hamden L.; McKim, Margaret G.; and
Passow, A. Harry. *Developing a Curriculum for Modern Living.* Second
edition, revised and enlarged. New York: Bureau of Publications,
Teachers College, Columbia University, 1957. Pp. xii+740.

* Taylor, Marvin J. (ed.) *An Introduction to Christian Education.* Nashville:
Abingdon Press, 1966. Pp. 412.

* ———. (ed.) *Religious Education: A Comprehensive Survey.* Nashville:
Abingdon Press, 1960. Pp. 446.

* *Tools of Curriculum Development for the Church's Educational Ministry.*
The Work of the Cooperative Curriculum Development. Anderson,
Ind.: Warner Press, Inc., 1967. Pp. 224.

* Tracy, David. *The Achievement of Bernard Lonergan.* New York: Herder and Herder, 1970. Pp. xvii+302.
* van Caster, Marcel. *The Structure of Catechetics.* Trans. by Edward J. Dirkswager, Jr. *et al.* New York: Herder and Herder, 1965. Pp. 253.
* Vieth Paul H. (ed.) *The Church and Christian Education.* St. Louis: The Bethany Press, 1947. Pp. 314.
* ———. *Objectives in Religious Education.* New York: Harper & Brothers, 1930. Pp. xiv+331.
 White, James Asa (ed.). *Christian Education Objectives.* A Symposium Assembled under the Auspices of a California Council of Religious Education, Berkeley, Cal. New York: Fleming H. Revell Company, 1932. Pp. 142.
* Wyckoff, D. Campbell. *The Gospel and Christian Education.* Philadelphia: The Westminster Press, 1959. Pp. 191.
* ———. *Learning Tasks in the Curriculum.* Edited and Published by the Department of Curriculum Research and Development, American Baptist Board of Education and Publication. Valley Forge, Pa., 1965. Pp. 68.
* ———. *The Task of Christian Education.* Philadelphia: The Westminster Press, 1955. Pp. 172.
* ———. *Theory and Design of Christian Education Curriculum.* Philadelphia: The Westminster Press, 1961. Pp. 219.
 Yearbook of the American Baptist Convention, 1967-68. Valley Forge, Pa.: The Judson Press, n.d. [1968]. Pp. 578.
 Zeigler, Earl F. *Christian Education of Adults.* Philadelphia: The Westminster Press, 1958. Pp. 142.
 ———. *The Way of Adult Education.* Philadelphia: The Westminster Press, 1938. Pp. 320.
 Ziegler, Jesse H. *Focus on Adults.* Elgin, Ill.: The Brethren Press, 1965. Pp. 128.

ARTICLES

* Arntz, Joseph. "Natural Law and its History," *Concilium,* V, No. 1 (May, 1965), 23-32.
* Asquith, Glenn H. "Contemporizing Curriculum," *International Journal of Religious Education,* XLI (June, 1965), 16-17.
 Bacik, James and Lynch, Rosemary. "A New Venture in Adult Education," *The Living Light,* V, No. 4 (Winter 1968-69), 82-92.
 Barrosse, Thomas. "Mission to the Gentiles," *The Bible Today,* No. 24 (April, 1966), pp. 1583-92.
* Baum, Gregory. "The Magisterium in a Changing Church," *Concilium,* 21 (January, 1967) 67-83.
* Bornkamm, Gunther. "mystērion" in *Theological Dictionary of the New*

Testament, Vol. IV; *L-N.* Ed. by Gerhard Kittel. Trans. and ed. by
Geoffrey W. Bromily. Grand Rapids, Michigan: Wm. B. Eerdmans
Publishing Company, 1967, 817-28.

* Brown, Raymond E. "The Resurrection and Biblical Criticism," *Commonweal,* LXXXVII, No. 8 (November 24, 1967) *(Jesus: Commonweal
Papers: 2),* 232-36.

* Chenu, M. D.—"The History of Salvation and the Historicity of Man in
the Renewal of Theology" in *Theology of Renewal,* Vol. I: *Renewal
of Religious Thought.* Ed. by L. K. Shook. New York Herder and
Herder, 1968, 153-66.

* Cobb, John B., Jr. "The Intrapsychic Structure of Christian Existence"
in *To Be a Man.* Ed. by George Devine. Englewood Cliffs, N.J.:
Prentice-Hall, Inc., 1969, Pp. 24-40.

* Curran, Charles E. "The Ethical Teaching of Jesus," *Commonweal,*
LXXXVII, No. 8 (November, 1967) *(Jesus: Commonweal Papers:
2),* 248-58.

* Dolch, Heimo. "Sin in an Evolutive World," *Concilium,* VI, No. 3 (June,
1967), 36-40.

* Drummond, Richard. "Authority in the Church: An Ecumenical Inquiry,"
The Journal of Bible and Religion, XXXIV (October, 1966), 329-45.

* Hammans, Herbert. "Recent Catholic Views on Development of Dogma,"
Concilium, I, No. 3 (January, 1967), 53-63.

* Hubbard, Celia. "Corita—Myth or Maid," *The Living Light,* V, No. 4
(Winter, 1968-69), 101-09.

* Kasper, Walter. "The Relationship between Gospel and Dogma: An Historical Approach," *Concilium,* 21, 153-167.

* Keefe, Jeffrey. "Considerations on Maturity and the Catholic Priest,"
Worship, XLIII, No. 2 (February, 1969), 82-99.

+ Knowles, Malcolm S. "Androgogy, Not Pedagogy!" *Adult Leadership,* XVI,
No. 10 (April, 1968), 350-52 and 386.

* ————. "Program Planning for Adults as Learners," *Adult Leadership,*
XV (February, 1967), 267-68, 278-79.

* Larnicol, C. "Infallibilité de l'Église, du Corps épisopal, du Pape," *L'ami
du clerge,* LXXVI, 1966, 246-55, 257-59.

* Lawlor Francis "Infallibility" in *New Catholic Encyclopedia,* Vol. VII:
His to Jub. New York: McGraw Hill, 1967, 496-98.

+ Lee, James Michael. "Behavioral Objectives in Religious Education," *The
Living Light,* VII, No. 4 (Winter, 1970), 12-19.

* Lindbeck, George. "The Problem of Doctrinal Development and Contemporary Protestant Theology," *Concilium,* 21, 133-149.

* Lonergan, Bernard. "The Dehellenization of Dogma," *Theological Studies,*
XXVIII (June, 1967), 336-51.

* ————. "Functional Specialties in Theology." *Gregorianum,* L, No. 3-4
(1969), 485-505.

* ————. "Natural Knowledge of God," in *Proceedings of the Twenty-Third*

Annual Convention. The Catholic Theological Society of America. Yonkers, New York: St. Joseph's Seminary, 1969, pp. 54-69.

* ———. "Theology in Its New Context" in *Theology of Renewal*, Vol. I: *Renewal of Religious Thought.* Ed. by L. K. Shook. New York: Herder and Herder, 1968, 34-46.

* ———. "The Transition from a Classicist World View to Historical Mind-edness" in *Law for Liberty: The Role of Law in the Church Today.* Ed. by James E. Biechler. Baltimore: Helicon Press, 1967, pp. 126-33.

* Maguire, Daniel. "Holy Spirit and Church Authority," *Commonweal,* LXXXIX, No. 6 (November 8, 1968) (*Holy Spirit: Commonweal Papers: 3*), 213-20.

* ———. "Moral Absolutes and the Magisterium," in *Absolutes in Moral Theology?* Ed. by Charles E. Curran. Washington, D.C.: Corpus Books, 1968, pp. 57-107.

Martin, George A. "Dialogue Dilemma," *Today's Parish,* I, No. 2 (March-April, 1969), 2-4. Entitled "Adult Education in the Parish" in manuscript.

* Metz, Johannes Baptist. "The Church's Social Function in the Light of 'Political Theology,'" *Concilium,* VI, No. 4 (June, 1968), 3-11.

* Moran, Gabriel. "The Future of Catechetics." *The Living Light,* V, No. 1 (Spring, 1968), 6-22.

* ———. "The God of Revelation," *Commonweal,* LXXXV, No. 18 (February 10, 1967) (*God: Commonweal Papers: 1*), 499-503.

* ———. "The Time for a Theology," *The Living Light,* III, No. 2 (Summer 1966, 6-21.

* Moule, C. F. D. "Mystery" in *The Interpreter's Dictionary of the Bible,* Vol. III: *K-Q,* Ed. by G. A. Buttrick. New York: Abingdon Press, 1962, 479-81.

Nelson, C. Ellis. "The ABC's of a New Venture in Church Education" in *A New Venture in Church Education* (also known as *Christian Faith and Action: Designs for an Educational System*). Distributed by the Board of Christian Education, The United Presbyterian Church, U.S.A., Philadelphia, 1967. Pp. 26-32.

* Pannenberg, Wolfhart. "Redemptive Event and History" in *Essays on Old Testament Hermeneutics.* Ed. by C. Westermann, trans. and ed. by J. L. Mays. Richmond, Virginia: John Knox Press, 1963. Pp. 314-35.

* Pfeiffer, Carl. "The Role of the Catechist in Religious Education." Know Your Faith Series. Distributed by N. C. News Service, Washington, D.C., 1969.

"Response to Crisis," *Herder Correspondence,* VI, No. 6 (June, 1969), 175-77.

Reuther, Rosemary. "St. Stephen's Educational Program," *The Living Light,* V, No. 1 (Spring, 1968), 30-43.

* Richard, Robert. "Contribution to a Theory of Doctrinal Development," *Continuum,* II (1964), 505-27.

Ryan, Mary Perkins. "The Identity Crisis of Religious Educators," *The Living Light,* V, No. 4 (Winter, 1968-69), 6-18.

+ Schaefer, James R. "Baltimore's GIFT Program," *Today's Parish,* III, No. 4 (July/August, 1971), pp. 3-5.

+ ————. "Diocesan Coordination of Adult Christian Education," *The Living Light,* VII, No. 4 (Winter, 1970), 85-95.

ə + ————. "GIFT—An Adult Program That Works," *The Living Light,* VIII, No. 3 (Fall, 1971), 77-88.

+ ————. "Questions to Ask Before [In] Planning a Program" in *PACE—Professional Approaches for Christian Educators.* Ed. by Sheila Moriarty. Winona, Minn.: St. Mary's College Press, 1970.

————. "What Catholic Religious Education Can Learn from the 'Long-Range Program of Parish Education' of the Lutheran Church in America," *The Living Light,* IV, No. 2 (Summer, 1967), 57-76.

Snyder, Richard L. "Adult Education: Patterns and Planning," *Church School Worker,* XVIII, No. 1 (September, 1967), 38-41.

* Tracy, David. "Holy Spirit as Philosophical Problem," *Commonweal,* LXXXIX, No. 6 (November 8, 1968) (*Holy Spirit: Commonweal Papers: 3*), 205-13.

* ————. "Horizon Analysis and Eschatology," *Continuum,* VI (Summer, 1968), 166-79.

* van Caster, Marcel. "Catechetical Renewal and the Renewal of Theology" in *Theology of Renewal,* Vol. II: *Renewal of Religious Structures.* Ed. by L. K. Shook. New York: Herder and Herder, 1968, 222-41.

* Wyckoff, D. Campbell. "Christian Education Redefined" in *The Church in the Modern World: Essays in Honour of James Sutherland Thomson.* Ed. by George Johnston and Wolfgang Roth. Toronto: The Ryerson Press, 1967, pp. 203-23.

* ————. "Design in Protestant Curriculum." *Religious Education,* LXI (May-June, 1966), 169-73.

* ————. "Finding a Sound Design," *World Christian Education,* XIX, No. 4 (1964), 118-19.

* ————. "Instruction, the Person and the Group," *Religious Education,* LXI (January-February, 1966), 11-12.

* ————. "Learning—Planning—Goals," *Church School Worker,* XVIII (September 1967), 9-17.

* ————. "Putting the Objective of Christian Education into Practice," *Children's Religion,* XXVIII (June, 1967), 3-5.

* ————. "Toward a Definition of Religious Education as a Discipline," *Religious Education,* LXII (September-October, 1967), 387-94.

CURRICULUM RESOURCES AND
PROMOTIONAL LITERATURE USED BY THE
DENOMINATIONS AND DIOCESES STUDIED

Adult Education Courses and [Discussion] Programs. Distributed for Spring and Fall semesters annually by the Department of Adult Education, Office of Education, Diocese of Lansing, 311 Seymour Ave., Lansing, Michigan. Pp. 4.

Adult Times. A quarterly periodical issued by the General Division of Parish Education, Board of Christian Education, The United Presbyterian Church, U.S.A., Philadelphia, Vol. I (1956)—Vol. XII (1968). Discontinued.

Benson, Burton L. *The Divine Life in Your Home: Holy Family Program Manual, Phase I.* Minneapolis, Minn.: Education Incorporated, 1968. Pp. ii+41.

Bowman, Locke E., Jr. *Planning Teacher Education in the Parish.* Philadelphia: The Geneva Press, 1967. Pp. 95.

Carroll, James P. *Feed My Lambs.* Parent Education Series. Dayton, Ohio: Geo. A. Pflaum, Publisher, Inc., 1966. Pp. 126.

Christian Commitment Series. New York: Herder and Herder, 1968.
Braun, Theodore A. *Witnessing in the World.* Pp. vi+71.
Brueggemann, Walter. *Confronting the Bible.* Pp. iv+75.
Gilliom, James O. *Sent on a Mission.* Pp. iv+59.
West, Richard F. *Christian Decision and Action.* Pp. iv+76.
Williams, Alfred E. *Dilemmas & Decisions.* Pp. iv+76.
Dewey, Robert D. and Murphy, Charles. *Commitment: A Parent-Teacher Manual.* Pp. iv+76.

Christian Experience Series. Ed. by Mary Perkins Ryan. Dayton, Ohio: Geo. A. Pflaum, Publisher, Inc., 1965—.
Allemand, Edward. *About Hoping.* 1967. Pp. 125.
Gray, Donald P. *Where is Your God.* 1966. Pp. 123.
McBrien, Richard M. *What Do We Really Believe?* 1969. Pp. 125.
O'Neill, David P. *About Loving.* 1966. Pp. 123.
Ryan, Mary Perkins. *Through Death to Life.* 1965. Pp. 125.
Sloyan, Gerard S. *How Do I Know I'm Doing Right?* 1966. Pp. 126.

Clark, Sr. Mary Josepha *et al. Worship & Witness.* Distributed by the Mission Helpers of the Sacred Heart, 1001 West Joppa Road, Baltimore, Maryland 1967. Pp. iv+211.

Colloquy: Education in Church and Society. A monthly periodical (bimonthly July-August) continuing *Children's Religion* and *Church School Worker,* published by the United Church Press, Philadelphia, beginning Vol. I, No. 8 (September, 1968).

Conway, Thomas D. and Anderson, Eileen E. *Forming Catechists: An Introduction to CCD Teaching.* Contributing ed. Anthony T. Prete. New York: W. H. Sadlier, Inc., 1966. Pp. 117.

* The Decade Book Series. Ed. by Lindell Sawyers and Ray T. Woods. Philadelphia: The Geneva Press, 1968.
Bull, Robert J. *Tradition in the Making.* Pp. 128.
Cole, William G. *Sex and Selfhood.* Pp. 126.
Cully, Kendig B. *Decisions and Your Future.* Pp. 126.
Jansen, John Frederick. *Exercises in Interpreting Scripture.* Pp. 128.
LeFevre, Perry. *Man: Six Modern Interpretations.* Pp. 128.

McGill, Arthur C. *Suffering: A Test of Theological Method.* Pp. 128.

Moldovan, Stanley. *Youth in Contemporary Society.* Pp. 126.

Nelson, J. Robert. *Crisis in Unity and Witness.* Pp. 126.

Slusser, Gerald H. *A Dynamic Approach to Church Education.* Pp. 124.

Stotts, Jack L. *Believing, Deciding, Acting.* Pp. 126.

Szikszai, Stephen. *The Covenants in Faith and History.* Pp. 128.

White, O Z. *Changing Society.* Pp. 126.

Design for Teacher Education Series. Philadelphia: The Geneva Press, 1968.

Peebles, M. Agnes. *Practice Teaching.* Pp. 23.

Sawyers, Lindell L. *Guided Group Study.* Pp. 23.

Simpson, James E. *Repeatable Teacher Education.* Pp. 23.

The Teacher Education Study Group of the Synod of Ohio. *Teaching Teachers to Teach Inductively.* Pp. 23.

Design for Teaching-Learning: Prospectus I—1969-70. Valley Forge, Pa.: American Baptist Board of Education and Publication, n.d. [1969]. Pp. 47.

* *Enquiry: Studies for Christian Laity.* A quarterly periodical published by the Geneva Press, Philadelphia, beginning Vol. I, No. 1 (September-November, 1968).

Equipping Teachers to Teach: Preparing Leaders to Lead. Distributed by the General Division of Parish Education, Board of Christian Education, United Presbyterian Church in the U.S.A., Philadelphia, 1968. No pagination.

Greenspun, William B. and Norgren, William A. (edd.) *Living Room Dialogues.* Glen Rock, New Jersey: Paulist Press, 1965. Pp. 256.

———— and Wedel, Cynthia C. (edd.) *Second Living Room Dialogues.* Glen Rock, New Jersey: Paulist Press, 1967. Pp. xiv+270.

Haughton, Rosemary. *What Makes Children Saints.* St. Meinrad, Indiana: Abbey Press Publications, 1965. Pp. 31.

Hill, Doris J. and Jones, Louise M. *Planning for CFA.* Distributed by the Board of Christian Education, The United Presbyterian Church U.S.A., 1968. Pp. 48.

Hoag, Joy Marie. *How to Prepare Your Child for Confession.* St. Meinrad, Indiana: Abbey Press Publications, 1965. Pp. 32.

* Kempes, Robert H. *Lay Education in the Parish.* Philadelphia: The Geneva Press, 1968. Pp. 93.

Letters to the Churches. Twelve display cards. Valley Forge, Pa.: The American Baptist Board of Education and Publication, n.d. [1968].

Material Resources for Lay Education and Teacher Education. Distributed by the Board of Christian Education, The United Presbyterian Church U.S.A., Philadelphia, 1967. Pp. 25.

A New Approach to Lay Education. Distributed by the General Division of Parish Education, Board of Christian Education, United Presbyterian Church, U.S.A., Philadelphia, 1968. No pagination.

The New Testament in Modern English. Trans. by J. B. Phillips. New York: The Macmillan Company, 1958. Pp. xii+574.

* *A New Venture in Church Education* (also known as *Christian Faith and*

Action: Designs for an Educational System). Distributed by the Board of Christian Education, The United Presbyterian Church U.S.A., Philadelphia, 1967. Pp. 32.

+ *An Overview of the Steps in Program Planning.* Distributed by United Church of Christ, Council for Lay Life and Work, P. O. Box 7286, St. Louis, Mo. 65177. [n.d.]

+ *Planning Curriculum Locally—A Situational Approach to Lay Education— A Training Design for Presbyterians and Synods.* Distributed by Board of Christian Education, Presbyterian Church, U.S., Richmond, Va., 1970.

Parents as Teachers. A series of eight pamphlets. Notre Dame, Indiana: Ave Maria Press, 1964-66.

Carroll, James P. *Preparing Your Child for the Sacraments.* 1965. Pp. 32.

———. *Teaching Your Child about Sex.* 1966. Pp. 32.

Newland, Mary Reed. *Scripture in the Home.* 1964. Pp. 32.

Pottebaum, Gerard A. *Religion in the Home.* 1964. Pp. 32.

———. *Teaching Your Child about God.* 1964. Pp. 32.

———. *Your Child's Conscience.* 1965. Pp. 32.

Shea, James M. and Catherine D. *Forming Christian Attitudes in Your Child.* 1965. Pp. 32.

Tuomey, Magdalene Wise. *Liturgy for the Home.* 1964. Pp. 32.

Patterns of Promise. Ed. by the Christian Brothers. Winona, Minnesota: St. Mary's College Press, 1968. Pp. vi+248.

Pottebaum, Gerard A. Little Peoples' Paperbacks. A series of booklets for young children illustrated by Robert Strobridge. Dayton, Ohio: Geo. A. Pflaum, Inc., 1963-67.

Report of the National Advisory Commission on Civil Disorders [Kerner Report], *Summary of Report.* A Reprint from the Bantam Books edition. Published by the National Council of Catholic Men, Washington, D.C., n.d. [1968]. Pp. 29.

Reuther, Rosemary. *Communion Is Life Together.* New York: Herder and Herder, 1968. Pp. 48.

———. *Communion: A Parent-Teacher Manual with Record.* New York: Herder and Herder, 1968. Pp. 32.

Social Action Seminars. Series 101-10, Parish Participation Program. Distributed by Downs/Associate Services, 814 Thayer Ave., Silver Spring, Maryland, 1968. No pagination.

* *Trends: A Journal of Resources.* A monthly periodical (bi-monthly May-June and July-August) published by the Geneva Press, Philadelphia, beginning Vol. I, No. 1 (September, 1968).

Whats Happening—New Directions in Lay Education. Distributed by the General Division of Parish Education, Board of Christian Education, United Presbyterian Church, U.S.A., Philadelphia, 1967. Pp. 8.

Your Board of Education and Publication Works for You! Valley Forge, Pa.: American Baptist Board of Education and Publication, n.d. Pp. 20.

UNPUBLISHED WORKS

"ABCD Curriculum Plan: Writer's Manual (Perspective I)." An unpublished Resource for a Writer's Conference, May 22-27, 1966 produced by ABCD Curriculum Group #1. Distributed by American Baptist Board of Education and Publication, Valley Forge, Pa., n.d. [1966]. (Mimeographed.) Pp. 254 (each section separately paginated).

"ABCD Curriculum Plan: Writer's Manual (Perspective II)." An unpublished Resource for a Writers' Conference November 7-11, 1966 produced by ABCD Curriculum Group #1. Distributed by American Baptist Board of Education and Publication, Valley Forge, Pa., n.d. [1966] (Mimeographed.) Pp. 76 (each section separately paginated).

[ABCD] "Writer's Manual: Perspective III: ABCD Curriculum Plan for American Baptist Church Schools, the Church's School of the Christian Churches (Disciples of Christ)." An unpublished Resource for a Writers' Conference August 28-31, 1967 produced by ABCD Curriculum Group #1. Distributed by the American Baptist Board of Education and Publication, Valley Forge, Pa., n.d. [1967]. (Mimeographed.) Pp. 76 (each section separately paginated).

"Adult Church School Curriculum, 1969-1978." An unpublished prospectus of adult curriculum. Distributed by the American Baptist Board of Education and Publication, Valley Forge, Pa., 1967. (Mimeographed.) Pp. 6.

"Adult Education in the Diocese of Lansing." An unpublished paper distributed by the Department of Adult Education, Office of Education, Diocese of Lansing, 311 Seymour Ave., Lansing, Michigan, 1968. (Mimeographed.) Pp. 10.

* "Bibliography in Christian Education for Presbyterian College Libraries." Submitted by the Joint Committee of Nine for use in the program for the preparation of Certified Church Educators (Assistants in Christian Education). Unpublished papers distributed by D. Campbell Wyckoff, Princeton Theological Seminary, Princeton, N.J., 1960. (Mimeographed.) Pp. iii+23. (Addenda annually.)

* "A Case for Resourceful Freedom in Lay Education." An unpublished paper distributed among members of the Board of Christian Education, The United Presbyterian Church in the U.S.A., by members of the Division of Lay Education, Philadelphia, October 24, 1966. (Spirit duplicated.) Pp. 8.

"CCD Notes." An unpublished, bimonthly newsletter circulated among parish Confraternities of Christian Doctrine throughout the Archdiocese of Baltimore. (Mimeographed.)

"Communion in the Family: A Program of Preparation for Parents Who Prepare Their Children for First Communion." An unpublished booklet compiled and edited by Sister Teresa Mary [Dolan], for the Confraternity of Christian Doctrine, Archdiocese of Baltimore, January, 1969. (Mimeographed.) Pp. 29.

Cook, Paul G. "Confraternity of Christian Doctrine, Archdiocese of Baltimore: Doctrine Course." An unpublished series of fifteen lectures for
private use available in the files of the Archdiocesan Confraternity of
Christian Doctrine, 320 Cathedral Street, Baltimore, Maryland, 1967.
Pp. 66 (each lesson separately paginated).

"Current State of Adult Education and Future Possibilities." An unpublished memorandum submitted by the Director of Adult Education,
George A. Martin, to the Diocesan Superintendent of Education,
William Meyers, February 17, 1969. Files, Office of Education, Diocese
of Lansing, 311 Seymour Ave., Lansing, Michigan. Pp. 9.

"A Curriculum Plan for the Church's School: Working Document of Curriculum Group #1 as of January 7, 1966." An unpublished description
of the church school as a setting (incomplete), distributed by Christian Board of Publication, Christian Churches (Disciples of Christ),
St. Louis, Missouri. (Mimeographed.) Pp. 20.

"Cycle for the Church School: Christian Faith and Work Plan: Graded
Series." An unpublished outline of the curriculum plan distributed
by the American Baptist Board of Education and Publication, Valley
Forge, Pa., n.d. (Multilithed). Pp. 12.

"Cycle for the Church's School: Curriculum Group I, February 1, 1966."
An unpublished outline of the curriculum plan distributed by the
Christian Board of Publication, Christian Churches (Disciples of
Christ), St. Louis, Missouri. (Multilithed.) Pp. 11+1a.

* Description of the Units for a Basic Course of Study for Teacher Education and Lay Study." An unpublished paper issued by the Division
of Lay Education, Board of Christian Education, United Presbyterian
Church in the U.S.A., Witherspoon Building, Philadelphia, 1966.
(Spirit duplicated.) Pp. 3.

"The Design for the Curriculum of the Church's Educational Ministry
(ABC/CCP)." An unpublished draft composed by the American Bap-
tist Board of Education and Publication, Valley Forge, Pa., 1962.
(Mimeographed.) Pp. 24.

"A Discussion/Action Program Focusing on Race Relations Today: Based
on the *Report of the National Advisory Commission on Civil Disorders*." An unpublished guide distributed by the Office of Social and
Community Services, Department of Adult Education, and Renewal
through Vatican II Office, Diocese of Lansing, 311 Seymour Ave.,
Lansing, Michigan, n.d. (Mimeographed.) Pp. 18.

"The Divine Life in Your Home: Revised Reading Assignment List."
An unpublished reading guide distributed by the Department of
Adult Education, Office of Education, Diocese of Lansing, Michigan.
n.d. P. 1.

"First Confession and First Communion: A Study Issued for Pastors,
Principals and Religion Teachers of the Archdiocese of Baltimore."
An unpublished paper distributed by the Department of Education
and the Confraternity of Christian Doctrine, Archdiocese of Baltimore,
n.d [1968]. Pp. 10+4+4.

"Forgiveness in the Family: A Program of Preparation for Parents Who Prepare Their Children for First Confession." An unpublished booklet compiled and edited by Sr. Teresa Mary [Dolan] for the Confraternity of Christian Doctrine, Archdiocese of Baltimore, September, 1969. (Multilithed.) Pp. iii+43.

"God's Word in Your Life: Suggestions for the Parish Bible-Study Group." An unpublished paper distributed by the Department of Religious Education, Office of Education, Diocese of Lansing, 311 Seymour Ave., Lansing, Michigan, n.d. (Mimeographed.) Pp. 23.

Henthorne, Ray L. "Random Thoughts on Meanings and Experiences." An unpublished address delivered to Curriculum Group I, Writer's Conference, May 24, 1966. Distributed by the American Baptist Board of Education and Publication, Valley Forge, Pa. (Mimeographed.) Pp. 16.

"History of the Development of Our Method and Catechetical Apostolate." An unpublished paper in the archives of the Mission Helpers Generalate, 1001 West Joppa Road, Baltimore, Maryland, n.d. Pp. 7.

"Leading a Small Discussion Group." An unpublished guide distributed by the Department of Adult Education, Office of Education, Diocese of Lansing, Michigan, 311 Seymour Ave., Lansing, Michigan, n.d. (Mimeogrphed.) Pp. 5.

"Learning, Instruction, and the ABCD Curriculum Plan." An unpublished collection of papers prepared for: ABCD Writers Conference, Conrad Hilton Hotel, Chicago, Illinois, May 25, 1966. Distributed by Department of Curriculum Research and Development, American Baptist Board of Education and Publication, Valley Forge, Pa. (Mimeographed.) Pp. 25+G6+2 diagrams.

* McCarter, Neely D. "The Appropriation of Revelation and Its Implications for Christian Education." An unpublished doctoral dissertation. Yale University, New Haven, Conn., 1961. Pp. 348.

"A New Look at CCD Adult Education." For Use of Parish CCD Directors. An unpublished paper distributed by the National Center of the Confraternity of Christian Doctrine, 1312 Massachusetts Ave. N.W., Washington, D.C., n.d. Pp. 5.

* "Outline for Lay Studies Book on Instruction in Church Education." An unpublished paper available in "Decade Books" file, Division of Lay Education, Board of Christian Education, United Presbyterian Church in the U.S.A., Witherspoon Building, Philadelphia, Pa., October 24, 1966. (Spirit duplicated.) Pp. 2.

+ Schaefer, James R. "A Proposed Curriculum Design for Adult Christian Education for Use in Catholic Dioceses." An unpublished doctoral dissertation. The Catholic University of America, Washington, D.C., 1971. Pp. ix+612.

"Seminar in Catechetics: Discussion Leaders Guide." An unpublished guide distributed by the Department of Adult Education, Office of Education, Diocese of Lansing, 311 Seymour Ave., Lansing, Michigan, n.d. (Mimeographed.) Pp. 22.

"Some Comments on Proposals Submitted in the Lansing Renewal through Vatican II Program." An unpublished report circulated by the Department of Adult Education, Office of Education, Diocese of Lansing, 311 Seymour Ave., Lansing, Michigan, n.d. Pp. 2+chart.

* Wyckoff, D. Campbell. "An Organizing Principle for the Curriculum." An unpublished address delivered at the World Consultation of the Curriculum of Christian Education, Fürigen, Switzerland, June 13-July 4, 1964. (Mimeographed.) Pp. 14. Reported in synopsis under the title, "Finding a Sound Design," *World Christian Education*, XIX, (4th Quarter, 1964), 118-19.

————. "Toward a Definition of Religious Education as a Discipline." An address delivered at the annual meeting of the Professors and Research Section, Division of Christian Education, National Council of Churches, Dallas, Texas, February 14-16, 1967. (Mimeographed.) Published in an abridged form under the same title in *Religious Education*, LXII, (September-October, 1967), 387-94.

"The Young Church in Action: Scripture Parish and Home Small-Group Program." An unpublished guide distributed by the Office of Education, Diocese of Lansing, 311 Seymour Ave., Lansing, Michigan, n.d. (Mimeographed.) Pp. 22.

Index

Technically speaking, this is an index of concepts rather than an index of subjects or of subjects and authors. The table of contents, pp. vii-ix, will serve as an index of subjects and the bibliography, pp. 232-51, as a source of authors and their works. Several of the concepts, e.g. the categories of inquiry (objective, personnel, etc.) run through the whole book. For ease in finding specific concepts, then, the following code of subheadings, will be followed:

    0—basic concepts: natures, definitions, descriptions
    1—questions to consider: starting points
    2—foundations: argumentation, justification, basic input
    3—input from other sources
    4—details: variations, forms, aspects
    5—principles: results of theory and experience
    6—application to practice
    7—miscellany: related material not provided in previous subheadings
    8—illustrations, cases, and examples
    9—bibliography: by source not content

If the reader intends to make frequent or extensive use of this book, he may find it advisable to select one of the categories of inquiry, read through its entry in the index, and refer to the text itself for at least some of the references. This exercise should familiarize the reader with the methodology, specialized nature, and usefulness of the index.

252

appropriation
  0—definition 148-50
  4—affective 156-7
    deliberative 157
    interpersonal 157
  6—application to learning 153-7
  9—B. Lonergan on 149-50
assent 155
assignment of sites 57
availability, as determining factor of
  context 178

Baltimore (Archdiocese)
  involvement in this study 10
  on context 169-70, 173, 175-6, 177,
    (quoted) 169, 173, 175, 177
  on objective 76-7, 82, 84, (quoted)
    76-7, 84
  on personnel 88, 90, (quoted) 92,
    97, 98, 99, 102
  on process (quoted) 148, 158, 160
  on scope 108, 116, 118, 119, 142,
    143, (quoted) 108, 118, 119, 142,
    143
  on timing 180, 181, 183-4, 186, 187,
    (quoted) 180, 181, 187
Baptism 133
Barr, James, on the mystery of Christ
  as event (quoted) 122-3
Betts, George Herbert, *The Curriculum of Religious Education* 52
Bible
  on "Church's experience" 114-5
  on faith (quoted) 150
bishop of Rome 93-4
Bishops
  infallibility 92-4, 95
  role in adult Christian education
    36, 91-6, 103
  teaching authority 92, 95
Board of Christian Education 71, 88,
  99
Body of Christ *see* Mystical Body
Boelke, Robert R.
  on faith (quoted) 152
  on process 44, (quoted) 45
  *Theories of Learning in Christian
    Education* 107
Bornkamm, Gunther, on mystery
  (quoted) 132

Bower, William Clayton, *The Curriculum of Religious Education* 52
budgeting 57
Bultmann, Rudolph, on the mystery
  of Christ as event 121

CCP see Cooperative Curriculum
  Project
care, custodial 57
Caster, Marcel *see* van Caster, Marcel
catechists
  training 96
catechetical signs (four) 139-40
categories of inquiry *see* inquiry, categories of
Catholic Church
  Pope 93-4
  purpose 33-4, 83-5
celebration (definition) 131
  see also mystery of Christ as celebration
charity 135-7
Christ *see* Jesus Christ, Mystery of
  Christ, Mystical Body
Christian (definition) 8
Christian education *see* education,
  Christian
Church (definition) 101 *see also*
  Catholic Church
"Church's experience" 114-5
cognition 155-6
cognitive understanding *see* understanding, cognitive
College of Bishops *see* bishops
Commission of General Christian Education 28
  on scope 38
Committee on the Study of Religious
  Education 52
community 170
complacency 5
comprehensiveness 40, 116-8
conceptual systems 16, 19-22
confusion in modern world 5
context 168-78
  0—definition 46, 168, 219
    description 25-6, 66
  1—major question: Where does
    learning happen? 46, 67, 168-70,
    224

on categories on inquiry (quoted)
16, 19-22
on curricular questions 65
The Gospel 80
grouping 46-7, 171-4
Growth in Faith Together see GIFT
Guided Group Study (quoted) 172
Guided Group Study (quoted) 172
Gustafson, James, *Christ and the
Moral Life* 107
on morality 137-8 (quoted) 138

Häring, Bernard, *The Law of Christ*
107
on morality 136-7, (quoted) 137
hermeneutic, new 129-30
9—G. Ebeling on 130
historical knowledge see knowledge,
historical
Holy Spirit 77
horizon
0—definition 124-5
4—relative 125
9—B. Lonergan on 124, 125n, 126n
D. Tracy on 124, 125n
see also mystery of Christ as horizon
how? see Process

identification
as a way of learning 153
definition 152
with other persons 45
9—D. C. Wyckoff on 152
imperative see mystery of Christ as
moral imperative
imprimatur 96
infallibility 92, 94, 95
"initiating objective" 86
initiation 163-4
9—van Caster on 163
inquiry (learning mode) 162-3
inquiry, categories of 16-26
general concerns 50-60
related to administration 57-8
related to evaluation 56-7
related to organization 55
sequence 25-6
summary 65-9
9—J. Goodlad on 16, 19-22

Horace Mann—Lincoln Institute
on 17
D. C. Wyckoff on 23-5
see also context, objective, personnel, process, scope, timing
insight 155-6
intention of participants 8
interdependence
of aspects of scope 140-1, 142, 144-5
of kinds of learning 154
of modes of teaching 161
interpersonal (definition) 149 see also
learning, interpersonal
interrelationship
of personnel 87-9
of scope and process 165-6
of teacher and learner 36
intervention, divine 41

Jesus Christ
as norm 138
death and resurrection 123
person of 77
see also mystery of Christ, Mystical
Body
John, Saint
on mystery of Christ as horizon
(quoted) 127
on mystery of Christ as moral imperative (quoted) 135

KAIROS 48
KERYGMA 80, 121, 123, 162
Kingdom of God 80
knowledge, historical 155
developed by disclosure 161-2
Knowles, Malcolm S., on Christian
adult education methodology
(quoted) 18-19

Lansing (Diocese)
involvement in this study 10
on context 169-70, 173, 174-5, 176,
177, (quoted) 169, 174-5, 177
on objective 76-7, 82, 84-5,
(quoted) 76, 84
on personnel 88, 90, 91, 92, 97, 98,
99, 102, (quoted) 90, 91, 98, 102
on process 147-8, 158, 160,
(quoted) 147-8, 160